The Advancement of Theological Education

The Advancement of Theological Education

By

H. RICHARD NIEBUHR

DANIEL DAY WILLIAMS

JAMES M. GUSTAFSON

NEW YORK

HARPER & BROTHERS, PUBLISHERS

Library of Congress catalog card number: 56–12071

Contents

v

Foreword

The book herewith presented to readers concerned with the advancement of theological education in American and Canadian Protestantism is the second and final part of the report of a study of the graduate seminaries in the two nations. The first part was published in April, 1956, under the title *The Purpose of the Church and Its Ministry, Reflections on the Aims of Theological Education.* The present work might well bear the subtitle *Reflections on the Methods of Theological Education.* Since methods, though directed by aims, are rarely directly deducible from them the two parts of the study are relatively independent of each other.

These two books, together with a series of five bulletins distributed to the seminaries between April, 1954, and April, 1956, represent the documentary results of an inquiry which was set in motion by the American Association of Theological Schools and financed by the Carnegie Corporation of New York.[1] The general plan for the study agreed upon by these two organizations provided that "the primary focus of the study is upon the work which the theological schools do in the preparation of persons for the parish ministry," though it was recognized that "around this primary focus lie a large number of subsidiary questions which need to be examined in order to throw further light on the work of the theological schools." It was agreed that one of these "principal subsidiary questions has to do with the role of the minister in contemporary life" and that there was also "urgent need for a comprehensive collection of data about the seminaries and their qualitative assessment." The plan further provided for the appointment of a director, who was to be "entirely responsible for the administration of the research project, including the appointment of the staff" and for the appointment of a small advisory committee "to frame terms of reference for study of the role of the minister," "to bring lay perspective to bear on the study as well as that of clergymen and educators, to advise with regard to methodology and research procedures, to assist in the effective promulgation and implementation of

[1] A volume of essays, *The Ministry in Historical Perspectives,* was edited by members of the Study staff and its publication financed from Study funds, but it does not constitute a part of the report.

the study." Objectives and audiences were described in the plan as follows: "The eventual objective of the study is the improvement of the work done by the theological schools. This objective is of concern eventually to many audiences," including faculties and boards of trustees responsible for theological education, conferences such as the American Association of Theological Schools and groups of seminaries organized in denominational councils for theological education, colleges and universities, denominational leaders, church members in general, and the American public. Finally, the plan provided that the period to be devoted to the research by the director and his staff should be approximately fifteen months in length.

In accordance with these provisions H. Richard Niebuhr of the Divinity School of Yale University was appointed director in December, 1953. His nominations of Daniel Day Williams, then of the Federated Theological Faculty of the University of Chicago, as associate director, and of James M. Gustafson, then pastor of the Northford (Connecticut) Congregational Church and graduate student at Yale, as assistant director were approved by the Administrative Committee of the American Association of Theological Schools. The Advisory Committee, similarly nominated and approved, consisted of the following: Theodore Ferris, rector of Trinity Episcopal Church, Boston, Massachusetts; Paul N. Garber, resident Methodist bishop of the Richmond Area, Virginia; Ralph W. Loew, pastor of Holy Trinity Lutheran Church, Buffalo, New York; Frank McCluer, president of Lindenwood College, St. Charles, Missouri; Walter N. Roberts, president of United Theological Seminary, Dayton, Ohio; Lewis J. Sherrill, professor at Union Theological Seminary, New York, New York; Charles L. Taylor, Jr., dean of the Episcopal Theological School, Cambridge, Massachusetts; Gordon M. Torgersen, minister of the First Baptist Church, Worcester, Massachusetts. This committee organized in September, 1954, choosing President Walter Roberts as chairman and Mr. Gustafson of the staff as secretary.

The study began intensively on July 1, 1954. The early months were devoted by the staff to their self-orientation in the field and to the development of study procedures. Responsibility was partly divided so that the associate director gave primary attention to the faculties, courses of study, and teaching methods of the seminaries, the assistant director to the qualifications, the selection, and the experiences of students, the director to the churches and the ministry. Eventually information was gathered by means of questionnaires from all the accredited members of the American Association, from almost all of the associate members, and from a considerable number of seminaries not affiliated with that organization. Thirty-six of these schools were selected so that the list would be representative of the denominational and regional pattern of American church life, of large and small, well-endowed and economically poor institutions, of Negro and white enrollment. These schools were asked to supply data about changes that had taken place in their status and work during the twenty-year period from 1934 to 1954. Another line of inquiry was pursued by means of school visitations that offered members of the staff opportunities for interviews with administrators, teachers, and students and allowed them to make more of a qualitative study than the quantitative data submitted by the schools permitted. Ninety schools were so visited. Participation by staff members in three regional seminary conferences and in six denominational consultations on theological education supplemented the insights they received from the visitation program. As has previously been described in *The Purpose of the Church* the interview method was also followed in the effort to gain understanding of the role and problems of the modern Protestant minister as well as of the types and experiences of theological students. It would be as wearisome to the reader as it is to the writer to detail all the other lines of inquiry that were followed and all the methods that were used. Whether they were well chosen can be judged only by their results.

The present report of the findings of this inquiry is a product of joint authorship in the sense that it was planned by the staff as a whole, that the material used was gathered in the course of common inquiry, and that every section was reviewed by all the members of the group. Responsibility for the sections, however, was allocated to the individual staff members. The director bears primary responsibility for Chapters One, Two, Three and Nine and for editing the volume; the associate director for Chapters Four, Five and Six; the assistant director for Chapters Seven and Eight and the Appendix.

The authors desire here again to express their thanks to those many individuals and institutions to whom they are indebted and whom they mentioned in the Foreword of *The Purpose of the Church*. Special mention is due to the members of the Advisory Committee, to the presidents, deans, and registrars of the seminaries who faithfully and patiently responded to requests for information, to the denominational executives, theological professors, and students who shared their observations and reflections with us, to the ministers who gave us time for interviews or wrote painstaking letters on their work, to the lay educators who advised us on many difficult points. Among these scores and hundreds it is scarcely fair to name individuals, yet we are particularly conscious of the assistance given by Professor Lewis Sherrill, President Walter Roberts, and Dean Charles Taylor who are all officers of the American Association of Theological Schools as well as members of the Advisory Committee; by Professor Raymond Morris who was our chief consultant on library matters; by Professor Samuel Blizzard who shared with us some of the early results of his study of the ministry; by Marcus Robbins, the Comptroller of Yale University which administered the funds; by Dean Liston Pope of the Yale University Divinity School; by James A. Perkins of the Carnegie Corporation.

The Carnegie Corporation, though providing the funds that made the study possible, is not the author, owner, publisher, or proprietor of these or of the other publications issued by the staff of *The Study of Theological Education in the United States and Canada,* and is not to be understood as approving by virtue of its grant any of the statements made or views expressed therein.

For her work on the present book the directors are greatly indebted to Mrs. Fleur Kinney Ferm. She has typed and retyped the manuscript many times, has supplied the index and has efficiently managed the office of the inquiry. Robert Gessert during a brief period of employment made some of the statistical studies eventually used by the director in the first two chapters. Mrs. Miriam Smith assisted the directors during the major part of the inquiry both as secretary and in research.

As the study is brought to its conclusion the directors are keenly aware of its deficiencies. The answers to many questions remain incomplete; many others remain unanswered; new lines of inquiry have opened up that could not be pursued. They hope, however, that they have been able to present some information and advice that will contribute to the advancement of theological education in the United States and Canada. Believing as they do that self-examination and improvement in education must be continuous they are gratified by the establishment of a new central office of the American Association of Theological Schools. That office and its director will be able to continue on a year-by-year basis what has been intermittently done to date by such inquiries as this and its predecessors.

H. RICHARD NIEBUHR
DANIEL DAY WILLIAMS
JAMES M. GUSTAFSON

The Advancement of Theological Education

CHAPTER ONE

Some Recent Trends in Theological Education

I. The Historical Background

Insofar as the present study of theological education is historical it is primarily concerned with recent trends: with the growth of graduate schools of theology, of their enrollment and faculties; with changes in the curriculum, in the denominational character and in the financing of this education. These developments can be sketched without much reference to long-range historical movements. Nevertheless, since readers as well as writers will have in mind some ideas of the background of such recent developments and since these ideas may conflict it seems desirable that the authors state their understanding of the larger historical scene.

That understanding differs from a widely accepted interpretation. In each previous study of theological education in the United States and Canada as well as in many other treatments of the subject the historical background in view was that of the decline of this education from the high position it had gained in Puritan New England. So Professor Mark A. May in his book on *The Profession of the Ministry* interpreted trends in the education of the ministers by reference first to the changing educational status of Congregational ministers in New England from the earliest Colonial period to the twentieth century and, secondly, to the proportion of college graduates entering the ministry from 1642 to 1930. He found that "the proportion of college graduates among Congregational ministers in New England has been declining steadily for 200 years. Presumably the educational level of the Protestant ministry in the United States in 1926 was below that of 100 years ago and well below that of 200 years ago. Second, the proportion of college-graduate men entering the ministry has been declining irregularly for 300 years. In the last fifty years there has been a very severe drop in the number of college graduates entering the ministry directly and without seminary training." [1] Such statements have helped to establish the widespread impression to which a sociologist has given typical utterance in the following statement:

[1] W. A. Brown, and Mark A. May, *The Education of American Ministers*, 4 vols., 1934; Vol. II, 33.

In the long run the quality of the men who enter into the various existing professions depends in considerable part on the relative morale of each of those professions. A hundred years ago the Protestant ministry was a profession of high prestige and equally high morale; it then drew to it men of intellectual vigor and strong ambition. Today the ministry is a profession as low in prestige as in income, and the general level of morale among ministers is lower still; today, therefore, the university training centers for the ministry get the culls of the academic crop.[2]

With the facts stated by Professor May one cannot quarrel, though the assertions made by Professor La Piere are unsubstantiated. It is the interpretation of the facts that needs to be challenged. To deal with the history of the Protestant ministry and with the history of education as though they were continuous from Puritan New England to the twentieth century is to ignore the radical revolutions which took place in both areas in the nineteenth century. Historians are pointing out increasingly that the matrix of American religious life as we now know it is not to be found in the seventeenth century but in the nineteenth, not in New England only but also on the frontier; that the origins of those denominations which exercise a large influence in the twentieth century are to be found in the revivals of the eighteenth and nineteenth centuries more than in the Puritan movement; that all of the churches, even those which originated in the Reformation, have been deeply influenced by the experimental religion of the revival period; that American college and theological seminary systems had their effective beginnings in the nineteenth century.[3] Professor Richard C. Wolf after describing the standard, i.e., New England, version of American history writes: "Based upon a thorough knowledge and appreciation of the Colonial Period, and detracting nothing from the importance of that period as the foundational section of the history, a new interpretation has been constructed (by newer historians) in which the Middle Period is seen as the truly formative period out of which has come modern America." Religiously this Middle Period is marked by the rise of those denominations which had their roots in the revival, by the development of an experimental and highly practical theology, by the increased participation of the churches in the democratic movement and the increased participation of the democratic masses in the life of the churches. As Professor Wolf points out, between 1800 and 1870 the Baptists grew from a membership of 103,000 to almost 1,500,000; the Methodists from 65,000 to 2,500,000; the Disciples from nonexistence to a membership of 450,000; but those denominations which had been

[2] Richard A. La Piere, *Theory of Social Control,* New York, 1954, 409; cf. 84, 497.

[3] Richard C. Wolf, "The Middle Period, 1800–1870, The Matrix of Modern American Christianity," *Religion in Life,* Vol. 22, 72 ff.

strongest in the eighteenth century showed a much smaller rate of growth. The Presbyterian Church "advanced from 40,000 members in 1800 to 713,000 in 1870." The Congregationalists increased from 75,000 to 306,000; the Episcopal Church from a membership of 12,000 in 1800 to almost 208,000 in 1870. (A different factor was introduced into the situation by German immigration and the growth of the Lutheran Church in America from 15,000 members in 1800 to about 400,000 in 1870.) The increase in membership of the newer denominations was probably not so much at the expense of the older churches as it marked a net gain in Protestant church membership. It is to be noted, further, that the type of experimental religion represented by the revival churches greatly affected the ideas and practices of the older denominations. This experimental faith, emphasizing conversion and personal experience of reconciliation to God, differed markedly from the older type of more rational, creedal and sometimes liturgical conceptions of Christianity. Its popular appeal was greater; the gifts it required in the preachers who disseminated it were different.

From this point of view the history of the denominations in the twentieth century must be understood as a development of the faith engendered and popularized by revivalism and Pietism. As these churches now function they represent the modification of empirical religion by intellectual and cultural influences more than a decline from the Puritan norm. The educational status of ministers must be assessed in the light of this movement. The question is not so much what has happened in the course of three hundred years to the education of Congregational ministers as what has happened since 1800 to the educational status of ministers in America in general, including first of all the ministers of the very large and popular denominations that began their American history long after the Puritan founding of New England. Furthermore one must ask what happened among Congregationalists, Presbyterians, Episcopalians, and Lutherans in their understanding of Christian faith and life before one asks what happened to their practices of theological education.

A second factor too much ignored by the exponents of the doctrine of decline is the educational revolution that occurred in the nineteenth century. The democratic and religious movements of the time were accompanied by the founding of hundreds of church colleges, the development of the public school and state university systems, the steadily increasing demand for college education by American youth, eventually by the unprecedented influx of youth into higher education in the twentieth century, the increase in the number of professions, and the growth of professional training. This educational revolution also began in the Middle Period and not in Colonial times. Hence the direct comparison of the proportion of college graduates entering the ministries of a few eighteenth-century denominations from three or four colleges with the proportion entering all the present American denominations from six or seven hundred colleges and state universities ignores many important factors in social and religious history and yields little helpful insight into the contemporary situation.

If we consider theological education against the background of the developments in the Middle Period and later, the following factors seem significant: 1) The kind of practical Christianity which had its roots in the revivals had little interest in theology as a direct expression of human faith in God and love of neighbor. If love and faith were not conceived wholly in emotional terms they were nevertheless regarded from a highly practical point of view. Theology as such was often subject to religious contempt. Empirical religion in the churches frequently joined hands with anti-intellectualism in equalitarian democracy. 2) The primary conditions for the exercise of the ministry were the reception by the individual of a spiritual call and the experience of personal conversion. 3) Interest in education in the churches was great, as the founding of many colleges indicates, but was not directed toward theological education as such but rather toward a Christian general education. The colleges founded by the churches were designed to prepare men for the ministry by the study of the Bible and of the humanities. 4) Finally, insofar as ministers received a special preparation for carrying on their tasks, they were trained in practical work more than in theological disciplines.

In the light of this history we see that the Protestant seminaries of today like the denominations have their roots in two related but differing conceptions of Protestant faith. The first of these is the one developed in the churches of the Reformation and in Puritan England. The second is the conception which grew up in the period of the revivals. The two movements have greatly influenced each other and seminaries today often show the traces of both origins, but the distinction needs nevertheless to be kept in mind. Further, we note that the present situation in theological education may be regarded as representing modification of the convictions and measures of revival Christianity at least as much as continuation and decline of the Reformation tradition. In the third place, the development of theological education in modern times has much in common with the educational movement in democracy in general. Protestant Christianity in the United States and Canada has influenced the culture considerably, not least through the founding of colleges and theological seminaries. However, it is also true that these institutions have been deeply influenced by the cultural development. One reason frequently mentioned in recent times for the founding of theological schools is that Protestant churches need ministers at least as well trained as their laymen are. Finally, it is noteworthy that the participation of the denominations in the recent growth of theological education has been very unequal. While certain denominations, such as the Presbyterian, Lutheran and Episcopal churches, are continuing a long-established tradition when they maintain theological schools, others such as the Methodist Church, the Baptist conventions, the Disciples and similar groups entered into the field of theological education in later periods; the development of their schools is often more rapid and otherwise participates more in the popular educational movement than is the case in the churches of the sixteenth-century Reformation. In this connection it seems pertinent that many of the more recently organized denominations, such as the Church of the Nazarene and the Seventh-Day Adventists, are now engaged in a movement toward improved education of their ministers comparable to that on which Methodists, Baptists, and Disciples embarked in earlier decades. Furthermore, the growth of the Bible School movement in the twentieth century is not always to be regarded as a phenomenon of the opposition of "conservatives" to "liberals"; it is an indication of the increased participation of certain groups in the United States and Canada in the general movement toward education. The conservative schools seem to have their origin less in antagonism to the "liberal" schools than in the desire of conservative groups to provide higher education of a Christian type for their young people and particularly for their ministers. The alternative for them is not at present the sending of their youth to the older schools but no higher education at all, since, as they see it, education is either secular or biblical.

A special feature of the present situation when we consider it against the background of nineteenth-century Christianity is the strong tendency in all of the churches, whatever their origin, toward the development of a Christian theology, that is, toward the development of a comprehensive Christian understanding of man and his destiny, of creation, sin, and salvation, of God, Jesus Christ, the Holy Spirit, and the Church. Conversion and spiritual experience continue to be important but the understanding of Christianity as a reasoning and reasoned faith, as an intelligible conviction about God and salvation, is gaining ground. Such rational religion is far removed from rationalism; it remains religion but has become faith that seeks understanding. Theological schools are being founded and are growing not only because American Protestants desire a well-educated ministry, but because ministers want theology.[4]

---

[4] There are differences between the two countries covered in this survey. Canada doubtless has been less affected by the revival movement and by certain forms of what is called in America the "democratic way of life" than has the United States. Its schools are strongly influenced by the pattern of the English theological colleges. Yet in both countries the theological education movement needs to be traced

II. The Graduate Schools of Theology in the United States and Canada

Forgoing further reflections on general background we shall concentrate in this study, so far as history is concerned, on the trends in theological education that have become manifest during the time from 1920 to 1955 and particularly on the last twenty years of that period. Approximate comparisons between the status of theological education in the 1950's and the 1920's or 1930's can be made because studies of theological education, largely as it was going on in 1920 to 1923 and in 1929 to 1933 were published in 1924 and in 1934.[5] Further data on trends in this period have been made available to the present study by thirty-six typical schools in the United States. These institutions, cooperating with the study, furnished data concerning changes in enrollment, curriculum, finances, et cetera during the years from 1935 to 1955.[6] The schools, selected as more or less typical, represent many denominations and most regions in the United States; some are interdenominational; they range in size from small to very large seminaries.

A striking characteristic of the development from 1920 to 1955 is the growth of graduate education in theology.[7] According to Dr. Kelly 161 schools were called seminaries in the early 1920's by their supporting constituencies. Of these, 131 were located in the United States, the other thirty were in Canada. In 1934 Professor May listed 224 Protestant seminaries in the United States and Canada, of which 198 were in the former country, twenty-six in the latter. The present study has classified 180 institutions as Protestant theological schools, twenty-nine of these being in Canada, the remaining 151 in the United States. Since three of the schools in Canada are so closely affiliated that their statistical data must be classified together, we shall ordinarily be dealing with twenty-seven schools in Canada rather than with twenty-nine, and with a total of 178 rather than 180 schools.[8] On the surface this appears

---

back not only to the days of colonialism but even more to the national periods in which the religious life in each nation as well as its political life gained independence and a definite character of its own.

[5] Cf. Robert L. Kelly, *Theological Education in America*. A Study of 161 Theological Schools in the United States and Canada, New York, 1924.

William Adams Brown, Mark A. May, and Frank K. Shuttleworth, *The Education of American Ministers*, 4 vols., New York, 1934. Hereafter this work will be cited as *American Ministers*.

[6] Since not all of the schools were able to give information on all of the subjects, in ensuing statements it will always be noted what number of schools of the typical group supplied usable data on a particular topic.

[7] The term "graduate" is used in two senses in theological circles: 1) as applying to all post-A.B. or B.S. theological education; 2) as applying to post-B.D. theological education. It is here used in the first sense.

[8] Two Canadian schools, Diocesan College and United Theological College in Montreal, are federated with the McGill University Faculty of Theology. The statistics available to the Study are those of the McGill Faculty of Theology. The

to mean that the number of theological schools has declined since 1934 but this is probably an illusion. Professor May listed institutions which were preparing men for the ministry. If the present study had used this definition a large number of Bible colleges and Bible institutes would have been included and the number of schools would therefore be far greater than 178 or 180. The number 180 in 1955 is comparable with the number 161 in 1924 since our definition of a theological school approximates that of Dr. Kelly; it is hardly comparable with the 224 of 1934.

More significant than the number of schools called seminaries by their constituencies or themselves is the number of those carrying on theological education at the graduate level. Among 131 seminaries in the United States in 1923, Dr. Kelly found there were only sixty that sought to work specifically as graduate schools; six others required some college work for admission; fourteen required only high school graduation or its equivalent while fifteen appeared "to adhere to no definite scholastic standards for admission." [9] Moreover, the tabulation of the information he received from the schools revealed that only five out of the sixty—or the 131—actually admitted only college graduates and only twenty-eight were able to list 75 per cent or more of their students as holding college degrees.[10] A decade later Professor May found the situation somewhat improved but not radically so.[11] In the present study only schools which were known or were reputed to offer graduate work were included. Some of them, to be sure, were found not to require college graduation for entrance while others are evidently very lenient in their enforcement of this standard of admission. Nevertheless, out of 178 schools, 134 reported on this point with sufficient accuracy to enable us to summarize their returns. The result is presented in the table on page 8.

As the table indicates there were in 1955 at least 119 schools with 75 per cent or more of college graduate enrollment while Dr. Kelly could count only twenty-eight in this group. More significant may be the fact that forty-five of these 119 schools (compared with five in the Kelly report) indicated that all their students were college graduates, while another fifty-eight reported that 90 per cent or more of their enrollment fell in this classification.

The enrollment statistics of schools need also to be taken into consideration. The 134 reporting schools of 1955 account for about nine-tenths of the total Protestant theological registration. A third of their students (or

problems arising from the federation of four schools at the University of Chicago are not quite comparable; these are counted as four schools.

[9] Kelly, *op. cit.*, 29–30.

[10] *Ibid.*, 412–15.

[11] *American Ministers*, Vol. III. 15, 64 ff.

Pretheological Education of Students in 134 Seminaries
1954–55

Percentage of school enrollment consisting of college graduates	Number of schools reporting	Enrollment of these schools	Percentage of reporting schools	Percentage of reported enrollment
100%	45	7,543	33.5	34.8
90–99%	58	10,966	43.3	50.6
75–89%	16	1,095	12	5
Below 75%	15	2,068	11.2	9.6
Totals	134	21,672	100	100

The 134 reporting schools may be arranged in the following groups:

College Graduate Enrollment

	100%	90–99%	75–89%	Below 75%	Totals
A.A.T.S. members *	30	38	5	2	75
Enrollment	6,159	9,550	416	923	
A.A.T.S. associates	7	10	7	5	29
Enrollment	1,045	828	453	483	
Other schools	8	10	4	8	30
Enrollment	339	588	226	662	

* Those schools accredited by the American Association of Theological Schools.

30 per cent of total Protestant enrollment) were in the forty-five schools reporting only college graduates. More than 86 per cent of all reported students or 74 per cent of the total estimated number of Protestant theological students in the United States and Canada were in the 103 seminaries that had 90 to 100 per cent college graduate enrollment. The twenty-eight schools that reported 75 per cent or more college graduates in 1922–23 had a total enrollment of 2,515, 28 per cent of the 9,000 theological students estimated to be in all the schools at that time; our 119 comparable schools have 19,604 students, which is 78 per cent of the estimated total.

In general it appears that there were four times as many genuinely graduate schools of theology in the United States and Canada in 1955 as there were in 1923 and that such schools enroll almost eight times as many students as they did thirty-two years previously. Most of this increase in graduate work in theology has taken place since the time of the publication of the May-Brown report. The evidence is that not less than 80 per cent of the estimated total enrollment of theological students in the United States and Canada consists of college graduates.

This proportion is to be compared with the 1924 estimate that 44 per cent of seminary students had college degrees,[12] and with Professor May's statement that "for the country as a whole it is safe to say that in 1930 about half (plus or minus five per cent) of all theological students did not hold college degrees." [13]

It is to be noted that in these respects there are differences between the schools in Canada and those of the United States. Of the forty-five schools reporting that 100 per cent of their students are college graduates only one is located in Canada. Of the twenty-seven Canadian seminaries only three report that 90 per cent or more of their students are college graduates while eight indicate that less than 75 per cent of their enrollments can be so classified. The shortage of ministers in Canada poses so great a problem that variations of this sort are explicable. Moreover there are marked differences between the religious and educational traditions of the two nations.

In order that this development of graduate education in theology may be set in some perspective it must be remembered that in the United States as a whole the development of graduate schools since 1920 has been phenomenal. The general development of interest in professional education in the New World is perhaps the most important reason for the growth of graduate work in theology. Other factors, however, must not be underestimated. Among these the effect of the May-Brown study and the development of the American Association of Theological Schools during the period under consideration with the inauguration of its program of accreditation are doubtless of great importance. Another significant factor has been the increased interest of certain denominations in theological education. Among the 178 schools dealt with in the present study there are twenty-seven that were not listed in the 1934 survey. Five of these schools had indeed been founded in the 1920's but were not recognized in 1934 as theological seminaries. Of the remaining twenty-two, four were established in the 1930's, twelve in the 1940's and six have opened their doors since 1950. Nine of these twenty-seven new seminaries carry the name "Baptist" in their titles while at least six others are supported by groups that in the past looked somewhat askance at the theological education of the ministry. Those denominations which have had a long historical interest in theological education have founded only three of the twenty-seven new schools.

III. *The Students*

A. *Enrollment.* The increase in enrollment of theological schools in recent decades, though less remarkable than their progress toward graduate status, has also been considerable. The United States Office of Education (successor to the Bureau of Education) reported in the fall of 1954 that 114 "separately organized theological schools in the continental United States and outlying parts" had a total enrollment of

---

[12] Kelly, *op. cit.*, 164.
[13] *American Ministers*, III, 325.

28,760 students. This number, presumably, is to be compared with the 109 institutions that reported to the Bureau of Education an enrollment of 8,216 in 1919–20, and with the 164 schools of 1929–30 reporting 13,074 students. The government list includes Roman Catholic and Jewish schools but excludes those seminaries or divinity schools which are parts of universities. Available statistics, however, indicate that the increase of enrollment in the Protestant theological seminaries of all types in the United States and Canada is on the whole comparable to that recorded by the government offices.[14]

Dr. Kelly reported that the 161 theological seminaries in the United States and Canada enrolled 10,750 students in 1922–23. Professors Brown and May dealing with 224 Protestant seminaries in both nations estimated that their students approximated 10,000 in number in 1930.[15] In the present study 178 seminaries were requested to send reports on enrollment. The 144 that responded reported a total enrollment in 1954–55 of 23,595 students. Available statistical data for nineteen of the nonreporting schools indicated that they had an enrollment of 1,177 students. Hence 163 theological schools in 1954–55 enrolled some 24,772 students. Even though the fifteen seminaries for which no data were available may be very small it still seems likely that not less than 25,000 students were enrolled in Protestant theological seminaries in 1954–55. Insofar as these numbers are comparable with those furnished by the Kelly study and with those of Professor May's inquiry it appears that the number of Protestant theological students in the United States and Canada is two and a half times larger in 1955 than it was twenty and thirty years earlier.

The upward trend in theological enrollment indicated in these rough comparisons comes to appearance also in the statistics of those "typical" seminaries that supplied the present Study with reports on their development from 1935 to 1955. Thirty-two of these schools gave relatively complete information on their enrollment. A compilation of their returns yields the following results:

Enrollment Increase in Thirty-two Seminaries
1934–35 to 1954–55

	1934–35	1939–40	1944–45	1949–50	1954–55
Total enrollment	3,884	4,428	5,544	7,347	9,776
Per cent of increase		14	25	32	33
Per cent increase over '34–35		14	42.7	89	151

[14] Cf. *Biennial Survey of Education*, 1928–30, Vol. II, 321, 324, 328–29. Schedules for 1954 were supplied by the Office of Education. Cf. also *Biennial Survey*, 1934–36, Vol. I, ch. III, 66–68.

[15] Kelly, *op. cit.*, 172.
American Ministers, Vol. I, 85; cf. Vol. IV, Appendix to Vol. III, 139–40.

That increase in enrollment has been greatest since the end of the second World War while it was relatively modest during the 1930's as well as the 1920's is indicated also by other evidence. In order that such figures may be seen in the right perspective, it is to be remembered that student enrollment in higher education in the United States alone increased from 600,000 in 1919–20 to 2,300,000 in 1951–52, and that graduate school enrollment during the same period increased from 10,000 to 172,000.

While the increase in theological enrollment has not kept up with the increases in graduate school or college enrollment, nevertheless it has exceeded the rate of growth recorded in Protestant church membership which advanced from 31,500,000 in 1926 to 57,000,000 in 1953. The ratio of theological student enrollment to Protestant church membership indicates that the increase has been real. In 1924 Dr. Kelly estimated that for every 2,600 church members one person was preparing for the ministry.[16] If we take into view that the Protestant churches in the United States reported some 57,000,000 members in 1954 and that there were about 24,000 students in their seminaries, the present proportion is one theological student in a graduate school of theology per 2,375 church members. More significant may be the fact that the average size of local churches has increased greatly in recent decades so that the ratio of theological student enrollment to the number of organized Protestant churches shows great improvement since 1930.[17] The rate of increase in enrollment varies greatly in the different sectors of North American Protestantism. Thirty Canadian seminaries listed in Dr. Kelly's report had an enrollment of approximately 1,000 students in 1922–23.[18] Data available for 1954–55 indicate that not much more than 1,000 students were enrolled in that year in the twenty-seven Canadian schools. Twenty-three schools in Canada reported a total enrollment of 938 students; since the four schools for which no data were available are small the Canadian total is not likely greatly to exceed 1,000. The ninth census of Canada reported that some 7,300,000 persons belonged to Protestant groups, but it is probably not fair to compute that in Canada only one theological student is in residence for every 7,300 Protestant church members. Data gathered from such various sources are not comparable. Yet many reports make it evident that in view of their responsibilities and opportunities the Canadian churches are facing a great shortage of ministers and theological students. In the case of both countries, it is to be remembered, the number of students in theological schools is far smaller than the number of men and women who are preparing for the ministry. Several large denominations prepare young people for the ministry in Bible institutes and Bible colleges only. In other instances only graduation from a liberal arts college is necessary as academic preparation for entrance on the profession.

Other differences in rate of growth appear when denominations are compared with each other. The Southern Baptist Convention has probably increased its graduate seminary enrollment more rapidly during the

16 Kelly, *op. cit.*, 172.
17 Cf. *Yearbook of American Churches* for 1956, 267–68.
18 Kelly, *op. cit.*, 410–11, 414–15.

last decades than any other denomination, partly no doubt because it is a
rapidly growing body, but mostly because the theological education of its
ministers has only recently become a widely accepted requirement or expectation in its churches. The schools of the Presbyterian Church in the
United States of America, a denomination with a long tradition of theological education, probably represent a more normal or average pattern
of growth. From a total enrollment of 659 in 1920 they advanced to 850
in 1925 and 868 in 1930, dropped back to 775 in 1935 and to 699 in
1940; in 1945 they enrolled 796 students, in 1950, 1,067 and in 1954,
1,398.[19] In view of the wide variations that obtain among the denominations in their rates of growth and their concern for the theological education of their ministers the over-all averages cannot be applied to any
individual system of schools. Variations are encountered within the denominations and within the group of interdenominational schools. In
general the strong schools have increased most rapidly, even when policies
of limitation of enrollment regulated their growth. The small schools have
profited somewhat from the general increase of enrollment but not proportionately.

Three other questions about the enrollment tendencies are frequently
raised: to what extent are women ministers being prepared in theological
schools? Is the theological education of Negro ministers keeping pace
with the general movement? What new provisions are the seminaries
needing to make for married students?

Since the end of the first World War and particularly since the end of
the second, a strong demand has arisen in the churches for trained women
workers especially in religious education. In a number of denominations
movements toward the ordination of women to the ministry have been
accelerated. Despite these tendencies the enrollment of women in theological schools does not seem to have increased at a higher rate than
general enrollment. Out of thirty-two "typical" schools that reported on
enrollment trends eighteen stated that they enrolled women students in
1934–35; twenty-four listed women students in 1954–55. The total number of women enrolled in this group of schools had doubled during the
twenty years (390 to 805). In these schools the rate of increase in women
students' enrollment had lagged somewhat behind the rate of total enrollment increase. The tendency indicated is not out of line with the experience of professional schools in general.[20]

It is difficult to discover reliable data on the increase of Negro student
enrollment in theological schools. Among the 178 seminaries on the master
list, sixteen are primarily schools for Negro students; of these two are
accredited schools. The total enrollment of the sixteen schools does not
exceed 600. (Nine of the schools reported 276 students in 1954–55; the
catalogues of four others list 225 students). Twenty-nine of the "typical"

[19] Cf. *Minutes of the General Assembly of the Presbyterian Church in the
United States of America*. Fifth Series, Vol. III, 1954, Pt.I, 386. The enrollment
of a Puerto Rican seminary has been subtracted from the totals reported in the
Minutes.

[20] *Biennial Survey, 1951–52*, Ch. I, 40; cf. Ch. IV, Pt. I, 36.

schools reported on the number of Negro students enrolled during the period 1935 to 1955. (Several schools in the special list did not report on this item because they keep no records of the "race" of their students. In the case of one school that recently dropped the practice of keeping such records an estimate of the number of Negro students in 1954–55 was used in the table.) Their figures yield the following table:

			Negro Students Enrolled in Twenty-nine Seminaries		
			1935–55		
	1934–35	1939–40	1944–45	1949–50	1954–55
Enrollment in 3 Negro schools	109	109	106	110	95
Negro enrollment in other schools	18(7)*	43(12)	65(14)	83(14)	122(19)
Total Enrollment	127	152	171	193	217

* Figures in parentheses indicate the number of schools enrolling Negro students during the specified year.

Insofar as these schools are really typical one can conclude that the number of Negro theological students has not increased at the same rate as the number of theological students in general. *In principle* few seminaries, even in the South, follow a segregation policy; actually the number of Negroes in the integrated schools is very small.[21]

A special feature of recent trends in the theological enrollment is the marked increase of the number of married students. This trend, of course, is by no means unique to seminaries since all other professional schools, not to speak of colleges, must make their adjustments to the lower age of marriage on the part of American youth. Yet it is clear that the semi-monastic character of theological schools prevalent in some places in years past has vanished. Statistics from the schools which reported on trends in enrollment indicate that while in 1934–35 15 per cent of their students were married the percentage had risen to thirty-six by 1954–55. In any typical seminary in the United States in the 1950's from 30 to 60 per cent of the students are married, though in some instances the percentage drops as low as eighteen and in others rises as high as eighty. What this tendency has meant for the schools in pressures to provide new types of housing will be pointed out later when the financing of theological education is discussed.

B. *Recruitment and Selection of Students.* No radical changes have taken place during the last twenty or thirty years in the recruitment practices of the schools and the denominations. Insofar as increased enrollments are due to recruitment programs it is the intensification and organization of such programs in several denominations that may be held accountable. The extension of recruitment activity into state

21 See below, Appendix on the Theological Education of Negro Ministers.

and municipal universities together with the development of student Christian work on such campuses may be the most significant change that has occurred. One denomination reports that it can trace the increase in its theological student body almost wholly to these sources; it is receiving as many applications for admission to seminaries from denominational colleges as it has in the past, but not many more; it has doubled its theological enrollment because of the influx of students from schools not church related.

Greater emphasis is being placed in several quarters on selective recruiting. In this connection the inauguration of the Rockefeller Brothers Theological Fellowship Program may become important. Under the general direction of the American Association of Theological Schools "this program is designed for those who are not already committed to the Christian ministry. It is intended for students who are uncertain in regard to their vocation, young persons preparing for careers in other fields, and recent graduates presently in other occupations or in the military services, who are interested in giving serious consideration to the possibility of entering the ministry. It is not a general theological fellowship program, but one designed for a particular purpose, namely to discover and develop new talent for the Christian ministry." The program which provides one-year fellowships to some fifty students, was instituted in 1954; some years must elapse before its effectiveness can be evaluated.

Concern for high quality in the student bodies rather than increase of numbers marks the activities of a growing number of denominations and schools. Few indeed follow Gideon's principles and strategy, but many are concerned to maintain somewhat high standards in the schools and in the ministry. The problems arising from selection policies must be dealt with below. Here it is sufficient to chronicle a few recent developments. In a number of denominations closer bonds have been fashioned or old bonds have been strengthened between schools and such church bodies as presbyteries, associations and dioceses. These church bodies are occasionally taking very seriously their duties in accepting young men and women as candidates for the ministry and in recommending them to the schools. Several denominations, notably the Presbyterian Church in the United States of America, the United Lutheran Church, and the Protestant Episcopal Church, are developing testing and interview procedures designed to enable church authorities and schools to advise applicants for admission to theological study and ministry more wisely for their own and the Church's good. Admission applications in most schools are now being more carefully examined by faculty committees than was customary in the past, though there remain many institutions in which the judgment of a single, very busy man is deemed sufficient. A very considerable number of schools are now requiring their students to take special tests of academic achievement, personality traits, vocational interest, emotional stability, intelligence, et cetera. In a study made by Rev. Elmer G. Million of the National Council of Churches in 1954 it was found that almost half of the seminaries affiliated with the American Association of Theological Schools were using such tests. Of the thirty-six typical seminaries especially studied in the present survey all but eight reported the use of psychological or achievement tests, though in three instances they were administered by a denominational agency or university rather than directly. In two-thirds of the institutions the tests had been introduced since the end of the second World War; most of the seminaries emphasized the experimental nature of their use and their relevance to the counseling rather than the admission of students. Only four of the schools use them somewhat in deciding on applications for admission. In general these schools lack sufficient or adequately trained staff members to make fruitful use of tests either in counseling or admissions procedures.

IV.   *The Theological Faculties*

A. *Number of Teachers and Student-Faculty Ratios.* Has the increase in the number of schools requiring college graduation for admission been accompanied by corollary advances in methods of instruction, in the number and in the training of the teachers in these schools? Several sets of data are available from which one may venture to extract a partial answer to this question.

Out of the 178 schools of the 1955 list, 142 with an enrollment of 23,486 students reported 1,384 full-time and 536 part-time faculty members. Thus the average school had 165 students, between nine and ten full-time, three and four part-time faculty members. The ratio of students to full-time faculty members was 17 to 1, to all teachers 12.2 to 1. The ratios may be compared with those of 1929–30, which were 12.9 to 1 and 9 to 1, sixty seminaries being considered in that calculation.[22] The range in 1954–55 was much greater than in the earlier year. The seminary with the largest enrollment in 1955 (it is an accredited school) had a ratio of sixty-one students to each full-time teacher, while a ratio 7 to 1 was not uncommon among schools with small enrollments.

Information from thirty-three schools that gave a detailed statement of trends in their development from 1935 to 1955 supports these findings and adds some additional insight. These seminaries reported in 1934–35 they had employed 357 full-time faculty members and enrolled 4,984 students; in 1954–55 their 474 full-time faculty members supervised the studies of 10,758 men and women. The number of students per faculty member had increased in the twenty years from 14 to 22.7. If part-time faculty members are counted the ratio had increased from 10.5 to 1 to 15.7 to 1. These

[22] *American Ministers,* III, 110–11.

crude averages do not tell the whole story for it is made clear by the information that a larger proportion of the full-time faculty is now charged with administrative work than was the case twenty years earlier. The proportion of the full-time faculty members in these schools who are engaged wholly or partly in administrative work rose from 22 to 31 per cent, while the ratio of students to those faculty members who give all their time to teaching increased from 18 to 1 to 25 to 1. It seems that the schools have maintained administrative staffs proportionate to the number of students enrolled but have not employed commensurate teaching staffs.

B. *Age and Rank.* The teachers in the theological schools in 1955 were slightly younger on the average than they were at the time of the May-Brown study.Although the average age has dropped by only one year (from fifty-two to fifty-one) only 22 per cent of those who have attained full professorial rank are now above sixty while 30.5 per cent were in the same category in 1929–30.[23] At the same time a smaller percentage of men under forty now have professorial rank. Retirement rules and provisions on the one hand, the adoption by seminaries of university patterns of ranking and promoting faculty members seem to account for these differences. A larger proportion of teachers is classified in associate and assistant professorial ranking (28 per cent of the total faculties) than in 1929–30 (14.4 per cent). The average age of the members of this group is forty. The age range of the faculties as a whole runs from twenty-four to seventy-four years, and the median age is forty-seven.

C. *Preparation: Academic.* Insofar as earned academic degrees are an index of the preparation of teachers for their task the contemporary seminary professor seems somewhat better equipped than was his immediate predecessor. A comparison of Professor May's analysis of the records of 366 teachers in 1929–30 with our examination of the records of 471 theological faculty members in 1954–55 yields the following results:

Percentage of Theological Teachers Holding Various Earned Degrees
1929–30 to 1954–55

	1929–30	1954–55
Collegiate Bachelor (A.B., B.S.)	89.1%	87.7%
Divinity Bachelor (B.D., S.T.B.)	62.6	69.2
Collegiate Master (M.A., M.S.)	56.6	42.2
Collegiate Doctor (Ph.D.)	33.3	46.3
Divinity Doctor (S.T.D., Th.D.)	6.8	18.9
Divinity Master (S.T.M., Th.M.)	6.3	24.4[24]

Some apparent discrepancies in the table are doubtless due to differences in the methods of sampling used in the two studies. Many of the

[23] *American Ministers,* III, 90, 94; IV, Appendix to Vol. III, 143.
[24] *American Ministers,* III, 97.

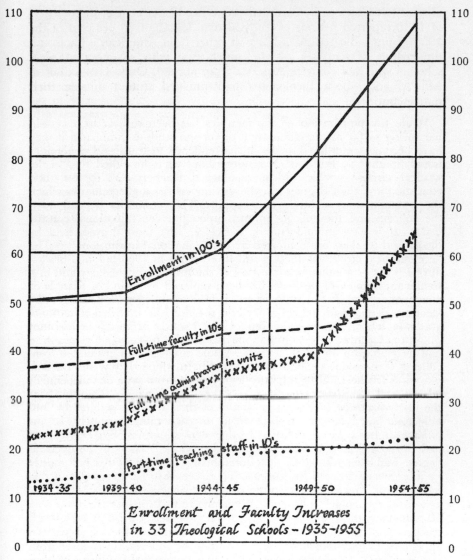

Enrollment and Faculty Increases in 33 Theological Schools - 1935-1955

men on the 1955 list who have no collegiate bachelor's degrees are teachers in the schools of a few denominations which until recently followed certain European patterns in the development of their colleges and seminaries. Such schools granted no degrees. In any event the comparison makes clear that a considerably higher proportion of theological teachers now have earned the highest academic degree, the doctorate, than was the case in the earlier period.

It must be noted at the same time that opportunities for study abroad have been sadly curtailed. Whereas 42 per cent of the teachers of 1930 reported periods of study abroad less than 20 per cent of the 1955 group indicated attendance at other than American schools and universities. Twenty-six of the ninety-two who so reported were scholars who had come to America from abroad. Only sixty-six out of 445 American-born theologians had pursued studies outside their native continent.

While the preparation of the faculties has been subject to a certain narrowing so far as the elimination of foreign study is concerned it may have become somewhat broader in its tendency to transcend denominational limitations. Professor May, describing what he called the "ecclesiastical circle," wrote: "Most theological teachers . . . receive their education and their degrees in colleges, universities and seminaries which the denominations maintain and support. The seminaries depend upon the colleges and the colleges in turn upon the denominational constituency. It is easy to understand, therefore, why most degrees held by theological teachers are conferred by denominational institutions." [25] The "ecclesiastical circle" of 1930 is still in evidence in 1955 but it is broken at one point or another by almost all of the teachers of theology and in a significant number of instances has been replaced by a kind of triangle of which one point is the state or municipal or independent college, the second a denominational seminary and the third an interdenominational graduate school. An examination of the records of thirty-six assistant professors teaching in denominational seminaries revealed only four who had never broken out of their circle. While nineteen had graduated from colleges of the same denominational family in which they were now employed as teachers, thirteen had college degrees from state or independent schools and four from colleges of another denomination. Two-thirds of the thirty-six to be sure were graduates of their church's seminaries, and only four had received the B.D. from interdenominational schools, another four from the seminaries of other denominations. But twenty-four had pursued graduate studies outside the "circle." Half of the doctoral degrees had been granted by denominational schools, the other half mostly by interdenominational institutions. There seems to be no significant difference in this respect between the younger teachers—the assistant professors—and their older colleagues. When the records of forty-six professors of systematic theology, philosophy of religion and Christian ethics—all teachers in denominational schools—were examined the same pattern appeared. Twenty-four had graduated from the colleges, thirty-three from the seminaries of their denomination or denominational family and fifteen had earned the doctor's degrees in such institutions. But twenty-one were graduates of colleges of other denominations or of independent and state schools, and twenty-four had earned the doctorate outside the denominational circle—for the most part (sixteen) in interdenominational schools. So it appears that while a large proportion—approximately two-thirds—of the teachers in denominational seminaries have done their B.D. work

25 *Ibid.*, 99.

under denominational auspices, not much more than half prepared for it in denominational colleges, and less than half continued their graduate work within the same confines. A rough computation gives reason to believe that on the average teachers of theology have spent about nine years in study since leaving high school and of these nine have given four to work outside the "ecclesiastical circle."

D. *Preparation: Professional.* The members of the faculties in theological schools, as in the case of all professional schools, are members of two professions and continue for the most part to function as such. Of 461 whose records were examined in 1955, 88 per cent were ordained clergymen and 77 per cent had had some experience in the parish ministry. Almost two-fifths of the number had served churches for eight or more years. Their teaching experience was also considerable. Two-fifths had taught in colleges for periods ranging from one to thirty years. About three-fourths had taught in seminaries four years or more.

Reliable comparisons with the faculties of 1930 are difficult but there are many indications that theological education is regarded now as more of a profession for which men and women must prepare especially and that while some parish experience is thought to be desirable for most teachers, the pastoral office as such is not regarded as supplying the background most faculty members need; the practical fields, and, in part, administrative positions being exceptions.

The analysis of four groups of faculty members of the 1955 list indicated the following situation so far as general preparation was concerned:

	Presidents and Deans	New Testament Professors	Theology Professors	Practical Theology Professors
Number	30	37	54	49
Number with earned doctorates	15	27	42	21
Number with previous teaching experience *	23	22	40	23
Average years previous teaching †	13	8	9	6
Number with pastoral experience	27	25	44	49
Average years pastoral experience	14.5	8	9	14.5
Foreign study	3	11	23	3

* Only teaching experience prior to employment in present school was considered.

† The averages were computed not for the whole group but only for those reporting such experience.

Such indices do not reflect the varieties of experience in professional work represented in the theological faculties. A significant number of men have served in the military and hospital chaplaincies, in executive positions in church work; a few have been public school teachers. The administrative officers could be divided into three almost equal groups: those who had been chosen from the professors in the school they were now supervising; those who had come directly out of the pastorate; and those who had been called from some other denominational executive position, usually a college presidency.

E. *Summary.* The general situation seems to be that theological teachers in 1955 are on the whole better prepared for their work than they were in 1930, that more is required of them: in the number of students to be instructed per teacher, in amount of administrative work to be done, and in the quality of the work expected. There are exceptions. A school-by-school analysis would doubtless show a significant number of instances where none of these advances has been made; where, indeed, so far as the intellectual climate of the institution is concerned, there has been retrogression. There is little room for complacency about the faculty situation; but there has been some progress. So far as *effectiveness* in teaching is the question there may have been retrogression. That retrogression is due to five factors: the increased student load per teacher; the increase of administrative duties of a large number of the teachers; the difficulties offered by the curricular dilemmas; the demands made on the theological faculties by increasingly active denominations, local churches, and other agencies; and, connected with all these, the financial difficulties under which the schools labor, difficulties that are sharply reflected in faculty salaries, stipends for students preparing for theological education, and in the temptations of professors to supplement income by activities outside the schools.

V. *What Has Happened to the Course of Study*

In 1934 it seemed to Professor May that four important changes had taken place in the theological curriculum during the previous generation. Subject matter had been greatly enlarged, partly by the subdivision of traditional studies, partly by the introduction of new courses; the elective system had been generally adopted; provision was being made for a differentiated ministry; changes in educational theory had emphasized the importance of "learning by doing" and so led to the development of field work programs.[26] Of these four changes only the first and last seem characteristic of the movement from 1934 to 1954. The development of the elective system has been stopped and in part reversed, in theological as in general education. The provisions

26 *American Ministers,* III, 35–36.

made for a differentiated ministry in the 1920's continue in force in those schools which then accepted the plan but have not been imitated widely.

Impressions gained from many sources and the analysis of information supplied by the seminaries indicate that five main tendencies characterize recent changes in the course of study: 1) the tendency to re-establish or maintain, to integrate and to relate to contemporary life the traditionally basic theological studies; 2) the trend toward the introduction of nontheological disciplines which seem necessary both for the interpretation of theology and as background for the practical disciplines; 3) the response of the seminaries to changes in emphasis in pastoral work by the introduction of new disciplines in practical theology; 4) an accelerated movement toward the increase of "learning by doing" and of the participation of the schools in the work of the churches; 5) the tendency consequent on the previous movements to develop prescribed curricula consisting of many introductory courses.

1) Emphasis on the importance of the traditional disciplines of theological study in the biblical, church-historical and systematic fields has been reinforced after a period in which their values were frequently questioned. Religious and theological movements in churches and schools, the interests of students and alumni, the concern for "professional" understanding of principles versus the interest in purely vocational skills, have led in this direction. The desire to correlate these studies with each other more effectively has resulted in efforts in a number of schools to develop "core courses." The interest in relevant interpretation of Bible and doctrine and in relating theological understanding to contemporary culture has encouraged the development of studies in Christian ethics, the history of doctrine, the philosophy of religion and the "theology of culture." Thus biblical, church-historical and theological studies have been re-established or re-emphasized as the stable but not static basis of theological education.

2) In many schools nontheological subjects, particularly psychology, but also the history of philosophy and sociology, have been added to the curriculum. In part this movement seems to reflect the concern that theology be studied in a large context and in continuous dialogue with the ideas that most affect contemporary secular thought; in part it is due to the need to supply background knowledge for practical studies in pastoral work and social ethics; in part it has been made necessary by the entrance into the seminaries of many students who, despite college graduation, are poorly prepared in those humanistic disciplines and social sciences that are most germane to theological study.

3) The life of the churches in recent decades has been marked by heightened interest in the priestly character of their mission, as wor-

shiping, confessing, and interceding communities, by growing concern for their pastoral work to individuals, by the increasingly rapid change of an institution responsible for preaching the gospel to the highly organized educational and eleemosynary as well as priestly society, and by the development of interdenominationalism. These and corollary changes have been reflected in the demands made on the practical theology departments for more adequate preparation of students for the conduct of worship, the administration of the church, Christian education, and ecumenical activity. Hence new courses in practical theology have been added or older courses augmented and reconstructed.

4) The requirement that academic work in classroom and library be accompanied by active participation in church work has been increasingly accepted during the past twenty years. A majority of the schools now require their students to do "field work" on weekends during the school year, during the summer months, and, occasionally, during an "internship" year. To an increasing extent, though still inadequately, schools are employing faculty members whose chief responsibility is supervision of this field work. Some few denominational boards also have begun to take seriously their responsibilities for the education of the students they employ in summer vacation periods. Two organizations, The Council for Clinical Training and the Institute of Pastoral Care (the former founded in the late 1920's, the latter in 1944), supplement the work of the seminaries by providing for students and clergymen programs of in-service training in mental and general hospitals. This whole movement—the development of field work, internship, and clinical training—during the last twenty or thiry years has been so rapid that its organization and direction remain somewhat in arrear.

5) The combination of pressures resulting from these various movements have had the consequence that the typical theological curriculum now consists mostly of required courses, that most of these courses are of an introductory nature and that time for independent and advanced study has been curtailed. By 1955 the problem of the curriculum had become very acute in many schools and many reorganizations were being contemplated, among them in particular the addition of a fourth year either of academic study or of "internship" in a church.

Some of these movements and their consequences can be quantitatively illustrated, as in the table on pages 24 and 25. It is based on the reports made by twenty-five of the "typical" schools. Since three schools that offered highly diversified programs of study could not be included, the computation is somewhat weighted in favor of seminaries adhering more closely to traditional patterns.

VI. *Denominationalism and Interdenominationalism in Theological Education*

Contradictory movements toward union and toward division have marked the history of American Protestantism almost from its beginnings and have deeply affected its educational institutions. These movements have continued during the recent period covered by this report. The history of theological education since the end of the first World War shows the effects of both tendencies. New seminaries have been founded as new denominations or ecclesiastical parties have been organized by evangelistic groups or protesters against dominant ideas in older denominations or by dissenters from church unions. The merging of denominations (as in the cases of the United Lutheran Church, the United Church of Canada, the American Lutheran Church, the Congregational Christian, the Evangelical and Reformed, the Methodist and the Evangelical United Brethren Churches) have usually resulted in the union of seminaries. If number of schools only is considered then the tendency toward division seems to have been stronger than the tendency toward union.

It is not apparent from available data that the established schools have become significantly more interdenominational in recent decades in the composition of their faculties and student bodies. Out of thirty-five "typical" schools reporting on this item eighteen stated that all of their faculty members belonged to the denomination administering the institution; three additional schools, each of them supported by two co-operating denominations, also had no faculty members belonging to other denominations; in eight more the faculties were at least 80 per cent denominational. Only six out of the thirty-five had recognizably interdenominational corps of teachers, and only one of these six was affiliated with a denomination. Four out of thirty-two schools reported a 100 per cent denominational student enrollment in 1954–55; twenty others recorded student registrations that were from 80 to 99 per cent denominational; of the remaining eight schools three were nondenominational university schools. The records of the individual schools over the course of twenty years indicate a modest movement toward more interdenominational student bodies, though a few seminaries (four out of thirty-two) were more denominational in the composition of their student bodies in 1955 than they had been in 1935. Measured by the standard of the church affiliation of students the Episcopal schools in the group were the most consistently denominational. They were followed closely by the Lutheran seminaries, and those of the Southern Baptist Convention. The four denominational schools with the most diversified student bodies were Methodist, Congregationalist, Disciple, and Presbyterian, U.S.A. Other seminaries, however, representing the same national organizations, with the

The Required Theological Curriculum in 25 Schools 1935–1955

Subject	No. Schools Requiring		Requirements in Percentage Points of Total Units Required for Graduation			
			Median		Low	High
	1934–35	1954–55	1934–35	1954–55	1954–55	1954–55
Old Testament	25	25	10.1	8.8	3.6	14.8
New Testament	25	25	11.0	10.4	3.6	20.4
Church History	24	25	10.0	9.4	3.6	13.7
Systematic Theology	25	25	8.4	6.6	3.2	14.6
Preaching	25	25	8.1	6.2	3.1	13.2
Group totals	—		47.6	41.4	17.1	76.7
Christian Education	19	23	6.0	5.6	3.1	9.9
Church Administration	21	23	4.0	3.3	1.9	16.0
Field Work *	2	21		2.8	2.1	4.8
Group totals	—		10.0	11.7	7.1	30.7
Christian Ethics	9	17	3.0	3.3	1.9	5.6
Missions	16	17	4.0	3.1	2.0	7.7
Conduct of Worship	13	17	2.2	2.8	1.0	5.1
Philosophy of Religion	15	16	3.9	3.3	1.9	6.4
Group totals	—		13.1	12.5	6.8	24.8

Psychology	7	14	3.3	3.8	1.0	5.6
Greek	11	12	8.1	7.3	4.1	14.3
Pastoral Theology	4	10	4.3	3.2	1.5	6.0
History of Doctrine	5	9	2.2	3.2	1.9	4.1
Social Ethics	7	9	3.6	3.2	1.9	9.4
Hebrew	9	8	8.3	6.1	4.4	8.5
Music	4	8	2.0	2.0	1.1	4.2
History of Religion	8	7	3.3	2.8	1.9	3.6
Group totals	—	—	35.1	31.6	17.8	55.7
Speech	4	6	3.0	2.1	1.9	6.6
Evangelism	2	5	5.9	3.4	2.1	4.5
Sociology	5	3	4.0	3.6	2.2	5.6
Group totals	—	—	12.9	9.1	6.2	16.7
Electives	18	24	24.2	20.1	2.1	40.6
Grand Total	—	—	142.9	126.4	57.1	245.2

25

* Field Work is now required in 21 schools but only four give academic credit.

exception of Congregationalism, had highly homogeneous denominational student bodies. Denominationalism and interdenominationalism in theological seminaries depend in part it seems on the ethos of the national organization, but in part on the spirit of the school itself or of the region in which it works.

The nondenominational divinity schools, a varied group, have enjoyed consistent growth during the period since 1920 but at no accelerated rate when compared with the denominational seminaries. Now, as then, their enrollments account for about 15 per cent of the total theological student registration. The university schools that form a significant part of the interdenominational group have come to play an increasingly significant role in providing specialized graduate education of doctoral grade for teachers in seminaries and colleges but they have in general been concerned to maintain strong B.D. curricula and enrollments. The extent to which their work in graduate or doctoral education tends to break the "ecclesiastical circle" in the training of seminary faculties has been pointed out above.

As in the churches so in the schools the unitive movement tends to take the form of co-operation more than of interpenetration and merger. The most significant co-operative venture in theological education in the recent period has been the one conducted by the American Association of Theological Schools which succeeded the more loosely organized Conference of Theological Seminaries in 1936. The Association has functioned primarily as an accrediting organization, enforcing through its membership provisions certain minimal standards. Its work as a counseling agency and as a means for promoting co-operative endeavors, always in view since its inception but hampered by lack of funds, promised to enter on a new phase in 1956 with its receipt of a sizable grant from the Sealantic Fund, Inc., founded by John D. Rockefeller, Jr., in 1953 for the promotion of theological education. Other nondenominational organizations, such as the organizations of teachers in the practical fields, of field work directors, of teachers of Christian ethics, and discussion groups of theologians have provided for mutual stimulation and exchange of information on the part of individual faculty members rather than for institutional co-operation. The formation of denominational councils of theological education or of seminary departments in boards of education has been a relatively significant feature in the recent history of theological education, but this development indicates a strengthening of denominational control and an increase of denominational self-consciousness rather than a movement toward ecumenicity and interdenominationalism.

CHAPTER TWO

Trends in the Economics of Theological Education

The financial history of the schools during the period under consideration has been mainly affected by four factors: the economic demands incident on increased enrollment and higher standards; the participation of the schools in the fluctuations of national prosperity and monetary values; their relation to the movement of economic centralization in the denominations; and the economic decline of the teaching profession in general. The influence of these and other movements comes to appearance when the reports of schools concerning their construction of buildings, expenditures, income, sources of support and salary scales are examined.

I. *Physical Plant*

The seminaries, particularly in the period from 1946 to 1954, have added many buildings to their physical equipment. Eighty-eight schools, about half of the total number and two-thirds of those that reported, stated that they had undertaken new construction or major renovation during the decade since the end of World War II spending almost fifty million dollars on these projects. Ten out of these eighty-eight had built completely new plants, usually on new sites. Of the remaining seventy-eight institutions, seventeen had built or purchased apartment houses for married students, sixteen had erected new dormitories, thirteen each libraries, classroom buildings and office quarters. Six had constructed new chapels and seven provided additional faculty houses or apartments. Many new buildings were in prospect and the need for additional accommodations was felt to be pressing in most seminaries. Of the seventy-eight accredited schools thirty-three stated that they needed additional apartments for married students; twenty needed to expand or construct libraries; twelve each complained of inadequate chapels, classroom buildings and men's dormitories; eleven needed office space, nine new or enlarged refectories. Four believed that they could not solve their problems without building complete new plants— a judgment with which outside observers were inclined to agree.

The general impression gained from reports and observation is that apart from a few sad exceptions, the theological schools with the support of the churches are making a creditable showing in supplying the physical equipment required by increased enrollment and graduate

27

status; that, however, the pressure for additional dormitories and housing for married students has taken precedence over the demand for better instructional equipment. Though interest in library improvement is conspicuous, certain defects in contemporary theological education appear in the lack in school after school of sufficient seminar rooms, and, perhaps even more, in the failure of many schools to feel pressure at this point.

II. *Current Expenditures*

In 1954–55 the Protestant seminaries of the United States and Canada expended about $26,000,000 of current funds in carrying on their work.[1] No comparable estimates for earlier periods are available but it is likely that the expenditures reported by twenty-six typical schools give some measure of the increase which has taken place since 1934–35. These schools enrolled 3,768 students in that year against 7,951 in 1954–55, an increase of 211 per cent. Their annual current expenditures in the twenty-year period mounted from $2,725,263 to $8,214,999, an increase of 301 per cent. In the same period, however, the consumer's price index doubled—from 57.2 in 1934 to 114.8 in 1954. Expenditures on parity with 1934–35, taking into account the increased enrollment, would have reached more than $11,000,000. With increase of enrollment, expenditures per student have dropped, not absolutely but in view of the increase of cost of living.

Of greater significance than changes in total current expenditures are changes in the proportions of current funds spent for the various items of the school budget. Some comparisons can be made on the basis of the analysis of thirty-seven financial statements for the year 1928–29 by the May study and of twenty similar statements for 1953–54.[2] This comparison indicates the following changes in the percentages of total expenditures devoted to certain items:

	1928–29	1953–54
Administration	3.5	15
Instruction (salaries in 1928)	44	33
Library	3.4	6
Maintenance	22.2	19
Total educational and general	83.1	73

[1] The Biennial Report of the American Association of Theological Schools reports gross expenditures of $18,537,097 in 1954–55 by seventy-eight accredited schools enrolling 17,650 students; of $3,411,679 by thirty-six associate schools with 3,568 students. Twenty-one nonaffiliated schools with 2,846 students reported total expenditures of $2,808,000. It is estimated that these 135 schools account for about 96 per cent of the total graduate theological enrollment and that the remaining forty-three schools do not spend more on the average per student than do the reporting schools.

[2] *American Ministers,* IV, Appendix to III, 227.

Student subsidies	5.7	6.6
Pensions and annuities	1.8	2.8
Auxiliary enterprises	no report	11

That large increases in the percentage of current funds expended for administrative and library purposes have been accompanied by significant decreases in the percentage of budget expended for teachers' salaries and other instructional purposes is borne out by the reports of the typical schools, though their reports are less detailed than those found in the financial statements and more subject to errors of interpretation. These twenty-six schools reported that from 1934–35 to 1954–55 the percentage of current funds spent for administration had increased from 17.3 per cent to 22 per cent, for libraries from 5.4 per cent to 7 per cent; at the same time their instructional expenditures declined from 41 to 37.6 per cent.

There are, as in all cases, very great differences among the schools. On the whole the institutions which publish detailed financial reports are strong and well-managed schools. Yet one of them spends only 18 per cent of its budget for instruction, several devote 25 per cent or less to it while in a few cases 50 per cent of the current funds are expended for teachers' salaries and minor expenses incident to instruction. In general it appears that while administrative expenses have kept pace with increases in enrollment and cost of living and while library expenditures reflect these influences and the attainment of graduate status by the schools, instructional expenditures lag behind in conspicuous fashion. While some of the difference is due to the greater efficiency of larger schools, this factor does not account for the discrepancy entirely. The difference appears in schools that have increased greatly in enrollment, in others that have made moderate gains and again in schools that have stood still so far as enrollment is concerned.

It is somewhat alarming that in theological education the percentage of expenditures devoted to educational and general purposes has declined in the recent past while the general trend in higher education has been in the opposite direction. The Office of Education of the U.S. Department of Health, Education and Welfare reported in 1955 that 77.8 per cent of the total current expenditures by institutions of higher education in 1951–52 had been for educational and general purposes. "A gradually increasing emphasis on the educational and general functions of a college or university, as contrasted with those of an auxiliary or other non-educational character, is seen in the fact that the corresponding percentages for this item in earlier years were: 1945–46, 70.3; 1947–48, 73.0; and 1949–50, 76.0." At the same time the Office reported that independent theological schools on its list spent only 68.8 per cent of their total expenditures for educational and general purposes, that an insignificant part of this portion was devoted to research, an unusually large part to administration.[3] While the government list of independent theological schools differs significantly from the one used in the present study, all analyses made by the latter of financial reports and of data furnished by "typical" schools lead to a similar conclusion: theological schools devote only 70 per cent of their total expenditures to meeting educational and general needs and of this portion they give an unusually large amount to administration, a conspicuously small amount to research.

III. *Income*

In 1928–29 theological schools as Professor May pointed out were exceptionally well endowed when compared with other educational institutions of similar size. His analysis indicated that on the whole they derived 60 per cent of their income from the yield of permanent funds, receiving the remainder from student fees, board, et cetera. (11.4 per cent), gifts (10.5), churches (3.1), denominational boards (1.0) and miscellaneous sources.[4] The situation had not changed radically by 1934–35, despite the depression. In that year, according to the reports of our "typical" schools 54 per cent of their income came from endowments, 13 per cent from payments by students, 13 per cent from gifts. However, the contributions made to these particular schools by churches (3.3 per cent) and denominational boards (8.6) were somewhat higher than the schools of 1928–29 had reported. These increases apparently indicated a trend which has carried forward to 1955. An analysis of the data furnished by 27 "typical" schools yields the following table:

Percentage of Income from Various Sources in 27 Schools

	1934–35	1954–55
From permanent investments	54	32
From students	13	18
From denominational boards	8.6	20
From gifts	13	12
From churches	3.3	3.6

The radical changes in proportions of income derived from endowments and from denominational boards are the most striking features

---

[3] *Biennial Survey of Education in the United States,* 1950–52; Ch. IV, Sec. II, 34–39.

[4] *American Ministers,* III, 481–83; IV, Appendix to III, 227.

called to attention by the table, though the increase in student payments is also significant.[5]

Income	1928–29	1953–54
From endowments	61%	34
From students	11.4	30.7
From denominational boards	1	16
From gifts	10.5	12
From churches	3.1	1.5

Averages, however, do not tell the story. Endowments on the one hand, income from denominational boards or similar sources on the other hand, are very unequally distributed among the schools. While the seventy-eight accredited schools held $127,000,000 in invested funds in 1954–55, thirty-three of them claimed more than four-fifths of that total. These thirty-three seminaries had increased their total endowments from $74,000,000 in 1944–45 to $104,000,000 in 1954–55. Their average of $3,000,000 of invested funds per school is to be compared with the average of half a million each for the remaining forty-five accredited seminaries.[6]

The schools' shares in funds provided by the denominations are unequal to the same degree. Not only do interdenominational schools fail to receive any of these appropriations but many denominational schools receive little support from national church budgets. Out of 147 seminaries that answered questionnaires more or less completely, eighty-seven reported receipts from denominational boards while in the case of twenty-six others it was quite clear that no such funds formed part of the income. The total amount reported as received from denominations was a little over five million dollars.[7] Thirteen schools, however, accounted for half of this total, forty-one for more than 80 per cent. The average receipts from denominational boards were $200,000 in the case of the thirteen schools, $100,000 in the case of the forty-one, less than $20,000 apiece for the other forty-five seminaries reporting such income.

[5] The same trends in sources of income appear when thirty-seven financial reports of 1928–29 are compared with twenty of 1953–54, though there are some important percentage differences between the financial report analysis and the "typical" school analysis.

[6] Source: Biennial Reports of the A.A.T.S. Thirty-six associate schools report endowments totaling $10,624,000 in 1954–55, averaging less than $300,000 per school.

[7] Certain ambiguities in questions and answers led to confusion in some cases regarding the amounts given by denominations and by local churches, particularly in the case of two denominations. There is reason to believe that total income from denominations is very nearly equal to total income from endowments.

It begins to be clear that in theological education, so far as support is concerned, three patterns of financing may be distinguished: there are schools depending primarily on endowment income, supplemented by fees from students and private gifts; there are the schools financed largely by appropriations from denominational budgets, and there are the mixed schools that derive their main income about equally from endowments and from denominations. Thus the seminaries offer a rough parallel to the publicly and privately financed universities and colleges of the United States.

An analysis of the reports submitted by the group of representative or typical schools revealed the presence of these three groups, though the number of institutions falling into the third category was too small to encourage any effort at generalizations. The following tables indicate the differences in the amount and percentage of income from various sources in two of the groups.

Twelve Seminaries Supported by Church Boards

Income	1934–35	Percent of Expenditure Covered	1954–55	Percent of Expenditure Covered
Endowment	170,000	27	417,000	14
Denominational boards	235,000	37	1,345,000	47
Churches	76,000	12	139,000	5
Gifts	52,000	8	162,000	3.5
Students	68,000	11	462,000	16
Enrollment	1,545		5,075	

Nine Endowed Seminaries

Income	1934–35	Percent of Expenditure Covered	1954–55	Percent of Expenditure Covered
Endowment	1,086,000	65	1,949,000	53
Denominational boards	4,000	0.2	11,000	0.3
Churches	19,000	1	201,000	5
Gifts	235,000	14	660,000	18
Students	229,000	14	693,000	19
Enrollment	1,779		2,286	

Several significant points are indicated by these tables: the more rapid increase of enrollment in the denominationally supported schools; the extent to which income from denominations keeps pace with increased demands while endowment increases fall behind such demands; the extent to which endowed schools are dependent on special gifts; the differences in cost to student between the two kinds of schools.

It must, however, also be pointed out that these nine endowed schools maintained a better student-faculty ratio (fourteen students to each full-time faculty member in 1954–55) than the denominationally supported schools (thirty-six to one). Further, several of them followed selective procedures in admission of students not characteristic of the seminaries in general.

In 1934 Professor May found that "theological seminaries as a whole, in comparison with other institutions of comparable size, are well equipped, exceptionally well endowed, and favorably situated with respect to current income." So far as equipment is concerned the same statement can be made in 1956, but how do theological schools now compare with other institutions when endowment and current income are considered? As has been noted, some are very well endowed and some receive excellent support without having much endowment. In 1955 theological schools still held first rank among the various groups of institutions in amount of endowment held per student but they had lost some ground. The government report of 1927–28 on which Professor May's judgment was based [8] showed that independent Protestant seminaries held productive funds of $6,739 per resident student while the comparable amounts for all privately controlled institutions in the country was $1,818, for all publicly controlled institutions $318. The Biennial Report of the Office of Education for 1950–52 lists theological schools as having $2,909 endowment per resident student, while privately controlled institutions of all types hold $2,040 and publicly controlled ones $455.[9] The average endowment per enrolled student among those seminaries in the United States that are members or associates of the A.A.T.S. was $6,103 in 1954–55, a drop of $600 from 1927–28.[10]

The May analysis also regarded theological schools as favorably situated with respect to current income. Their total receipts per student were found to be uniformly in excess of those of other institutions of comparable size.[11] However, there was indication that they had lost some ground since 1900. By 1955 the position of the seminaries was less favorable than it had been in 1927–28. Endowment earnings on which the seminaries depend to a considerable degree had shrunk, both with respect to percentage of yield on invested capital and on proportion of expenditures covered by such yield. While grants from denominations

[8] Cf. *American Ministers,* IV, Appendix to III, 228.
[9] *Ibid.,* Ch. IV, Sec. II, 45.
[10] The average endowment funds per student held by the eight Canadian institutions of the A.A.T.S. was $20,804.
[11] *American Ministers,* III, 482, 487.

had greatly increased, these contributions had not kept pace with the increased grants made by federal and state governments to other types of education. In 1951–52, all institutions of higher education in the United States being considered, 48.8 per cent of their educational and general income came from federal, state, and local governments (veterans' tuitions and fees not included). Even in the case of privately controlled institutions it appears that 19.7 per cent of such income was derived from these sources. In the case of the theological schools less than .05 per cent came from governments.[12] While higher education in the United States in general was being increasingly financed by public funds, the theological schools more than any other group of institutions were excluded from such benefits. (The Canadian schools were an exception since in that nation government grants are made on a per student capita basis to qualifying institutions including theological seminaries.) In the United States other types of professional education than theological received very considerable sums from federal and state sources. Out of 121 accredited law schools forty-eight are parts of publicly controlled and financed universities; [13] out of seventy-six medical schools studied in 1950–51, thirty-five were tax supported. Fifty per cent of the total income of all seventy-six schools "came from tax monies," the privately supported schools receiving a larger share of federal funds, the tax-supported schools a higher proportion of state, county, and city grants.[14] The professional education of teachers is even more heavily financed proportionately by tax monies than are medicine or law.

In view of this situation it is important to ask whether the churches, particularly in their denominational organizations, are supporting as actively the schools in which students are being prepared for the ministry, as the national community through its governmental institutions supports institutions in which workers are trained for other professions. Taking Protestant theological education as a whole, it is clear that the churches as organized denominations do not support the seminaries to the same extent that state and federal governments support other types of professional education.

There seems to have been some slight improvement in the contributions of the churches as organizations to their theological schools. Professor May reported that "theological institutions are not now receiving the same proportionate financial support from the churches" that they had received in earlier decades. He found that in the Presbyterian Church, U.S.A. the twelve seminaries had had an income of

---

[12] *Biennial Survey,* 1950–52, Ch. IV, Sec. II, 14, 16, 17.

[13] *American Universities and Colleges,* 6th ed., 1952, 99 ff.

[14] John E. Deitrick and Robert C. Berson, *Medical Schools in the United States.* 1953, 81 ff.

$26.11 for every $1000 of church expenditure in 1900 but only of $14.86 in 1926.[15] Insofar as our data are comparable it appears that the ratio in this denomination had climbed slightly by 1953 to $16.82.[16] A considerable number of denominations had begun by 1955 to make provision in their over-all budgets for grants to their theological schools. In some denominations this practice had begun with the founding of their seminaries; in many others, among them the largest, the claims of the schools had only recently been recognized. But many denominations continued to expect their schools to finance themselves.

The dependence of theological schools on the churches for financial support is further accentuated by the fact that so large a share of private giving has been channeled in recent times through foundations while these organizations, by and large, have been loath to support theological seminaries, probably because of fear that they will become involved in the rivalries among Catholics, Protestants, and Jews, and among the denominations. A few foundations make gifts to the schools of a single denomination; some to single schools. The large contribution made by John D. Rockefeller, Jr., to theological education in 1953 through the Sealantic Fund has so far accrued primarily to the benefit of the nondenominational schools, which indeed need such aid especially since they not only lack all state support but also receive no denominational aid. The wise administrators of the Fund have sought for fair ways to strengthen theological education in the denominational schools and have taken steps in this direction through the faculty-fellowship program they have inaugurated and through the aid given to the American Association of Theological Schools so that it can extend its counseling and promotional activities. Yet it remains true that the great majority of seminaries receive as little direct aid from the great foundations as from government. They remain responsibilities of the churches.

IV. *Expenditures per Student*

Two quantitative measurements derivable from financial reports are of some value in estimating trends and in making comparisons among schools or types of schools. One of these is the measurement of expenditure per student, the other is the professorial salary scale.

Expenditure per student is a very rough index of quality of performance. It is relatively high when the faculty-student ratio is favorable; it decreases as schools enroll more students without employing additional teachers. Excellent schools which follow the policy of the

---

[15] and [16] Cf. *American Ministers,* III, 486; IV, Appendix to III, 232; also *Minutes of the General Assembly of the Presbyterian Church in the United States of America,* May, 1954, Pt. I, 385 and 269; Pt. III, 493.

theological colleges of England and confine instruction to a small group of students show a high expenditure per student; on the other hand seminaries that have no such policy but are inefficiently managed, or are unattractive to students and so have small enrollments, show a similarly high per capita expenditure. Very low expenditure per student usually indicates an unfavorable faculty-student ratio or low salaries or both.

In 1954–55 the seventy-eight accredited schools of the A.A.T.S. enrolling 17,650 students reported total gross expenditures of $18,500,-000, averaging $1050 per student. The thirty-six associate schools spent an average of $956; twenty-one nonaffiliated schools averaged $987. These figures agree well with the reports of twenty-six schools, selected as a sample, who reported on the expenditures during a twenty-year period. Their reports and other information yield the following table:

Expenditures per Student in Twenty-six "Typical" Schools
1934–35 to 1954–55

	1934–35	1954–55	Percent increase
Consumers Price Index	57.2	114.8	200.7
Enrollment	3,768	7,951	211
Gross expenditures	$2,725,000	$8,215,000	301.5
Expenditure per student	$723	$1,033	142.7

Of somewhat greater significance are the expenditures for administration, instruction and libraries reported by the same group of schools.

Average expenditures per student (Twenty-six schools)*

	1934–35	1954–55	Percent increase
Administrative expenditures	$122	$218	178.7
Instructional	294	381	129.2
Library	38	76	200

* In the reports of the U.S. Office of Education educational and general expenses include, in addition to the three items listed in the above table, operation and maintenance of physical plant. If, as seems reasonable on the basis of the data submitted to the study, 17.5 per cent of gross expenditures are allowed for this item the average educational and general expenditure per student in the typical theological schools was $856 in 1954–55.

The most striking point in the comparison is the low increase in the strictly instructional budget of the schools, especially when both the advance of the seminaries to graduate status and the increased cost of living are considered. Theological schools, of course, have increased in average size during the course of twenty years, as indicated among other things by the growth of the twenty-six schools from an average enrollment of 145 to one of 306. Small schools, it is well known, are more expensive per student than larger ones. But such improvement in efficiency is scarcely an adequate explanation for the low increase in the instructional budget. The financial data serve to confirm impressions derived from other sources, namely, that the seminaries as a whole have made more advances in most other fields of their operation than they have in the central matter of improving instruction.

The range in this respect is very great indeed. In a group of thirty-four schools submitting data the instructional expenditure per student ranged from $170 to $1,345; the median was $365. Seven of these schools spent more than $500 per student for instruction only; seven less than $250. Six of the latter were accredited schools. It must also be said that among the seven schools spending above $500, four were suffering from difficulties in keeping up their enrollment and one was a school of relatively poor rank. In the low expenditure group were two of the largest schools on the continent with very high student faculty ratios. Library expenditures in the same group of schools ranged from a low of $22 per student to $222, nine schools spending more than $100 a year per student on this item. The median was $60, but six out of thirty-three schools spent less than $40 per student.

Differences between the endowed and the denominationally financed schools appeared in the comparison of the nine endowed with the twelve denominationally financed schools of the control group. The former had a range from $345 to $1,345, the latter from $217 to $620, in instructional expenditures per student. In library expenditures the range in the endowed schools was from $35 to $222 but seven of these nine schools spent above $100 per student; the range in the board financed schools extended from $27 to $140 but only one of the twelve schools spent above $100 per student for this item.

The final question we may undertake to answer in this connection is how theological schools compare with other institutions of higher education with respect to expenditure per resident student. The U.S. Office of Education in its *Biennial Survey of 1951–52* stated that theological schools and junior colleges were the least expensive institutions in the country per student enrolled when only educational and general expenditures were considered. The seminaries on its list with an average expenditure for these purposes of $589 stood in marked contrast to publicly controlled universities ($1,328) and privately controlled technological schools ($1,779); they fell far below the national average of $914 for all institutions of higher education. Even when research and extension expenses were deducted (a minute fraction in the case of the seminaries but an important item in the case of the universities and technical schools) the seminaries were still below the national average of $716.[17] These government statistics, however, are based on the reports of a group of schools significantly different from the list used in the present report. The Office of Education lists 114 independent theological schools, of which number thirty-two are institutions that we have classified as Bible colleges and institutes; nine are Roman Catholic and three Jewish seminaries. The official list does not include the theological schools administered as parts of universities. The available reports from the graduate schools of theology, with which this report is concerned, indicate that their average expenditures per student for educational and general purposes (excluding auxiliary enterprises such as operation of dining halls, dormitories, also student subsidies, research, and extension) was a little above $700 at the time when the national average of all schools of higher education was $716.[18]

V. *Professorial Salaries*

The final set of questions to which financial reports can give some answers concerns salaries of teachers in theological schools. The questions are: What salaries are being paid in theological schools? How well have they kept pace with increased cost of living and the demands for more extended preparation on the part of the teachers? How do seminary salaries compare with those paid in other institutions of higher education and with those obtaining in the professions, especially in the ministry?

Our data are derived largely from the information furnished by the "typical" schools. On the basis of their reports the average salaries paid to teachers of the various academic grades during the twenty-year period from 1934–35 to 1954–55 were as follows:

	1934–	1939–	1944–	1949–	1954–
Professor	4,185(25)*	4,160(28)	4,543(28)	5,795(31)	6,995(31)
Associate	3,790(10)	3,557(14)	3,825(13)	4,919(19)	5,911(25)
Assistant	2,864(8)	3,263(9)	3,209(10)	4,222(16)	5,185(20)
Instructor	1,681(10)	1,831(10)	1,814(10)	3,090(12)	4,162(14)

* The numbers in parentheses indicate how many of the thirty-six schools reported on the item. In the case of schools furnishing housing 20 per cent of the reported cash salary was added.

[17] Biennial Survey, 1950–52, Ch. IV, Sec. II, 34 ff.

[18] The Office of Education estimates that the theological schools reporting to it spent 68.4 per cent of their current expenditures for "educational and general" purposes in 1951. Analysis of twenty detailed financial reports of theological schools for 1953–54 shows that on the average 73 per cent of the current budget was used for these purposes. Various computations, using both the data supplied biennially by the A.A.T.S. schools and the special information given by twenty-six "typical" schools support the estimate that in 1951 the expenditure per student in Protestant graduate theological schools was above $700. As noted above the average "educational and general" expenditure in the "typical" schools seemed to be about $850.

The range of 1954–55 professors' salaries in the schools of this group extended from a low of $4,800 to a high of $9,500. The median school paid an average salary of $6,700. In a larger group of 101 schools that reported their salary scales for 1954–55 the range of individual salaries of faculty members of professorial rank extended from a minimum of $2,800 to a maximum of $15,000.

The range of salaries may best be represented by a table.

Professorial Salaries in Protestant Seminaries 1954–55

	Below $4500	$45–$4900	$50–$5400	$55–$5900	$60–$6400
A.A.T.S. members	0	3	6	8	23
Nonaccredited	3	4	4	4	6

	$65–$6900	$70–$7400	$75–$7900	$80–$8400	above $8500
A.A.T.S. members	9	6	5	8	6
Nonaccredited	1	3	1	0	1

That the salaries of theological faculty members have lagged behind the increase of the cost of living appears when the averages of the various ranks are computed in terms of 1939 dollars.

Average Salaries of Theological Teachers in 1939 Dollars
("Typical" Schools)

	1934	1939	1944	1949	1954
Consumers Price Index	57.2	59.4	75.2	101.8	114.8
Professors	4340	4160	3590	3380	3620
Associates	3930	3560	3020	2870	3060
Assistants	2970	3260	2535	2460	2680
Instructors	1745	1830	1430	1800	2100

If the increase of income and other taxes during the period were taken into account the loss of purchasing power of theological faculty salaries would appear in even more radical form.

So far as the averages of salaries are concerned theological seminaries do not compare unfavorably with other institutions of higher education. The Fund for the Advancement of Education estimated that in 1953 the salaries of faculty members in large universities (mostly state institutions) averaged $7000 for professors, $5,600 for associate professors, $4,600 for assistant professors and $3,700 for instructors.[19] The authors of the Bulletin in which these estimates were made were concerned,

[19] Beardsley Ruml and Sidney G. Tickton, *Teaching Salaries Then and Now. A 50-Year Comparison with Other Occupations and Industries.* The Fund for the Advancement of Education, 655 Madison Ave., New York 21, New York, 1955, 32.

however, to point out two things: that during the course of fifty years the teaching profession as a whole had lost economic status relative to other professions and that at the top, that is in the case of administrators and professors, not only a relative but an absolute deterioration had taken place. Since 1904 every classification of workers for which statistics were offered had increased its purchasing power, in most instances more than 100 per cent, but among educators only elementary schoolteachers and univeristy instructors had profited considerably from increase of national productivity. Principals of high schools, presidents and professors of large universities had suffered an actual loss in purchasing power of their salaries while associate and assistant professors had made only very small gains (6 and 3 per cent). Both types of deterioration—the absolute loss of purchasing power and the more general relative deterioration of economic status—were found to have been more rapid in the latter half of the fifty-year period than in the earlier twenty-five years. This period, from 1928 to 1953, is nearly identical with the one with which the present study of theological education is concerned. It has been the period in which the seminaries have been challenged to make their greatest advances in centuries, when the need for a well-educated ministry has been most widely recognized, when the requirement that teachers of theology be highly prepared professionally has been accepted. And this has also been the period when the teaching profession in the seminaries as well as elsewhere suffered a decline in compensation in terms of the purhasing power of the salaries paid.

Comparisons of seminary salaries with those obtaining in the ministry are difficult to make since available data have been gathered from too many noncomparable sources. The ministry like the teaching profession, considered as a whole, has suffered from inflation and the redistribution of national income so that it appears to have lost both purchasing power and relative economic status during the second quarter of the twentieth century. Nevertheless fully trained ministers appear to have done better than teachers in maintaining the standard of living customary to the profession.[20] Theological seminaries in general report great difficulty in securing for their practical departments the services of well-trained and experienced ministers, since the difference between the salaries the schools can offer and those which such men receive in the churches requires radical reduction of living standards. Of at least equal significance is the difference in compensation offered to B.D.

[20] Cf. "Ministers' Salaries in Three Religious Bodies, 1939–53" in *Yearbook of American Churches, Edition for 1956,* New York, 1955, 271–76; Fred S. Buschmeyer, *A Study of the Financial Support Given Ministers of the Congregational Christian Churches in the Year 1953,* pamphlet published by The General Council of Congregational Christian Churches, N. Y.

graduates who are entering parish work and to Ph.D. graduates in theology beginning a teaching career. Several seminaries report that their B.D. graduates are ordinarily placed in churches paying salaries of $3,600 and parsonage, which with a 20 per cent allowance amounts to $4,320. The young men who go on to do two or three more years of graduate work, usually incurring debts in the process, may at the end of that period expect employment in college departments of religion or in seminaries with a salary of $4,000 without free rent.

CHAPTER THREE

Problems of Government

Statistical information of the sort presented in the previous chapters cannot give an adequate picture of theological education as it is being carried on in the Protestant seminaries of the United States and Canada. The situations, achievements, and difficulties of the schools are so highly individual that generalizations, especially in numerical statements, are often irrelevant to particular institutions. The interactions in the educational process of administrators, teachers, and students, of denominations, their boards, and their schools, of universities, colleges, and seminaries, of traditional ideas, new experiences and in sights, are so complex that no statistical formulation can describe them. Hence an effort must be made to set forth the achievements and problems of theological education in America in such manner that some justice may be done to the complex dynamism of the educational process and to the individuality of the organizations and persons engaged in it. To this effort the following chapters are devoted. In them an account is to be given of the impressions made on observers by the administrations, the faculties, the students, the courses of study and the ways of teaching. Based in part on direct observation the account in larger part is derived from reports of participants in the life of the schools.

The question how to provide for good administration is of great importance to all the schools, of critical significance for many. It is, however, much less frequently the subject of close study by boards and faculties than are questions about faculties, students, and curricula, though often the key to the solution of problems in these areas lies in good administration. It is strange that this is so since the Protestant theological schools of North America operate for the most part within denominations that are greatly concerned with questions of church polity and in nations that have been preoccupied with problems of government.

I. *Patterns of Government*

The patterns of administration to be found in the seminaries are so various, so much the product of individual histories, that not much help toward understanding them, their successes, and failures can be

42

gained from efforts to classify them. The theological schools, to be sure, may be divided into the four groups that are governed respectively by 1) boards elected by national denominational bodies; 2) boards elected by regional church groups, such as dioceses, synods, presbyteries, associations, et cetera; 3) self-perpetuating boards; and 4) boards representing a number of organizations, such as educational societies, alumni, denominational education commissions, et cetera. The last group is the smallest, comprising apparently about 10 per cent of the total number of schools; the other three groups seem approximately equal in size. Representatives of each group encounter peculiar administrative difficulties or obstacles, for instance, in establishing good relationships with seminaries of other denominations, or even with those of the same denomination, or with the churches, or with the universities and colleges. One has the impression that in the case of the fourth group the machinery of government is often cumbersome and requires an unusual amount of attention, while the schools of the first group may be most subject to denominational isolation. But on the whole the classification is of little assistance in analyzing problems of administration.

The schools may also be distinguished from each other by taking the polity of the denominations with which they are affiliated into consideration. The constitutional patterns of the churches, however, are often irrelevant to their governmental arrangements for the schools. In an association of churches organized on congregational principles the seminaries may be excepted from the responsibilities and rights of free communities, being subjected to a more than episcopal supervision by the overseers of the denomination. In churches that adhere to the episcopal scheme of government seminaries may function as very independent congregations. The management of a school serving in a church with presbyterial polity may be so monarchic that the college of ministers constituted by the faculty exercises few of the rights of a presbytery.

Again one can divide the schools into the two groups of denominationally governed and the independent or interdenominational institutions. Yet independent schools, governed by self-perpetuating boards, maintain very close relations to a denomination; a few interdenominational seminaries are subject to stricter control by a theological party represented in several denominations than are other institutions directly governed by boards representing a single denomination.

II. *Defects of Government*

A. *Thought Control.* Such schemes of classification illuminate only slightly the problems of government in theological schools. More help may be gained by attending to the chief defects encountered in their administration. The first and most common of these seems to be due more to lack of good citizenship, of responsibility and freedom in the exercise of power, than of inadequate administrative arrangements. It appears in the denial of liberty to faculty and students by churches or theological parties for whom the Protestant principle of the freedom of the Christian man seems to be only a museum piece treasured for exhibition and not a gift to be exercised. Too many schools are subject to a close guardianship by defenders of a faith once and for all delivered to some special group of saints. Their faculties find themselves under the suspicious scrutiny of groups or parties or, less frequently, whole denominations, that are unimpressed by the wisdom of Gamaliel; certain that they possess not only a truth but the whole truth and nothing but the truth; yet at the same time they seem to have little confidence in the power of God to establish the victory of truth. Fearful of the new appearance of the kind of unconventional thought that marked the rise of the Reformation or subsequent revivals, such groups constantly examine youth and its instructors to see if there be any way of wickedness in their minds, to discover potential deniers not of the Lord but of some statement about him or to find out betrayers not of Christ but of his plenipotentiaries. The kind of fearfulness which became epidemic in various college and university faculties when political heresy was the subject of a grand inquisition has been endemic in some theological schools for many years, though the religious and social heterodoxies that are suspect in such seminaries have little in common with the opinions or conspiracies congressional committees condemned.

The devices by means of which defensive religion asserts its compulsions over theological faculties are as various as the orthodoxies it protects. The spirit behind these devices is always the same whether the convention defended is some sound form of words, some practice of worship, some set of folkways, some ancient or modern ecumenical or sectarian system of beliefs. One method of exercising coercion is through the requirement that teachers of theology affirm their adherence to a creed in more detailed fashion and more frequently than other ministers of the same denomination need to do. It is one thing to ask the person who assumes the office of teacher to make a solemn promise before witnesses to discharge his responsibility as one who is accountable to God; it is another thing to call him to account over and over again to a human court and to lay a burden of guilt upon him if he discovers in himself honest doubt of some of the specific affirmations he is required to make. The psychological and spiritual atmosphere of the society in which oaths of allegiance are required is of the greatest importance. In many cases where this requirement obtains there is genuine concern for individual responsibility to God, confidence in the teachers, respect for their integrity, and due humility on the part of those who are charged with oversight of the schools. In other instances, however, the spiritual climate is conducive to the growth of ungenerous suspicions, of rigidity in the interpretation of language and symbol, of coercive power over the minds of students and teachers.

Defensive, fearful religion frequently tries to exercise thought, control in more subtle ways than through the administration of loyalty oaths. Its pressures are exerted through the classroom visitations of official—but more frequently unofficial—guardians of faith, through students who listen to their instructors' lectures with ears attuned to departures from the sound form of words or the well-established train of ideas. Such students, it has been reported, have on occasion used tape-recording machines for the purpose of gathering sure evidence against suspected heretics. The pressures are usually less severe, but they may be the more stultifying in the long run in their milder and more pervasive forms. They may be more deadly when they are directed with great benevolence toward protecting faculty and students against all "foreign" influences than when they are exercised immediately on suspected heretics.

No specific governmental arrangement seems to offer guarantees that the responsibilities and the proper freedom of theological seminaries under God will be safeguarded. Though the loss of such liberty may be due in part in every instance to external pressure, it is also true that it never occurs without the consent of the governed. Timidity in the schools is no less at fault than is aggressiveness in their constituencies. Schools operating within the same denomination or region, subject to similar pressures, may differ widely from each other in the extent to which they exercise independent responsibility. The exercise of free and responsible citizenship in the schools and churches by officials, ministers, teachers, and laymen at the risk of occasional heresy trials and unofficial excommunications, seems to offer the only guarantee against abrogation of Christian liberty in the seminaries.

B. *One-Man Rule.* A defect that is more of an administrative character is found in those schools, too large in number, in which patriarchal or monarchic systems of rule place all power in the hands of a presiding officer. Such systems usually have grown up it seems because school administration has never been made the subject of careful consideration and legislative enactment. Occasionally the unconscious desire for power by some strong leader who felt the urge to achieve order and progress more than he desired liberty and justice may have been responsible for fastening the patriarchal pattern on a school. The general impression of the observer, however, is that where such government is established the present incumbent of the high office is as much its victim as his colleagues are. Unschooled in administrative procedures, save, perhaps, for those he learned in a parish ministry where he was the only and unquestioned leader and the center around which the community revolved, he seeks now to preside over an institution that has grown up from small beginnings without ever having organized itself in a rational manner. In such institutions the board of directors may look for its direction to the school executive; except occasionally in the matter of annual budgets it may feel that its function is to support the president. The members of the faculty confine themselves to their duties as teachers, including, perhaps, service on curriculum and library committees. They have no voice in the determination of broad policies or in new appointments to their ranks unless the president thinks it wise to consult one or another of them. Sometimes they have the feeling that all the important decisions are made at some tea table, that considerations too deep for their understanding are being weighed by the one responsible captain of the ship. They may even feel especially favored when their advice is asked. They have no access to the board of control except through the executive; no responsibility to counsel with the board on questions of policy; no stated procedures through which grievances can be transmitted. All relations are personal and unstructured. All lines of power and all lines of communication from and to boards, churches, and other schools run in and out of the one office. Morale in such schools is often low; the energies and ideas of competent men remain unused and dispersed. The faults of such a system of administration are magnified when an unperceptive successor follows a man whose *charismatic* gifts had been effective in building up a school which had become a kind of extension of his personality.

C. *Cumbersome Machinery.* A less common though not infrequent obstacle to good administration is encountered in the cumbersome, frictionful governmental arrangements that thwart the efforts of even good executive officers and wise faculties to conduct effective schools. Such cumbersome administrative machinery is usually the product of historic developments. The federation of previously separated schools, the separation of a seminary from a college or its union with a university, the merging of institutions as a result of church unions and similar movements, may lead to the multiplication of governmental devices. The need to maintain the legal provisions of advantageous charters, or the desire of groups to maintain control over schools with which they have been historically affiliated, or the wish of schools to cultivate the support of various constituencies, often lead to an amorphous proliferation of boards and interlocking directorates for which no clear lines of responsibility have been defined. The administrative officers of such schools need to take into account not one but several veto powers and must give a great deal of their time and energy to the removal of friction. In these complex organizations responsibility is so widely diffused that often it is scarcely exercised. The controlling boards may begin to accept their role as that of putting the rubber stamp of approval on the actions of an executive officer. Their loss of morale, of active concern for the development of the school, under these circumstances is intelligible.

Some case studies illustrating this failure in governmental arrangements may illuminate the point. A certain seminary, the product of a merger, has a board of seventy-three members which really consists of two boards that must take concurrent action. One of these boards, with twenty-five members, represents one of the merged schools, the other one with forty-eight represents the other institution. The first board is wholly self-perpetuating, the second partly so but some of its members are elected by a denominational education society, others by the alumni of the school. In addition to these two affiliated directing organizations there is a board of overseers which at present seems to perform only ritual functions; but even quiescent organizations have been known to rise from the dead. The school in question is well governed by its president and faculty, but the former seems to give an undue amount of time to the maintenance of proper lines of communication with his boards and overseers at the expense of his educational task in leading a faculty. More complex is the case of a federated school which is governed by a university administration, an executive council consisting of the deans of the four federated schools, a dean of the federation, four boards variously elected by groups representing denominational interests involved. In one of the four schools the dean with an administrative council constituted by faculty members works within the structure of the federated faculty with its responsibilities to the university. But he and his associates also adjust themselves to the direction of a Board of Directors (operating both under a permanent charter and a less permanent, revisable constitution) elected by a Triennial Convention, called by the Board and made up of representatives of sixteen state associations; of an Executive Committee drawn from the Board; a Board of Visitors chosen by the State Conferences; an Advisory Committee and a Board of Associates chosen by the Board of Directors. In addition to these five or six organizations mentioned in the school's description of its government the catalogue lists a State Superintendent's Council and an Alumni Association Council. Less spectacular but still remarkably complex systems of government are to be encountered in many other schools.

The effects of such awkward governmental arrangements are sometimes similar to those that follow from no arrangements at all. Direction may become concentrated in the hands of one or two men who form the connecting links between separate organizations of advisors and directors. More frequently cumbersomeness leads to dissipation of energies and the discouragement of a sense of responsibility in the plural organizations, none of which can function effectively.

D. *Teachers' Bureaucracies.* Wholly different from these defects is the one that occurs when a highly rationalized organization of a faculty into committees with carefully defined responsibilities is allowed so to develop that a large part of the time of many teachers is taken up with administrative duties. The more democratic the school, the more it participates in the life of the churches and the community, the more concerned it is about the careful screening of applicants for admission, about the maintenance of common standards, the improvement of the curriculum, the development of the library, of service to alumni, of student counseling programs, et cetera, the greater becomes the drain on the time of the faculty members who move from one committee meeting to another, from counseling session to in-service-training seminar for alumni. In a significant number of schools the faculty members feel harassed by administrative duties which they perform with grudging willingness. They do them willingly and even enthusiastically because the importance of the tasks is recognized, yet grudgingly because the work of scholarship which the teacher was primarily appointed to carry on must suffer.

III. *Principles of Good Government*

How such administrative defects may be eliminated is a question not easily answered. Good government seems to require the recognition of at least the following principles:

1) In the relations of a school to an ultimate governing body, such as a denomination, the responsible Christian liberty of the school must be safeguarded. Such liberty is not independence, for the freedom necessary to mature Christians who recognize that they must serve God rather than men—even when the men are men of the church—is not a freedom without responsibility to men. But in good government, in theological schools no less than in political democracies, the principle of direct responsibility to God requires that all master-servant relations among humans be highly modified in the direction of equality in service. A theological school can never be dealt with as merely the servant of a denomination without violation of its character and without interference with the Christian obligations of its members.

2) The various bodies responsible for the conduct of a school-board of directors, faculty and administrative staffs—each need the power required by their responsibilities; these powers as well as the functions need to be defined and publicly stated; they must also be brought into

such balance with each that abuse of power may be checked. A faculty which has no recognized right to participate more or less directly with the board of directors in the appointments of administrative officers and of new colleagues or with the dean in determining admissions policies is not enjoying powers commensurate with its responsibilities; for it is a college of teachers charged, not one by one but as a group, with the task of the theological education of youth. A board of directors which must look for all directives to higher posts of command does not possess power equal to its functions. The recognition that power must be correlate to responsibility has special application to the position of the librarians in many schools, who despite the very large responsibility they carry in the teaching program are frequently without voice or vote in faculty meetings.

3) While it is impracticable as well as undesirable wholly to separate governmental from teaching functions, yet the administrative work of the faculties should mostly be confined to the larger questions of policy-making. Detailed executive work needs to be carried on by an administrative staff sufficiently large for the needs and adequately correlated with the faculty. In too many schools the dean is so burdened with administrative detail that he cannot function as the director of a college of teachers and planner of policies; in others too many teachers spend too much time doing work administrative assistants could do more competently. The provision of adequate administrative staffs has, as was noted in the previous chapter, placed a heavy burden on the seminaries. But the fact that administrative costs have increased more rapidly than instructional expenses is not an argument for the reduction of the former.

IV. *The Relations of Seminaries to Colleges and Universities*

The establishment of educationally fruitful relations between theological schools and other institutions of higher education presents peculiar problems to these schools and to the churches. A surface indication of the significance of the problems appears in the fact that almost half of the seminaries in the United States and Canada are administratively closely connected with colleges or universities while the other larger half consists of independent institutions. A little inquiry into the history of the seminaries shows how involved they have been in movements of separation from and alliance with colleges and universities. The stories of Andover's relations to Harvard, of Princeton Seminary's relation to Princeton College and University, of Southwestern Seminary and Baylor, of Boston University's School of Theology, of the Divinity School of the University of Chicago, of the University of Southern California and its theological School, of Butler, of Transylvania and the College of the Bible—to mention only a few—indicate what attractions and repulsions, what complex interaction of many forces have been at work. Contemporary reorganizations of divinity schools in some universities; the separation of such schools from other universities; the building of new seminaries in close proximity to established universities; the removal of others to a distance, are symptomatic of the same attraction-repulsion pattern.

The questions which arise in this connection for the administrators of schools seem at first to be relatively simple: shall we seek or maintain close relations with a college or university? Can close relations be established without administrative correlation of college or university with divinity school government? Or, conversely, shall we become independent of government by college or university administration? But these simple questions open up a large number of complex issues, and they arise in peculiarly individual historical situations.

The historical situation in which the questions are raised may be marked by the secularization of education in a liberal arts school originally founded by a church as a preparatory school for the seminary, or by the change of such a school (under the persuasion or coercion of economic needs) from church to communal, municipal or state control, or by the victory of some dogmatic group that gained control of the college. It may be marked by the increase of intellectual vigor in a theological school mismatched with a humdrum college, or conversely by the need to break out of confining parochialism and to enter into more stimulating intellectual relations; or by the tendency of the one or the other partner to want to open its doors more widely to students of many denominations and theological parties or to both Negro and white students. When the seminary asks questions about its relations to college or university it is aware that both it and the other institution are subject to the operation of many forces. The theological school which is independent of a university is usually dependent on a denomination—though a university may be denominationally controlled; the school which is independent from denominational control is likely to be dependent on an apparently independent university. But neither denomination nor university is a sovereign power. They in turn have their dependences and their independences—on and from political powers, economic classes, regional climates of opinion, cultural groups.

Past historical situations of these sorts are reflected in the present organization and control of the theological schools. Out of 170 seminaries fifty-six are at present either functioning as graduate departments of colleges or as schools under the same board of control as the correlated college. Fourteen others are under the administrative control of universities.[1] Many of the nominally independent seminaries are

[1] Nomenclature is deceiving. Some universities are called colleges, many colleges

closely related to colleges controlled by the same denomination; often they have been administratively separated in some past period from such a college. Others have entered into more or less close affiliation with a university while maintaining independent status. Still others are not only administratively independent but also otherwise isolated from colleges or universities.

One may, with the question of college-university relations in view, divide the seminaries into six groups: 1) Those that are graduate departments of a college or which, located on a college campus, are under the same board of directors as the college (Phillips, Moravian, Anderson, et cetera); 2) the administratively independent schools operating as part of a denominational system of higher education and historically as well as actually allied with a denominational college or college system (the Southern Baptist schools, the Presbyterian, U. S. seminaries); 3) the independent denominational schools, drawing their students from a large number of denominational, private and state colleges (the Presbyterian, U. S. A., and most American Baptist seminaries); 4) the seminaries operating as schools within denominationally controlled universities (most Methodist seminaries); 5) university-affiliated denominational and interdenominational schools (Union, N. Y., Chicago Theological); 6) divinity schools controlled by independent nondenominational universities (Vanderbilt, Harvard, Howard, Yale, et cetera).

This great variety in organization—each group might well be divided into subgroups—indicates not only that educational institutions are the products of historical changes but that complex issues are involved and that no one desirable way has been found to meet all of them. The interests that lead to affiliation with and separation from colleges differ from those that are involved in the university-relations pattern. Close affiliation of seminary with a college is often due to concern for continuity between pretheological and theological education; it may also be due to the desire of a denomination to keep the whole process under control. Separation from a college may serve the interest of establishing seminary work on a graduate level, out of reach of the influences of collegiate environments, or it may issue from a concern to open the theological school to students representing a large variety of backgrounds so that its work may be less constricted by the limitations of regional or provincial climates of opinion.

In the case of university relations close contact is sought because seminaries left to themselves, controlled only by institutional churches,

go by the name of universities. In the above classification only those institutions are classed as universities which have at least one graduate division besides the theological school.

tend to neglect their functions as intellectual centers and to become vocational training schools, while, conversely, separation from university atmosphere is desired because university schools are believed subject to the temptation to neglect their function as teachers of pastors while devoting themselves to theological inquiry. Or again closeness of relation with universities is desirable in order that there may be fruitful conversation between Church and culture, while the divorce of seminary and university may be sought because all the old and modern incompatibilities of Church and world make such conversation difficult or put temptations in the seminary's way to abandon its confession.

The great variety in the patterns of seminary-college-university organization indicates that no way has been found of reconciling all the interests, that the situation of the schools as a whole in this respect is highly fluid and that individual schools face many difficult decisions in regulating their relations to other institutions. One may venture the following general observations: 1) that the movement of theological schools in general is from close connection with colleges through independence toward affiliation with universities; 2) that this movement is expedited by increased interest in the graduate character of theological education, increased interest in such education as more than a utilitarian training program, and by increased interest on the part of the universities in theological inquiry; 3) that with a few conspicuous exceptions the administrative arrangements for the affiliation of seminaries with universities have been either too sketchy or too cumbersome to provide for the achievement of the desired benefits; 4) that the fruitfulness of the movement of seminaries toward the establishment of closer relations with the universities depends in part on the recognition by the administrators of the latter institutions both of the intellectual significance of theology in the universe of learning and of the significance of the Church, for which under all circumstances theological schools must provide well-prepared leaders. At the present juncture of affairs university administrations on the whole seem more aware of the former than of the latter point.

Many schools, to be sure, are unable to enter into close relations with universities in which there is understanding of their work. Past decisions about the location of the school may preclude such a movement. The questions about the ways in which they can encourage their students and faculties to participate in conversation with the representatives of the humanities, sciences, and philosophies, and about the measures to be taken to bring the latter into relation to theological inquiries cannot be answered by administrative arrangements but only through curricular and other means. But even those schools that by charter or other arrangements are closely united with universities must deal with these questions. Physical or administrative closeness to a university community does not guarantee participation in the life of a university community nor university support of theological study.

CHAPTER FOUR

The Theological Faculties

Theological schools in general find it difficult to acquire and keep strong faculties. The number of available persons who meet all the specifications upon which the schools would like to insist is never large. Academic training for scholarly teaching is required in most cases, though for a few positions stress may be laid on solid accomplishment in pastoral work. The faculty member will in either case be expected to have skill in teaching, and to be able to win the confidence of students, not only as a specialist in his particular area, but as a person and as a Christian. In most cases active churchmanship is expected, and, as was noted above, most members of American theological faculties are ordained ministers who have had considerable pastoral experience before coming to the theological school.[1] In most denominational schools the faculty member is, by custom or rule, a member of the particular church, and this further limits the possible choices for positions. Each new appointment, furthermore, must be considered in relation to the existing faculty from the standpoint of the fields covered, the ages and anticipated retirement of present members; and the need for the whole faculty to work co-operatively together in good spirit.

When we consider these requirements in the light of the fact that the divinity schools do not train a large number of specialist scholars, and further, that the creative scholar able to do distinctive work is rare at best, we can understand why the securing of good faculties is a continuing problem to the schools. A considerable shuffling of faculties takes place as men are called from one seminary to another, particularly in this time of increasing enrollments and improving standards. Often schools select promising young men from their own denomination for particular fields of study and find ways to give them the training which will equip them to teach. Men called from the pastorate to theological faculties are occasionally allowed a period of study in order to prepare themselves for a designated post.

Schools may seek their faculty members anywhere in the country and indeed anywhere in the world. With the number of available faculty people fairly limited, the schools usually find themselves looking

[1] Cf. Ch. One, Sec. IV, D.

54

over their entire denomination and throughout the country before making a new appointment. It is important to observe the extent to which seminaries in the United States have secured their faculty members from Europe and other parts of the world. Out of the 471 professors whose records were analyzed, thirty-six had received their primary theological education (in most instances they had carried on all their studies) abroad. An unusually large number of these were biblical scholars. It is clear that American schools are deeply indebted not only to the scholarship of Europe and Asia made available in books but also to this supply of scholars and teachers. The question is at once raised how far the continuance of this inflow of trained people can be depended upon in the years ahead. If it cannot continue it is all the more urgent that sound and adequate programs of advanced scholarly training be provided for an increasing number of American students, as well as for students from other countries who may come here to obtain their theological education.

Not many faculty members leave teaching for other positions in the churches or outside them. Some exception to this statement is probably found in the tendency of the Episcopalians to find their bishops in theological schools. Generally speaking, the lure of teaching, and the work of the theological community, appear to offer a satisfying life, and few leave once they have become a part of it.

The two greatest practical needs concerning faculty are: first, the development of a greater number of teachers who are not only intellectually competent and imaginative Christian persons but who have secured the extensive theological training necessary; second, resources need to be increased in the schools to enlarge faculties, to raise standards of teaching, and to provide for faculties a life somewhat less distracted by too heavy teaching loads, administrative duties and economic worries.

I. *The Vocation of the Seminary Professor*

In order to understand the significance of these problems today we need to see what is expected of the theological teacher, and how he does his work.

The faculty member of a theological school finds himself working under many of the conditions which characterize the life of other American college and university teachers. In addition to teaching a considerable number of classes, he carries on the good tradition of friendly relations between students and faculty. He becomes counselor and adviser on academic and personal problems. He serves on several committees which do the work of the school in the democratic tradition. He is called on for speeches, discussions, and other activities within the school and he is frequently active in community projects and church work outside the school. This is the general order of life in which he must find time to prepare his courses and to do his reading and writing.

Amidst this variety of responsibilities which tends to introduce an element of distraction into all American academic life, the theological teacher finds some special demands and tensions in his position.

There is first the double responsibility of the theological teacher for scholarship and for churchmanship. He is a faculty member in a school and responsible first to the school. But he is usually also a minister of the church and of his denomination. He frequently serves on denominational boards in addition to his activities in a local church. He is often called upon for special services in the churches as lecturer, writer, or consultant, and sometimes for positions of denominational leadership.

Much of the professor's time for which the church makes requests is related to his special field of study. His training in Bible, or theology, or pastoral care is used at points of need in the churches and their programs. This means that he must not only keep up in his field but also develop some special skills in communicating and adapting his work to the interests and needs of various groups.

Sometimes the faculty member fulfills these church obligations as one way of enhancing the status and public relations of his seminary among the churches. Often he accepts this work out of his own sense of responsibility as a churchman. In many cases the supplementation of his income with some outside remuneration is a practical necessity. These activities increase his store of experience. They encourage him to keep his work in vital relation to human problems; but at the same time his own deeper mastery of his field of study may suffer from the amount of time and energy which goes into these services.[2]

The matter of scholarship involves a second problem which confronts every teacher. He must find the right apportionment of his time between the basic scholarship which produces results over a long period of time, and the immediate demands of teaching the students

[2] A study of the information submitted by 471 theological teachers revealed great variations in the amount of time devoted to classroom instruction, to nonacademic student counseling and to church or community activities. Class hours (full-time teachers only being considered) range from six to twenty, the median being nine; two-thirds of the teachers give an appreciable amount of time weekly (estimated at from two to twenty hours) to nonacademic counseling of students; about the same number report that they devote from one to twenty-five hours a week to church and community work. Somewhat more than half of the teachers are members of denominational committees or boards. The number of theological teachers who plainly (on the basis of such reports) are trying to do too much or are subject to overburdensome demands seems to constitute about a fourth of the total number reporting.

who are before him. This dilemma faced by all professors is heightened in certain ways in a theological school. Here men are being trained for a vocation of leadership in the church. They need intellectual training, and scholarly teaching, but they need many other things as well. While technical scholarship in biblical studies, church history, theology, psychology, ethics and many other fields is absolutely essential, the student who is preparing for the ministry can afford to leave some of this scholarship to others as he prepares himself for the varied tasks of the parish. He will use the fruits of the centuries of Christian scholarship, but he does not expect to be able to give much time to study of this kind. Hence the theological teacher who feels a responsibility to work at basic problems in his field with that sustained effort which may produce results only after many years, finds that he must decide how much of his time he can reserve for this work and how much he ought to give to the teaching, counseling, and guiding of the students who are immediately before him, how much, also, to writing books of a relatively popular sort for the benefit of general readers in the churches. The work of teaching itself intensifies this problem. Theological students need to be introduced to basic knowledge in the various fields. They need training in the methods of scholarship and critical thought. This requires of the teacher many hours spent in solitary reading and study. He must find time to work beyond the immediate demands of his teaching in order that the teaching itself may become more nearly what it ought to be.

The existence of these tensions explains the fact that theological faculty groups frequently engage in a lively discussion of the "vocation of the seminary professor." In what sense is he minister, in what sense scholar? What is the right decision between the many legitimate demands which press upon him? How shall priorities of value be assigned so that the whole church is served in its long-range needs and its immediate circumstances? Is there a special calling to the teaching ministry?

In deciding such questions faculty members find themselves in situations where both personal interests and prestige factors are involved. There is the question of advancement and recognition. In American academic circles there is an old discussion concerning the high estimate placed upon publication as a condition for promotion, or other recognition, as over against good teaching. In the theological schools which are integrated into universities it may be said that theological faculties work within the same circumstances as other university faculties. Young men must make their way "up the academic ladder" to the professorships which give tenure and in which they are recognized as established in their fields of work. In some schools this may leave the men in the "practical fields," whose work does not allow of production of detailed scholarly studies, at a disadvantage. The problem of mutual recognition and respect among teachers in different fields may become intensified.

In most seminaries where there is no university connection the situation with respect to advancement and prestige is somewhat different. While there may be special recognition of men whose writings win them wide reputations, in most seminaries all faculty members are given full professorial rank, and there is a common salary scale except for a trial period for the younger men just coming onto the faculty.[3] This serves to lessen somewhat the competitive features sometimes found in university schools. On the other hand it is claimed that in this situation men find less incentive for devoting their energies to scholarly work. It is also true that theological faculties comprise men who have rather different conceptions of their vocation. For some the intellectual task has a high place; whereas for others the calling is to prepare men for the ministry through sound teaching but there is no special concern to work at the frontiers of intellectual problems. For still others the theological position is an opportunity to instruct, advise, and encourage theological students on the basis of the teachers' experience in the church. Here the teaching position is conceived primarily as an opportunity for personal inspiration and practical counsel. Back of this variety of definitions of the teaching vocation there lie the ultimate questions about the nature of the Christian faith itself. What is the relation of the intellect and its critical inquiries to the progress of the soul toward the Kingdom of God? What is the Church's responsibility for scholarship, and how much should be left to the secular sciences and the universities? How important in the preparation of the minister is his encounter with critical inquiry into ultimate problems? The answers given to these questions shape the theological professor's conception of his vocation.[4]

In this situation any vagueness in the school as to its purpose and its goals in theological education will increase the uncertainty of the faculty members as they try to discover the right use of their time. If schools put emphasis on the immediately useful training of ministers and allow students to spend a great deal of time on the field, with only minimal academic demands, the incentive for teaching which probes deeply into basic questions may be lost. If schools put too much demand on the teacher to carry a large number of hours and additional administrative duties, they may leave him without support in doing the reflective thinking which might be of greatest significance to students and to the churches in the long run. And undoubtedly there are

---

[3] A tendency in the schools in general to adopt the ranking and promotion procedures of the universities has been noted above, Ch. One, Sec. IV, B.

[4] See *The Purpose of the Church and Its Ministry*, 1956, Ch. III.

always some who retreat into their scholarly specialties and lose contact with the Christian cause.

It is our observation that some of the uncertainties of the schools as to their educational aims enter into the confusion of faculty members as to how to assign priorities amidst the conflicting demands placed upon them. The problem lies in discovering a right relation between the immediate demands of schools preparing Christian leaders for the contemporary world and the ultimate demands of the Christian community which in its pilgrimage through history must continually refresh, conserve and enhance its understanding of the truth of God and his world.

How these tensions are handled in the schools and their effect on the present state of theological teaching will become clearer as we look at the specific situations in the schools today.

II. *Typical Faculty Situations*

When we describe the typical situations of the faculty member we are concerned with the way in which his needs are provided for, the resources at his disposal to enable him to do good work and the important difficulties and obstacles which he encounters.

If we look first at the faculty member in those denominational schools which are not attached to or organically related to an independent university we find that the teacher is likely to have had one of two types of background. Either he has been a minister in his denomination for from ten to twenty years and has then come into the faculty to teach; or he has received his academic training fairly recently, has been ordained, has been pastor of a church, or a chaplain, or had some other pastoral duty for from two to five years and then has come into the theological faculty. Sometimes he may have taught for a few years in a college. The man who has had a long service in the pastorate is less likely to have completed a doctoral degree; though in a few cases he may complete this in middle life as he takes up his seminary teaching. The man who spends less years in the pastorate, or who is a college teacher, will in most cases have completed or very nearly completed a doctoral program, either the Ph.D. or Th.D., before he begins his teaching.[5]

The trend in theological seminaries at present is definitely toward the appointment of younger men, who have given most of their early years to securing academic training. Part of the explanation lies in an increasing emphasis on technical training in such fields as pastoral counseling. It may also reflect in part a raising of the standards within the schools so that the general preparation expected of the parish minister is no longer regarded as adequate for teaching in most fields in the schools. The circumstance should not be overlooked that when

[5] See above, Ch. One, Sec. IV, D.

schools seek an established minister for a teacher of homiletics, or pastoral care, two positions for which ministers are often favored, the school may discover that the salary received by the minister from his church so far exceeds the usual academic stipend that it would throw the school's salary scale entirely out of balance to pay him a salary comparable to that which he has been receiving.

The teacher in the denominational seminary usually finds that he shares the rank of professor with all other full-time faculty members. The salary scale is often fixed, though there may be minor flexibility in terms of years of service or other circumstances. If his house is provided as in many cases it is, his salary will usually be between $5,000 and $6,000 though he may receive less than $3,000 or more than $10,000. If house is not provided it may be between $6,000 and $7,000, but may be below $4,000 and, very, very rarely, up to $12,000 or $15,000. If the school has a summer session he is ordinarily paid extra for his services.[6]

In a very few instances schools make some adjustment of salary in relation to size of family and other need. Episcopal seminaries are the only group we have found which do this systematically. In these schools certain allowances are given for each child, and these increase as the children reach college age, after which the allowance is discontinued. Pension provisions are generally made.

The selection of the faculty member may come about in a variety of ways which are determined by the statutes and practices of the school or through informal and personal relationships. Generally appointments are made by the board of trustees or directors on recommendation of the president or dean of the school. Sometimes the school constitution calls for consultation with the faculty either as a whole or through a committee. Often when this provision is not explicitly stated such consultations are held. On this point some of the more serious difficulties we have discovered in the schools may arise. Doubtless there are occasions when good administration will require that faculties be rejuvenated by the introduction of new teachers not selected by their colleagues. But such occasions are rare, and it seems to be a fact that in the cases where faculty morale is at a low ebb and where there appear difficulties in realizing a genuine community of scholarship and devotion, one reason is that arbitrary appointments to the faculty have been made by president or boards without consulting the faculty. Sometimes the executive officer of the school regards the making of appointments as his personal prerogative, which by the letter of the constitution it often is; but it can be shown that the practice of making appointments on this basis is one way in which trouble may be created. In schools

[6] See above, Ch. Two, Sec. V.

with high morale new faculty members often stated that the element standing out prominently in their sense of security and hope in their position was the knowledge that the entire faculty had been consulted and had a voice in their election. It should be acknowledged that where there is serious disagreement in a faculty as to the nature of the appointment to be made, or over specific candidates, the exercise of overhead power in making the appointment may be the only way to resolve a deadlocked situation.

Once appointed the teacher finds himself expected to announce courses in certain subjects. The average teaching load is nine to ten hours per week. But in some schools it is only six or seven, in many it is twelve hours and in some cases reaches sixteen. That more than nine or ten hours is too many for graduate teaching will be agreed universally by educators. It should further be remembered that these many additional hours do not represent sections of elementary courses but usually mean courses at the advanced level often covering widely different fields. Heavy teaching loads may be made more burdensome in schools operating on the three-term system in which it is required that each term course be presented as an entity.

The teacher will have an office, usually not very spacious or efficiently equipped, but still an office. He will have the use of the school library, and while in most schools this means that he is relieved of the necessity of acquiring a large library of his own, he usually finds that he must develop an adequate working library at his own expense. He may have some secretarial help supplied by the school, but (a wellnigh universal complaint of faculty members) it will be inadequate for his needs. If he has at least some help he may remember that there are many schools in which the faculty member without administrative responsibility has no secretarial help at all.

In addition to teaching he will find three other major responsibilities which may be apportioned in various ways but none of which can be set aside. There is the administrative and committee work of the school in which he may share. In many schools he will find he has some responsibility for field work supervision. There is his individual counseling with students, and there are the requests for lectures and for writing from churches, and other groups.

Most schools carry on a large part of their program through faculty committees. These include admissions, instruction, student-faculty relations, policy, library, and other functions. In a few schools this committee load bears heavily on faculty time; in most it probably does not. The time spent with students in individual counseling both on academic matters and personal problems may consume a very large part of the faculty's energies. This responsibility is apt to be unevenly distributed; partly because there are some men to whom students go more readily; and partly because those in the field of psychology and pastoral counseling are more likely to have both the skills and the reputation of being good counselors.

It is in the demands from outside the school for preaching, speaking and writing that the average faculty member finds he has the most difficult decisions to make. These requests, except perhaps those in the summer period, usually take him away from his classes. Our study shows that to a considerable extent seminaries tend to be service institutions to denominations largely through use of the faculty as preachers and speakers. Administrative officers may find that a considerable part of their time goes into traveling and visiting, partly in the interests of the school and partly in fulfilling their responsibilities as churchmen.

Sometimes difficult decisions have to be made about requests for writing denominational literature. This writing of Christian education materials, editing of manuscripts, and writing for denominational journals may consume a great deal of time and may not contribute very much to the scholarly production in the faculty member's field. Such writing tends to be one of the activities which provides a fairly substantial financial return, and this is an additional pressure to take it in many cases.[7]

These outside demands involve genuine and important services to the church. This is what constitutes them such a real problem. They cannot be rejected on the ground that they are of no value. The question is, by what tests shall faculties decide what they should and should not do? It seems clear that if churches ask these many services from faculty, then careful provision should be made for a reasonable teaching load, sabbatical leave, and other means by which the faculty can be saved from losing its scholarly edge.

The professor in the independent university school finds himself in a situation very much like that of his colleague in the denominational school, but the fact that he is within the university system does present different aspects. He is more likely in the university to find that he is within the standard system of ranks and promotions, with his advancement in rank and salary dependent upon his demonstration of scholarly competence which means in most instances publishing of papers and books. If he is a young man he may find that he has many years of work as assistant or associate professor before he reaches the top grade and salary, and during this period he may be less well paid than are colleagues of the same age in denominational schools. In the university he will in nearly every instance have tenure after he attains the rank of

---

[7] The 471 professors who reported to the Study of Theological Education listed an impressive number of publications. Their literary production seems about equally divided between scholarly works and books written for the practical edification of the church. Many reported publications of the latter type only.

associate professor. In many denominational seminaries there is no explicit statement about tenure; though in many cases there is an understanding that all faculty members are appointed for an indefinite term, with the expectation that the appointment will hold permanently.

The university faculty is generally a fairly large one with some greater specialization in teaching assignments. In some respects the university offers greater stimulus to research and scholarly writing. At the same time the university teacher may discover that he is less free to work out the courses and the program of both teaching and writing according to his own interests.

The income of the university professor once he has reached the higher ranks is generally higher than that of the denominational school though there are a few church seminaries which provide salaries comparable with those of the universities. There is more likely to be some provision for sabbatical leave, and for additional research time than in the denominational seminary. Most university schools have advanced degree programs, and there is more graduate teaching, with supervision of dissertations. There is some greater opportunity for the university professor to discuss matters with men from other fields, though in seminaries which are located near universities and have co-operative relationships this opportunity also will be found.

Perhaps the most important difference between the school which has no relationships to a university and the one which has a co-operative relationship or is an organic part of a university is the intangible but potent factor of the intellectual and spiritual climate. The university offers the stimulus both of the general intellectual community and that of firsthand confrontation with the critical and rival expressions which modern culture poses against Christianity. The university offers a kind of microcosm of the most concentrated issues and criticisms regarding religion in the culture. At the same time and for this same reason the impact of a church tradition may be more difficult to realize than in the school which "keeps to itself."

We must raise the question as to whether there is a definitely "underprivileged group" of faculties in theological training. The problem is complex because many factors have to be taken into account, living costs in particular areas, opportunities to supplement income, the number of years of training required to prepare for a given post. It cannot be said that there is a simple picture. One of the lowest salary scales in the schools visited was found in an accredited school in a very large city. As was noted above the range of salary scales in the accredited schools is very great. There are unaccredited and unaffiliated denominational schools in which the faculty is very well paid. Generally speaking, however, there is a sliding scale downward as we move from the accredited university schools, to the independent denominational accredited seminary to the associate schools in the A.A.T.S. to the unaffiliated schools. The situation in the Bible schools shows that here the faculty salary scale is less than that in seminaries, even for men with equivalent training. The situation with respect to work load is similar. Seminaries with high teaching loads often also have low salary scales.

An analysis of the faculty salaries in a number of schools for Negroes shows that here there is a definite tendency downward. Very few professors or administrators in Negro schools reach the scale equivalent to that in comparable schools which are predominantly white. At the same time teaching loads are as heavy in the number of hours, fewer library facilities are available, and certainly there is less time for research and fewer provisions for sabbatical leave. There is at least one conspicuous exception to this general situation in the schools for Negroes, but on the whole the pattern prevails.

III. *The Well-balanced Faculty*

We need to examine certain aspects of the way in which faculties work, especially the kinds of personal and professional relationships which exist within the faculties, and some of the aids and obstacles to the most effective work. We shall examine the conception of the well-balanced faculty, the inner relationships of the faculty as a Christian community of scholars and teachers, the special hazards of the teaching position, and certain educational problems. We then consider conditions of good teaching.

The first need of a school is to have the major areas of instruction and counseling of students adequately taken care of by competent people in the various fields who have the talents and training required.

From the standpoint of covering the basic theological subjects most faculties are staffed with a few men who teach Bible, theology, religious education, and church history. The fields of pastoral work, church administration, and of preaching are often staffed by the president or by special lecturers. Several schools are now looking for a full-time appointee in homiletics for the first time in their history. This situation is due in part to the increased pressures on administrative officers who used to do much of the homiletical teaching. It also reflects the growing conviction that the task of instruction in preaching has become increasingly demanding in the contemporary period with new theological emphases, and with the growing complexity of the problems with which ministers must deal.

While it is obvious that the basic disciplines must be provided for it is not so obvious that there needs to be in the theological faculty some strong representation of scientific and cultural disciplines to act as a continual check and critic of the theological standpoint, and at the same time to provide for that vital discussion between theology and the cultural situation which is necessary if the faith is to be communicated to the world. In many faculties this introduction of a secular scientific discipline in addition to the classical linguistic disciplines is provided by the man in the psychological field; though in too many cases while this person may be an effective counselor he has not had sufficient basic training in psychological disciplines. Not many faculties have, in addition to a theologian, a man specifically trained in modern philosophy and able to deal with apologetic problems from a philosophical point of view. The sociological disciplines are even more poorly represented in spite of their great significance for Christian ethics, and indeed for all Christian thought.

The principle for which we believe a strong argument can be made is that no theological faculty is complete until it includes some men, who share the Christian outlook and faith and who are competent to explore scientific and cultural problems with the same rigor with which secular experts in those fields are trained. This principle would mean some radical rethinking of the problem of building a theological faculty. Far more needs to be done to make it possible for some theologically trained men to have the years of study necessary to make themselves competent in such disciplines as philosophy, law, sociology, psychology, literary criticism.

What we are arguing for is a new definition of the "minimum" theological faculty. Certainly not every discipline can be represented. The theological faculty is not a university; but it must encounter the methods and results of the special sciences and cultural studies in a firsthand way.

American theological faculties show a good representation of men with considerable experience in the church. Though it is often said that the seminaries are remote from the church, and that professors ought to take time off to "get out into the field," our study shows that this is usually a mistaken comment. Granted that remoteness from the practical life of the churches is a state of mind which may be found in some professors, generally speaking theological professors are in very close working relationship to the churches, so much so that one is more inclined to question whether they are always in a position to take a sufficiently long and critical view of the church's condition. The real difficulty faced by the schools in relation to church experience lies at another point. This is the question of how to use most effectively the experience of men who have spent most of their active lives in the pastorate. When these men become faculty members they enter a school situation which differs in many respects from the one in which they have had their major experience. They have not had the opportunity or stimulus in most instances to keep up a program of disciplined reading and scholarly work in a specialized field. Thus they may find themselves somewhat handicapped in the academic situation, and too often they discover that while they have a store of experience and practical wisdom they do not command a theoretical structure which can make this experience communicable and significant to another generation.

What can be done about this problem it is difficult to say. It may argue for not waiting too long to take men from the pastorate who are needed for the faculties. It also suggests finding ways to allow such men special periods of study with extra time to organize courses, and to develop the implications of the experience and thought which have been gathered in the pastorate.

All schools fill out their programs by use of special lecturers and part-time instructors. These arrangements are often satisfactory so far as instruction is concerned. They are comparatively inexpensive and when competent men are available often help to solve problems. The difficulty is that many schools find it financially desirable to carry such a large number of part-time instructors that the permanent and resident faculty is quite small. This means that a large amount of student counseling and of the general oversight of the school is left to the small group of permanent faculty.

Librarians sometimes are recognized as full-time faculty members, even when they have no teaching responsibilities; though there are still a good many schools where the librarian is not accorded faculty status. It appears from our study that schools ought seriously to consider making the librarians' position one of faculty status, seeking persons who understand the teaching responsibilities of the office, paying them accordingly, and enlisting them fully in the discussion and work of the teaching program. Where this is not done an important resource for criticism, guidance, and help to the faculties' teaching program is being overlooked.

It is impossible to lay down infallible rules for the building of a theological faculty. Each faculty member is a person with special talents and interests. Given the opportunity he will create his courses, develop his teaching, and shape the school fully as much as he is shaped by any prearranged scheme. Generally speaking, faculties seem to realize less than their full potentialities because the pressure of daily work is so great that there is not sufficient margin of time and opportunity for creative thinking about the general goals of the school. This suggestion leads us to some questions about the faculty as a community.

IV.   *The Faculty as a Community*

A strong argument is sometimes made for a *laissez-faire* theory of the theological faculty. In effect, let each man develop his own style, announce his own courses, go his own way. Students will choose the courses which are alive and significant. American faculty members do not readily come to a common outlook or agreement. Is it not better to consider the faculty as a collection of individuals who share the general aim of teaching theological students without trying to force them into any more co-operative or concerted outlook?

The tradition of individualism in American life undoubtedly has affected the spirit of the academic profession as it has others. There are professors who become established in positions and have a following who refuse to be bothered with wider demands upon their time. Many feel that much time spent in co-operative action and discussion is wasted. Further there is always the brilliant professor whose lectures and work are so important to the school that students demand his courses and the school must to some degree be built around him.

Yet in spite of these considerations the general tendency now in theological faculties, as in others, is toward a greater emphasis on co-operation and the achievement of a genuine community within the faculty. By this is meant something more than general good will. In many schools we were told that the faculty members "like one another," and get along splendidly, even that they have a great community of feeling. But all of this may be present without a faculty's tackling as a whole and with common responsibility its educational task. Elsewhere the desire of faculty members to function as a genuine college of teachers is thwarted by the lack of an administrative structure through which they could so operate.

There are imperatives in the Christian Gospel which call men out of their individualistic isolation, and these undoubtedly are operative in the tendency we are now describing. It should be remembered that however individualistic a faculty may be it is not the case that each lives to himself alone. There are elements of status, of the power of the established men, and the prestige of particular fields which from time to time need criticism and a fresh outlook. Decisions have to be made in a school about policy, educational matters, course requirements, and many other things. The question is whether these decisions are to be made by those who wield the power in a given situation or whether there is opportunity for continuing consultation within the whole faculty acting as a Christian community, and seeking to reach a shared clarification of goals and purposes.

In addition to the imperative to live and act in the spirit of the Christian community it is also clear that the pressures upon the schools have literally forced faculties to reconsider their programs to see if there are not more efficient and adequate ways of using time and resources. This does not mean that any less emphasis should be placed upon distinguished teaching; it simply means that with the pressure on the curriculum and on faculty and students nothing short of the wisest common counsel and mutual clarification of goals offers any hope for a solution.

In this move toward co-operation there is undoubtedly appearing a new definition of the Church and of the theological situation in which we are working. Co-operation among biblical scholars and theologians, among psychologists and theologians, between church historians and sociologists and between all these and the teachers who are dealing with Christian education, preaching, and other pastoral responsibilities is now a requirement for an adequate theological program. The discovery in our world and in the church that it is too easy and too dangerous to split apart realms of life which ought to be held together has become potent in redefining the collective responsibility of the theological faculty.

If we are right, if a movement toward internal communication and redefinition is taking place within the schools, it becomes pertinent to ask how it can be furthered. One suggestion is that the schools can make opportunities for faculties to have more time for free discussion among themselves. Several schools provide a retreat of several days for their faculties during the school year. A fair number of faculties meet for at least a few days before the school year opens.

It is important to ask who is responsible for developing such modes of faculty co-operation as may be required. We suggest that the role of the dean in many seminaries might well be underscored. Many seminary presidents are entirely too busy with the work of public relations and other responsibilities to give full attention to the internal development of the faculty's life. Further, many of the presidents are not especially prepared by experience or training for this role. The dean of the faculty, however, ought to be a trained academic person, fully able to give at least the prompting if not the leadership which might create new modes of communication within the faculty. In a good many schools the deans appear to us to be efficient and competent men, often with very long experience in the school. They see to it that the academic wheels turn smoothly, but not many of them take responsibility for a continual prodding of the faculty into self-examination and co-operation.

V.   *Educational Problems*

The effectiveness of a faculty in teaching and in developing the potentialities of students is not easy to judge. Certain distinguished teachers emerge from time to time and are known both through their reputation as teachers and through their books. The graduates of a school may over the years show that their training has placed a certain stamp upon them. The response of students to a school, and the degree of their own sense of being involved in a significant enterprise, may be an index. But the clue to the intellectual and spiritual vigor of a faculty which was most available to us was the judgment of the faculty members themselves expressed in the form of their own goals as they had defined them and their estimate as to whether or not they were able to realize their goals, and what obstacles they found.

Sometimes this faculty judgment takes the form of critical analysis of the students, their preparation, the time they have for their work, and their abilities. Probably the strongest obstacle felt by faculties to the achievement of high standards in the theological school is the inadequate preparation of students for theological work. If one discusses this problem in turn with college professors the point is at once made that the colleges have to deal with the limitations of high school training, and this in turn goes back to earliest schooling. There can be no doubt that theological schools must in large part deal with students as they come to them, without much opportunity to supplement earlier training, even in such matters as English composition, let alone the love of learning itself.

Granting all the special problems which schools must face in adjusting to the preparation of the students, the question still remains as to the intellectual tone of the theological schools. We ask, is there a continual movement in the classes and discussion to bring students to a sharper perception of ultimate issues, a broader grasp of what is involved in the Christian faith in its encounter with contemporary problems? Here the members of the study staff must speak out of their own impressions, and out of the many judgments which they heard expressed by individuals and in faculty groups. The answer given cannot be a simple yes or no. What can be said is that there are many circumstances in American seminaries which to some extent tend to restrict the full vigor of intellectual work. Some schools are in a better position to overcome these difficulties than others.

It appears to us that the greatest single difficulty in many schools is their tendency to become intellectually and spiritually "ingrown." Sometimes this is brought about by the weight of a denominational tradition. Sometimes it means that through certain teachers a school has come under the influence of a theological position which has been reproduced in students who later become faculty members. In its initial phases this doctrine may have represented a vigorous theological position, but it can become established as the dogma of a sect. The tendency of many schools to continue staffing their faculties with their own graduates can contribute to this ingrown and sterile atmosphere. The very small faculty, with each professor a "one-man department," tends, it seems to us, to reduce the intellectual potential of a school. This cannot be said without qualifications. One remembers visits to schools with such a faculty in which the situation of the school in its community and the reality of the issues faced by students and faculty alike produced an atmosphere electric with intellectual search and seriousness.

When a faculty tends to be a collection of individualists some significant opportunity for intellectual advance may be lost. We have said that any of the pressing issues in the Church today have to do with relationships between various aspects of the faith. The relationship of the Old Testament to the New is a central issue in biblical studies, and in the interpretation of the nature of Christianity. The relationship between knowledge in the sciences, physics, psychology, sociology on the one hand and the Christian doctrine of God, and his redemptive work, are among the crucial issues today. Neither the definition nor the resolution of these problems is possible without a continual co-operative discussion among specialists in various fields. Surely the theological faculty ought to provide for this meeting of minds.

Too many schools which are in a position to carry on significant co-operative work with colleges and universities in their area make very little use of this relationship. The most important reason is the pressure of time; but here is a place where some addition of teaching resources to the schools would make it possible for faculties to have more significant contacts with other teachers in the community. Students could be encouraged to take more work under good teachers in other disciplines if the theological curriculum were less rigid. Encounter with a major intellectual discipline, taught without specific reference to Christian presuppositions, can be a significant aspect of a theological education.

The fact that a divinity faculty exists within a university does not guarantee that there will be vital conversations between men in different fields. In many instances these are left to purely personal contacts and preferences. The question arises whether divinity faculties in universities ought not to take more definite and concerted action toward promoting discussion of basic issues with other faculties. The present ferment within the universities as to the crisis in our civilization and the aims of education offers a situation which is more open to significant interchange with theological thought than has been the case for generations.

In looking for indices of intellectual vigor one could make a case that grading practices offer important evidence. The survey of ten Methodist seminaries in 1944 disclosed that the grading in many schools generally was far higher than was warranted, and higher than would be the comparable grading in other graduate schools. A very heavy concentration of B's and A's was reported with very few C's and almost no failures. Our study shows that this is too frequently the case in a large number of seminaries. Too few schools make systematic studies of their grading practices, and in many grading is never reviewed. In some schools the faculty may have a discussion of the matter once in two or three years. Our observation would be that generally speaking schools which pay close attention to their grading practices and which seek to keep them in line with the general practices in graduate schools exhibit a higher level of academic performance.

The theological teacher who accepts responsibility for participating in the life of the school as a Christian community cannot define his work as narrowly as he might if he were devoted wholly to research, or to his preparation for the classroom. To a far greater extent than is often realized the life of a theological school presents the kinds of needs and problems which are found in the congregation of a church. Faculty and students are persons with a variety of needs. There is the concern for wholeness of life within a shared vocation. There is the continued search for the fuller meaning of Christian commitment. The richness of a theological faculty consists partly in the extent to which its members can bring to the community a ministry of Christian worship, personal counsel, and spiritual devotion in addition to intellectual competence and the ability to show the relationships between their particular fields of study and the life of the Christian and the Church in our kind of world.

One continuing problem which the teacher faces is the apportionment of his time between students who need the most help and those who need the least. Able and well-adjusted students are often left to make their way alone since they have no pressing needs. Students in grave difficulty may take a considerable part of the faculty's time. In a Christian community no one wants to leave the needy person without help. Yet a moral problem remains. What further growth in Christian maturity and in the effective service of the Church might come if more time were given to the students who show special promise? We find many faculty members who are troubled by this problem, none who have resolved it.

VI. *Toward the improvement of teaching*

Many measures suggest themselves as to how the work of the theological teacher may be made more efficient. Some of the obvious matters include the provision of more teachers in the schools with a consequent reduction in the size of classes or the number of hours of teaching required. If enough good and well-trained teachers can be found (which is a considerable condition in itself) the enlargement of faculties is a matter of financial resources. It must be remembered, however, that once the problem of a normal load of work is solved, the deeper problem of developing good teaching involves an escape from the dullness of routine, and the continual need to sharpen the mind against the harder problems of thought and action. There are ways in which schools can help to provide the situation in which the teacher who is willing to grow through continued exposure to critical probing can do so.

Schools can provide ways for teachers to have the stimulus of the learned societies in their fields. Many do allow some travel expense and other help. It still appears, however, that there are many theological teachers who have little opportunity for the kind of sustained discussion with other scholars which can be genuinely productive. This is especially true of schools which are at a considerable distance from places where such discussions are usually held. The theological discussion groups which have been developed and supported by the Hazen Foundation for many years have been of great value to several generations of theological teachers. The benefits of such discussion might be extended to a much larger number of faculty people who at present cannot participate in existing groups whose numbers are necessarily limited.

Periodic leaves, either on a sabbatical basis or otherwise, for advanced study and writing are a recognized part of academic procedure for the advancement of scholarly work and teaching. Provisions for such leave in a large number of seminaries are either not made, or are on such a limited basis as to be grossly inadequate. While many faculty members have their summers presumably free for independent work, this period in itself is often not sufficient for the study and work which ought to be done. This is especially true of the younger men who are likely to be under heavy pressure to supplement their salaries with summer lecturing and who especially need the time for further sustained study.[8]

The protection of faculties from too heavy a burden of outside work is partly of course a financial problem. More adequate salaries would not have to be supplemented with so much outside work, but in this matter we discover deans and presidents are likely to take a somewhat different view from the faculty. Some administrators claim that the faculty members take far more outside engagements than they need to and some teachers are highly critical of some colleagues on this point. There is the case of the teacher who finds his own need for response more deeply satisfied outside the school than within it. There

[8] Of the teachers of theology who furnished data to the Study approximately half indicated that they had never had leave of absence. A few answered the question, "When have you last had a sabbatical year?" with nostalgic reminiscences of semesters on leave more than twenty years ago. The relative rareness of sabbatical leaves among theological teachers may be partly due to their mobility. Of the first hundred who answered the question with a "never," "none," or "not yet" just half had been in their present positions less than seven years. The remaining fifty had been members of the same faculty from seven to thirty-eight years.

is also the continuing query about the vocation of the theological professor. Is he called primarily or exclusively to serve within the community of the school or is he committed to service of the whole Church? Some analysis of the decisions involved here by teachers and administrators might clarify situations in which faculty members feel they must go out more to the churches, ministers' groups, and young people's conferences, while the deans feel the faculty ought to stay home.

One of the least used but most effective methods of using a teaching staff efficiently is the provision for tutors. In a few Episcopal schools this system is in operation as a regular part of the teaching program. In a few other schools advanced students are used on a voluntary and informal basis in tutoring roles. Generally speaking, however, there is very little provision for this in theological education. The reasons are obvious. The program is expensive, and there must be advanced students on hand, or other mature and trained people in the community, to supply a tutorial staff. However, there are many schools where young scholars working on advanced degrees are available. At present many of them are pastors of churches or are carrying other outside work in order to make their way. Most of them could profit greatly from the tutoring experience. It could be the beginning of teaching experience, and a help to their own intellectual development. The advantage to theological students of personal attention from the tutor, and the opportunity to develop what has been too sketchily done in class lectures, is very great.

The needs for greater financial resources and for the training of more and better equipped teachers are plain. Unless more is done in this regard throughout our schools many of the circumstances which prevent good schools from being great ones, and fair schools from being good ones, cannot be cured. But once this is understood the further truth must be recognized that the climate within which a faculty works, the kind of stimulus which is being given by the school, by the church, and by the leaders of the faculty toward creative thinking, constitutes a matter of fundamental importance. If the teacher is left with the feeling that the turning out of an acceptable number of students from good average courses is sufficient, and there is no expectation that he will bring some original and distinctive thought to the traditional procedures, many will yield to the inclination to adjust quietly to the system, and do what is required without distinction. Further, if some faculty members feel that their subjects are looked down upon by others, or that they have no opportunity to make their own perspectives felt in the school as a whole, they will lack the sustaining sense of being contributors to the common enterprise.

The theological professor has his normal complement of problems both personal and intellectual. He has all the problems which other teachers, as well as professional men in general, have in American life—the pressure of activities, and the difficulty of concentration, the need to do a great many things as well as possible. He also may find he is struggling continually with the clarification of his vocation as scholar and teacher. With so many pressing needs about him it is natural for the teacher or writer who is dealing with ultimate problems to feel guilty about his own situation. He feels at times remote from the struggles of life about him, at least to some extent separated from them. He also feels the criticism from outside of his so-called "ivory-tower" existence. While he knows that the life of the mind is relevant to his time, and revolutionary in its implications for human living, still he sees the gap between critical thought and direct action. Not often is it given to scholars to see such an immediate relationship between theoretical research and practical power as in the case of nuclear physics or polio vaccine. Of course that kind of power leads to its own problems of self-searching and guilt. But we have no equivalent in the humanistic studies which deal with the ultimate dimensions of the human spirit. Here human powers are more diffuse, come to realization more slowly, make their impact more quietly.

We believe, however, that the self-definition of the vocation of the theological faculty member involves the special problems we have pointed out in the beginning of this chapter. It is of great importance that he attain clarity for himself as to what is needed from him as teacher, as member of a school, and representative of the Church. He needs to understand what he must do to train ministers for the kinds of problems which they will immediately face, and yet to have a clear view of how the maintenance, criticism, and restatement of the theological tradition depends upon the critical thought and sustained devotion of men working on problems which do not yield in years or even generations but which require the devoted study of the Christian community for centuries.

These ultimate and difficult questions can be escaped by the plunge into activity where results are immediately recognized, and reward is quickly bestowed. In the end, therefore, the most difficult problems facing American theological faculty members involve personal decision and commitment within the context of a responsible appraisal of the immediate and the ultimate needs of the Church.

No rules can be prescribed for meeting all these demands but we shall be more likely to have strong commitments and unconfused decisions if we bring the issues as to our goals into the open, and attain some common sense of obligation and destiny in the work we have to do in this specialized ministry. Churches and schools which are content with the routine performance of duties, however important, and which do not take care to look more radically at the resources needed to clarify, inform, and release the deeper vitalities of the Christian faith will someday find their spiritual energies drained away, and no replenishment available.

VII. *Future Needs for Teachers and for Christian Scholarship*

In assessing the over-all picture of the faculty needs in American theological schools we discover that the clearest directive is to increase the opportunities for able young students to get their advanced training and complete their doctoral work without too much loss of time and too much effort put on outside work. This responsibility does not fall in the first instance upon the schools but upon the churches. Only they can provide the resources for a significant advance in the graduate training of the future faculties. The Methodist program of graduate fellowships recently inaugurated is a promising development.

The question of the number and adequacy of the present schools offering graduate training for the preparation of teachers must be raised.[9] In some denominations, students may go to a graduate school of that church. Boston University trains many Methodist teachers; Princeton Seminary trains Presbyterians, but both of these schools also train men of other denominations. General Seminary is the only Episcopal school offering graduate training with a doctoral degree. Southern and Southwestern Baptist Seminaries graduate many teachers. Many schools, such as Iliff in Denver and Union in Richmond, offer Th.D. programs; but these are designed primarily for the pastor who wants to extend his training, rather than for the teacher. Standards for the Th.D. are notoriously variable. Much of the graduate training for future teachers is given either in interdenominational university schools, or in denominational schools which are identified with universities. In addition, a fair number of American students go to Scotland, England, or the Continent for advanced work.

The question occurs at once whether the pressing need is for an extension of the opportunities for graduate study in interdenomina-

[9] Earned doctoral degrees in theology or religion were awarded in 1955 by twenty-two accredited, three nonaccredited schools, as follows:

Th. D.s: Berkeley Baptist, 2; Boston, 5; Chicago Lutheran, 1; Emmanuel, 1; General, 2; Harvard, 2; Iliff, 2; New Orleans Baptist 10; Perkins, S. M. U., 1; Princeton Theological, 2; Southern Baptist, 36; Southwestern Baptist, 7; Temple, 6; Union, New York, 6; Union, Richmond, 5; University of Southern California, 1; Central Baptist, 10; Divinity School, P. E., Philadelphia, 2; Northern Baptist, 7. Total 107.

Ph.D.s: Drew, 3; Duke, 4; Harvard, 3; Union, New York (with Columbia Univ.), 11; University of Southern California, 3; Vanderbilt, 3; Yale, 12; McGill, 1. Total 50.

Of the 157 doctoral degrees awarded seventy-two were granted by six Baptist seminaries; twenty by six Methodist schools; seven by two Presbyterian seminaries; fifty-three by seven nondenominational university schools.

tional university schools, or whether individual denominations should seek to establish their own graduate schools. This question is being raised, for example, among several Lutheran bodies.

There is a strong argument for seeking the extension of graduate programs in university schools with interdenominational faculties and student bodies. The establishment of an adequate program for doctoral work is a complex and difficult task. Faculty, library, and variety of curricular offerings all require a development which is elaborate and expensive. It may be questioned whether in most cases any but well-established universities are able to provide the basis required. Further, the advantages to the students of education in the university setting where there is encounter with many types of Christian and secular thought are abundantly clear. Residence houses for particular denominational groups can, of course, be established at such graduate centers, so that the reinforcement of certain traditional values can be gained along with the values of the ecumenical setting.

We have been discussing the training of teachers, but the work of creative scholarship goes beyond the classroom, and the concern for the development of imaginative Christian scholarship on basic problems must be equally emphasized. The Church must explore new fields of thought as well as continue the tradition of thorough mastery of those subjects which are most directly related to the Church's self-understanding; such as the history and literature of the biblical sources and period, and the history of the thought and life of the Church. In order to keep such scholarly work alive provision must be made for extended periods of research and writing. Scholars in religion rarely receive grants equivalent to the Guggenheim fellowships for advanced work. Something akin to this provision for a few theological scholars who are ready to do some of the major work of their lives could be of great significance for the life of the Church.

Beyond this possibility for the specialized work in theological fields there needs to be much more thinking about the training of men who are able to relate the Christian faith to the growing body of human knowledge and method in other fields. We need some men who are trained both in theology and in psychiatry, both in theology and in law, in sociology, the physical and biological sciences, the humanities and the realm of art. Only a few men have the ability and persistence to achieve this double training under the best circumstances; but the practical obstacles may be too great even for the ablest. The Church could do nothing more significant for the relating of its Gospel to the problems of modern man than to make it possible for a few to achieve mastery in these fields and at the same time develop their theological resources. Further, the Church needs for its own sake to appropriate the best thought in many fields of inquiry and no greater challenge confronts the mind of the Church than to show the meaning of Christian faith in relation to the fundamental quests of the human spirit. Modern science, modern politics, indeed all of life in this world of great forces moving toward some new order present to Christianity a world to be understood, cared for, and won. This can be done, not by isolating the Gospel from the issues which emerge in the common life, but by a continual conversation in which the thought of contemporary man is met and understood in some intelligible relationship to the mind of Christ.

One way of assuming this responsibility would be to work for a much closer relationship between theological faculties and people from other fields and professions. This would not be a substitute for the training of some theologians in other specialized fields as well; but it could help to bring the entire theological community into a more significant meeting with issues as our contemporaries see them.

There is further the matter of our internal isolation from one another behind denominational walls. American faculties of theology would profit considerably in our judgment from a program of exchange professorships which would cross denominational and regional lines. There is also the intellectual isolation of many men within those faculties which are constituted as administrative and friendship groups but do not develop the life of a college of teachers and scholars. Many a faculty member has voiced ideas similar to those which one expressed in the statement, "In our faculty we do not meet often for the sort of brooding meditation and deep discussion which would be highly desirable. We probably do spend more time in discussion of student problems than do some faculties, but the main stress of our faculty meetings is on administrative and operational problems. Of course we do have good friendly discussions with individuals, but the faculty as a whole does not discuss the great issues deeply and at length. This it seems to me is our major weakness."

As we have talked with faculties throughout the United States and Canada we have found very few content with present standards and routines. There is a strong will to find some more adequate means to cope with the demands upon the Church and its ministry today. What is needed is more resource put at the disposal of the schools, but most of all encouragement from churches, from boards of control, and from the ministry to discover some new attacks on our common problems. Clearer vision of the vocation of the theological teacher, and the decision to provide conditions under which that vocation will be realized, would make possible a greater fulfillment of the faculties which are now doing good and often distinguished work but which have as yet unreleased powers of thought and spirit.

CHAPTER FIVE

The Course of Study

The curriculum of a theological school may be regarded both as an incarnation of the faith and spirit of the school and as the resultant of complex, material, psychological, and political factors which have combined to produce the decisions and compromises necessary in organizing the course of study.

The first chapter of this report has shown some of the major trends in the content of curriculum and the requirements made of students in the past twenty years. In this chapter we shall state some problems of the curriculum as it appears at present, and take note of some proposals for its reorganization. We shall then turn to the problems within each field of theological study and in their interrelationship, since the issues concerning the aim and content of theological study remain, whatever modifications in the length and form of the theological course may be made.

I. *Principles and Problems of the Curriculum*

A. *Factors Determining the Curriculum.* In some theological schools in general the curriculum has been established by tradition and has grown by accretion and accident. In some schools the faculties have no opportunity or channel for considering the curriculum as a whole. In others faculty members, and sometimes student committees, engage in a continual discussion of the problems. But whoever has to make decisions about the course of study deals with a complex of factors which almost defy systematic analysis.

Certain studies have always formed the foundation of the course because they stem from the Scripture and tradition of the Christian faith. Study of the Bible, the history of doctrine, the history of the Church, are established elements in all theological education. Through the centuries these disciplines have developed methods and standards of scholarship, and certain auxiliary studies. Biblical scholars study the original biblical languages and pursue archeological and anthropological studies which throw light upon the Bible. Church historians must take account of all other historical work. Systematic theologians have traditionally engaged in discussion with philosophy, and with scientific method and results. The preservation and development of these disciplines, appropriate to an understanding of Christian faith, has always been and surely will remain a responsibility of the Church and its theological schools.

The disciplines related to pastoral responsibilties, Homiletics, Pastoral Care, Church Administration, and Religious Education, are somewhat less sharply defined as to content and method of teaching. The relating of instruction in these functions of the ministry to the other studies is continually discussed. Does the student do best to get a foundation in the traditional disciplines first, or does he need to deal from the very beginning with the practical responsibilities of sermon preparation and pastoral care and so discover the questions which he should be asking of the Christian tradition? If motivation and insight may be clarified by a continual movement from specific human problems to ultimate issues and back again, where should the emphasis be placed? Faculties generally display a diversity of outlook on this question. There is an element of natural human bias, and, we can scarcely deny, an element of sin present as each faculty member tends to regard as most significant that approach to Christian faith in which he has his own training and in which he feels most secure.

The content of courses, and specific requirements, cannot be judged apart from the abilities and concerns of the faculty which is to do the teaching. One theory of theological education would hold that a school should select as able a faculty as possible representing the diversity of fields and then set each teacher free to offer such courses as he desires. In some schools each new faculty member must be assured of a class by making at least one of his courses required. When a school rejects this individualism and develops a curriculum which stresses the relationships of the various fields, the faculty must consider each course in the light of the pattern of the whole. Undoubtedly many new tensions are introduced by the present concern for an over-all strategy in theological teaching. Some men find themselves unable to do their best work within an established framework. Yet some kind of balance between complete freedom of the individual teacher and the need for an organically related education must be struck in our day.

Students' reaction to the courses required and provided is another important determinant of decisions on curriculum. Not uncommon student rebellions against particular courses often lead to adjustment. In several schools student committees give periodic reports on their reactions to courses and teaching. In two schools visited by members of the staff student committees working with faculty on curriculum secured additional requirements in historical theology. In several schools student reactions to first-year courses offer a particular problem. Yet not many schools provide effective channels through which such student reactions may regularly reach the faculty and be objectively considered.

Certain traditional and denominational expectations must also be considered in curriculum building. Obviously the school is expected to introduce students to the particular church tradition to which they belong. There are many denominational structures for the establishment of some measure of control over curriculum. Presbyteries determine standards for ordination; Episcopal students must pass canonical examinations set by the church, rather than by the school (though in cooperation with the schools); denominational or synodical visiting committees may make recommendations regarding curriculum, and in some instances legislate requirements. Denominational boards concerned with ministries such as chaplaincies, missions work, and the rural or city church often urge the giving of specialized courses. Alumni can exert considerable pressure for particular courses or emphases.

Unfortunately, in a not inconsiderable number of schools no effective provision is made for faculty discussion of curricular problems. In some schools the dean or president may alter or specify certain courses without consulting the faculty. Courses may be introduced not solely for their educational value but because they dramatize an interest and thus serve as means of enlisting students for special fields. Some courses may be given, partly because they serve a vocational aim, but partly also to symbolize the school's concern for that field.

B. *Some Problems of the Curriculum.* As a result of the operation of such inertias, pressures, and attractions the curriculum in most Protestant seminaries has so developed in recent decades that serious questioning about its adequacy has become the rule among the faculties and not a few student bodies. Four problems in particular, in addition to a host of minor ones, have become acute. The first of these is the problem of the goal or end of theological education; to this the present study group addressed itself in a former book, *The Purpose of the Church and Its Ministry,* and there is no need to repeat here a description of the present uncertainty about the nature and purpose of the ministry nor to offer again the reflections about the emerging new conception of the ministry there developed. What seems important is not that this study's definition of that aim be adopted but that schools clarify in their own way, with as much precision as possible, the unifying purpose that lies beyond all their special ends.

The second, third, and fourth problems, all closely interrelated with one another as well as with the first, are presented by the overloading of the curriculum, the extension of requirements, and the loss of unity among so many specialized courses. While the last of these will occupy us most in this section some reference must be made to the former two.

As the study of trends during the last twenty years has indicated, the curriculum in general has become overloaded in consequence of the proliferation of traditional studies, the necessity of maintaining the standard subjects, the desirability of adding new disciplines relevant to the new demands that are being made on the Protestant ministry, and the introduction of field work. The study of the curricula of twenty-five schools, reported in the first chapter, made evident that there was remarkable constancy so far as requirements in biblical studies, Church History, Systematic Theology and Preaching were concerned. But in the course of twenty years almost one-third of the schools had added Christian Ethics to their required curriculum, more than one-fourth had added Psychology. Other disciplines added to the requirements by a significant number of schools were Christian Education, Conduct of Worship, History of Doctrine, Music, and Evangelism. Slight upward trends could also be noted in required work in Church Administration, Social Ethics, Speech, Missions, Philosophy of Religion, and Greek. The most remarkable increase has occurred in the case of Field Work, which only two schools out of twenty-five required in 1934–35 but which was a part of the required program in twenty-one seminaries in 1954–55.[1]

Subject to all the objections which arise against a purely quantitative assessment of the curricular problem it may be said that if theological schools could teach everything that they regard as a desirable part of the curriculum and could give as much time to each subject as seems desirable the present period of study would need to be more than doubled. If, however, only the average or median percentages of the number of hours deemed necessary for each course be taken into consideration, then the present three-year course would need to be extended to four years if the overloading of the curriculum were to be taken care of within the framework of present teaching practices.

The second problem of the curriculum arises out of the tendency to prescribe a rigid course of study to all students. While there is some indication that this tendency has been increased by the movement toward overloading, on the whole the idea of the prescribed curriculum has been traditional in the seminaries. Some of the reasons for it will be pointed out below in the discussion of the unity of theological study. In part, however, the practice of prescribing the course of study derives from the days when all students could be expected to come to seminary with approximately the same background of humanistic studies in college; in part from theories of education and even of theology that are suspicious of the exercise of independence by students. Taking the seminaries as a whole it appears that four-fifths of the theological students' time is taken up by prescribed work.

[1] See Ch. One, sec. V.

Overloading of the curriculum and the tendency to require the mastery of disciplines one by one together have increased the urgency of the fourth problem, namely, that of the unity of theological study.

C. *The Structure of Theological Study.* There is today a strong demand for more order and unity in the theological course. Whether Christian truth can ever be described as an "organism" may be questioned; but there is no doubt of the widespread concern among students and faculty for some universal rationale and logic of internal relationships to order the diversity of the theological studies. This is partly a reaction against the piecemeal effect of the present curriculum and partly against the "free" system in which professors and departments compete for the attention of students. But mainly it stems from the conviction that the ministry must interpret the Christian life with a unified perspective on human problems. Preaching depends upon both biblical understanding and knowledge of the contemporary human situation. Practical church strategy should be based upon theological understanding of the church and upon a knowledge of Christianity's history in relation to culture. Pastoral care needs to unite the pastoral office with a more thorough understanding of mental health and illness.

The search for this internal consistency of the Christian understanding of life involves many subtle questions. Superficially it is possible to outline a scheme of studies in which each has its place and in which the relationships are formally stated. Such a theological encyclopedia can display a rational order and designate the relationships of all human inquiries to the theological themes. But the real key lies in the nature of the Christian faith itself and hence beneath the surface of any formal scheme. Because the Christian faith has at its center a personal response to the reality of the creative, redeeming, and inspiring God, the unity in our faith must be found through personal discovery of the ultimate reality which shapes the whole of life. What does the work of the Hebrew prophets as they assert the judgment and mercy of God have to do with decisions about the control of atomic energy today? How do we understand that when Paul speaks of dying and rising with Christ he is speaking a truth which is relevant to the sense of meaninglessness which may haunt a modern factory worker or executive? In answers to such questions we must discover the integrity of the Christian way of life as it binds God and man, past and present, together.

The Way of Personal Synthesis. The question of unity and direction in the curriculum involves the response of students to the personal demand implicit in their education. Though some professional studies may minimize issues of personal commitment and ethical responsibilty, most professional education today exhibits a lively concern with these matters. In theological education they are never peripheral. The student may have an intellectual grasp of Christian ideas and yet be far from having found the way in which this heritage bears upon his own place in the Christian cause. We have continually to seek the wedding of intellectual maturity to personal integrity and Christian commitment.

Unity then, in theological education, means more than logical unity, though that is a value to be prized. It is a matter of the interconnection of all topics in the curriculum and their being bound up with life experience in such a way that the student discovers exciting new possibilities through that central reality in his faith which gives meaning to the whole.

Because theological education has this personal dimension and because of the richness and diversity of interpretations of Christian faith, no one ideal pattern exists. There is always a strong argument for assembling a faculty of able individuals and setting them free, each to offer work in his own way, with the confidence that the teacher who can show the relation of his field to the Christian cause will communicate this relationship to his students.

In such a free system each student should be advised in his choices by a personal counselor to whom he can disclose his interests and feelings. Student and adviser together will work out a pattern of courses which make a logical whole, and observe some progression from basic work to advanced topics. Also students will be guarded against such concentration in one field as would prohibit a measure of acquaintance with the whole field. Where this plan is in use (as at Yale Divinity School) it includes requirements regarding the student's spread of courses through various fields. He has choices among courses within the prescribed fields. The plan also is adjusted to allow for different vocational aims. In the latter part of his study the student's choice of courses is related to his preparation for parish ministry, missions, college teaching, or for graduate study.

If this method of achieving unity by way of personal synthesis is to be successful it is of great importance that the faculty itself should, amidst all of its freedom, maintain continuous intellectual and spiritual contact among its members. This contact may, as in a few schools, appear in the form of lively and public debate among men who make very different approaches to the understanding of the Christian faith or of life in the light of faith, but yet demonstrate the unity of the Church in the midst of their differences. In other instances faculty members may give evidence of their awareness of what is going on in the classes or seminars of their colleagues without engaging in polemics. In any case the unity of theological study can be served in such a free atmosphere only if the faculty consists of a genuine *collegium* of teachers who have not only achieved personal syntheses for themselves but also realize as a group of intellectual workers the unity of the Church. To some groups it will appear that such unity can be realized and demonstrated only if all the teachers adhere to a common denominational confession; to others it seems that a common conviction and purpose does not need to be, or indeed cannot be, wholly or significantly conceptualized and verbalized.

The Core Curriculum. Another attempt to solve the problem of curriculum proceeds toward the establishment of a "core" of theological study. The proposal is to discover those basic contents and methods which are the foundation of all theological study and to provide these in an integrated and concentrated group of courses. When the student has completed his core work he is ready to choose further courses which will build upon the foundation now laid. The core curriculum has been developed in only a few theological schools, but many of the principles involved in its establishment are vital to any discussion of curriculum.

The core curriculum does not consist merely in any set of required courses which a faculty decides are necessary for the student. The attempt is to do in theological education something analogous to what is done in programs of general education at the college level, that is, to achieve a systematic analysis of the general elements which underlie all theological study and then to work out types of courses which will provide this general and integrated foundation for all students.

Two theological schools that have recently established core curricula on this basis may be considered here. The Federated Theological Faculty at the University of Chicago is organized in seven fields: Bible, Church History, Theology, Religion and Personality, Ethics and Society, Religion and Art, Christianity and the World Religions. Each of these fields offers a "core course" which varies in length from two to four quarters. This core course is intended not only to provide an introduction to the field but to provide the basic knowledge and essential methods which are involved in that area of interpretation of the Christian faith. Advanced work in a field presupposes mastery of the core material, and completion of the entire core is ideally intended to provide that "general education in religion" which should be expected of all ministers and teachers of religion. In practice, for the B.D. degree, students must take Bible, Church History, and Theology and then make some selections from the remaining fields. However, students may elect to cover the entire core in three years, and with some additional courses in preaching and church administration receive the B.D. degree. Graduate students who are candidates for the Ph.D. must cover the entire core (with some concessions to those who have already completed a B.D. degree). It is an essential part of the Chicago plan that students demonstrate their mastery at the core level not only by passing courses but also by passing comprehensive examinations set by the various fields.

The core curriculum of the Perkins School of Theology in Southern Methodist University is developed on a somewhat different pattern. Four basic areas are distinguished: the Bible, the Christian Heritage, Christianity and Culture, the Local Church. In each field a two-year course is offered which covers its basic work. Hence the student is free in his third year to choose among advanced courses. In the Perkins plan, preaching, worship, church administration, Christian education, and music are included within the local church area and offered as part of the core. In the Chicago plan these studies related to the specific functions of the ministry are not included in the core but are directed by a faculty committee on professional studies. In both plans the principle of the responsibility of the entire faculty, for interpretation and teaching of the specific functions of the ministry such as preaching and pastoral care is established.

That the core pattern is intended to break down rigid departmental lines is specifically stated by the Perkins faculty. Each division of studies is defined in relation to its place in achieving the major objectives of theological education:

I. To prepare the minister to understand and foster the program of the Church: the Life and Work of the Local Church.
II. To show that the Church exists within, not outside of, its society, and that, though molded by that society, it must nevertheless challenge its un-Christlike character: Christianity and Culture.
III. To show that the Church can accomplish its task in its society only as it knows clearly whereof it speaks: The Christian Heritage.
IV. To show that the heart of the heritage is the Bible, and the revelation of God in Christ which it contains: The Bible.

The Perkins plan allows an adjustment for the student who takes Hebrew and Greek, though he must use some of his elective time for this.

An immediate problem raised by the core curriculum proposal has to do with teaching. The Perkins faculty states that each teacher gives that portion of the core course for which he is prepared. Obviously such revision of curriculum requires each teacher to reconsider his offering in the light of the total pattern. In this departure from individualism, teachers may have to shift fields in order to staff the program. Courses have to be revised. Different styles of teaching complicate the attempt to work out a unified plan of courses. The existence of these difficulties emphasizes that this plan involves an acceptance by the entire faculty of responsibility for the order and rationale of the curriculm. This is acknowledged by the Perkins faculty:

Inter-divisional contact is not limited, however, to those whose own disciplines require it, but is engaged in by the whole faculty. To take two examples: "Homiletics," in the old departmental structure now falls, in the first instance, in Division I, but is properly a charge upon the interest and activity of the other three divisions, as well, to the extent that others than the instructors of homiletics should have an eye to the homiletical significance of their teaching and should bear a proper share of the responsibility for the laboratory work of practice preaching. "Systematic Theology" is in Division III, yet all instructors should be mindful of the inescapable theological implications with their students. Though such cross-fertilization is desirable in any kind of curriculum the new one at Perkins puts a special emphasis and premium upon it.

The two core programs here described of course are not the only efforts to establish a basic rationale for the theological curriculum. They illustrate the present concern to find such an order, and to provide a concentration of the curriculum which has principles of the structure of Christian faith and of educational theory behind it. They attempt to make explicit in the curriculum a conviction concerning the unity, order, and essential elements of the Christian faith.

It is not our purpose to make specific judgments upon this or any other curricular pattern. The two fundamental questions involved in the establishment of a core curriculum or indeed any system of requirements are first, the determination of the goals and content of theological education, and second, the discovery of how the meeting of student and teacher is to take place so that the vital current of personal interest and involvement is set in motion. The first question looks in the direction of the content of Christian faith and involves the order of Christian truth. The second question looks at the subjective and side of the appropriation of Christian truth in the life of the teacher and student. It is a sentimental reduction of the teaching process to say that it has to do solely with persons, not with subjects. At the same time those who study the subjects are persons who are to grow in Christian wisdom.

D. *Some Principles of Curriculum Construction.* The question of whether there is a specifiable content which constitutes the core of theological education is very difficult. Perhaps this core is not the same for all.

The "classical" disciplines, Bible, Church History, Theology, Pastoral Care, and Preaching, must certainly be included in any theological curriculum, though even if there were nothing else the problem would arise how much each of these should have of the student's time. But the situation today puts this question of allotment of time in a somewhat different light. If we ask how much time should be given to biblical studies, or to theology, the reply can only be, enough should be given to each so that it is seen in its significance in relation to the other subjects, and seen in the light of some organic perspective upon the

Christian faith with its implications for Christian life. Granted that each theological subject has its own integrity and that a student must learn in one sense to master such disciplines as biblical study or historical study "for their own sake," we find a widespread impatience today among both students and faculty with the tendency to leave each discipline to itself.

This search for the interrelations of the established disciplines includes also the search for the bearing of Christian knowledge upon the functions of the ministry. Christian preaching ought to draw upon the entire theological curriculum. Pastoral Care should be enriched with an understanding of the Church and of human life which comes from a knowledge of the care of souls in all ages.

The Dialogue between Sacred and Secular. It is not sufficient to specify these traditional subjects and the need for their interrelation. If the Christian faith must enter into a dialogue with contemporary thought and culture, a student has not been introduced to the core of theological education until he has entered into this conversation between Christian thought and the many disciplines which are concerned with man and his world.

If we grant that the theological school must become a center where this dialogue takes place, we have then to ask how this is to be provided and whether we can specify certain auxiliary disciplines which are essential to theological education today. What place is to be assigned to philosophy, psychology, and sociology, the study of world religions and literary criticism, is a topic of present discussion relevant to this issue.

It is necessary to underline just what is at stake here. It is not enough to say that philosophy, psychology, and sociology are necessary to the understanding of certain aspects of the minister's task; sociology, for example, for community analysis and social action, psychology for pastoral care and religious education. These and other disciplines are essential to the full understanding of the Christian faith itself. A professor of Old Testament said to one surveyor, "The problem of the nature of the Bible and its authority for the Christian is in one important aspect a psychological problem as well as a problem of literary and historical criticism." Knowledge of sociological patterns of the types of human groups and their structures of power and status becomes relevant to the whole of biblical and church history, as well as to an understanding of the Christian ministry. Psychology is not only an auxiliary discipline for the development of cure of souls, but it is one of the critical inquiries which bears upon the meaning of sin, guilt, and redemption. Philosophy offers a critical approach to understanding the ultimate questions and the relating of various fields of inquiry. It has usually been kept in a fairly close relationship to theology, though one of the common complaints of professors of theology today is the lack of adequate philosophical training among students. Further, with the present reign of positivistic philosophy in many universities, one is driven to ask whether it may not devolve upon theological schools to be among the centers which preserve the humanistic and spiritual tradition of Western philosophy against its dissipation.

It might seem that to insist on this conception of the theological curriculum as making a place for the mutual confrontation of sacred and secular studies makes an already difficult problem insoluble. Surely the most that can be expected from any student in the three years is a beginning of mastery of one limited field and some slight acquaintance with a few others.

We believe on the contrary that the point of view just taken will help in certain ways to ease the curricular problem. It is obvious that no student and for that matter no scholar in his lifetime will become conversant with all the possible fields and relevant knowledge. What is required from the theological student is something which is possible, and it is threefold: first, he should have a general acquaintance with the main areas of human thought. This is in part what his general education in college and his introduction to the theological fields should provide and there is no substitute for it. Second, the student should discover that angle of approach to Christian truth which is vital for him. This may come through his interest in one of the academic subjects; it may come through his attempt to become adequate in his preaching and pastoral duties, but there should be some avenue to Christian understanding which he has made his own and upon which he can spend intensive energies. Third, the student should begin to formulate his conception of the normative elements in Christian faith so that he has a principle of judgment which he brings to thought and action. But such a grasp of the normative character of Christian faith may become stereotyped and destructive unless it is related to a continuing process of criticism through those inquiries into human life of which we have been speaking. Therefore the student should not only have a view of the relation of Christian truth to the understanding which man derives from experience and critical inquiry, but he should have sufficient mastery of some particular discipline in science or the humanities so that the productive interchange between this field and Christian faith can take place in his mind.

The view taken here does not mean that any secular discipline can become a substitute for the theological center of the minister's work. The pastor is not first of all a psychologist or sociologist who happens to be working in a religious institution. He is a Christian minister who knows that the Christian understanding of life is continually made more fruitful when it is kept in close relation to that understanding of man and his world which comes from experience and critical inquiry and that the student or minister should continue to seek this understanding. Certainly the conception of theological education of which we are speaking does not envision that it is ever completed in a seminary course, or in a lifetime. What is important is that such a view of Christian understanding should be communicated to the student and that he should be equipped with the essentials for starting on the way toward it.

What has just been said about the discovery of interrelationships between disciplines has its bearing upon the view taken here of the ecumenical context of theological studies. The question of special courses in "ecumenics" has been often raised in our discussions. A few such courses exist, and in one American theological school there is a chair of ecumenical theology occupied by a distinguished theologian. There is no question of the value of such specific attention to ecumenical problems; but those most deeply concerned with the ecumenical movement see clearly that the life of the whole Church should become the context for all theological studies. When Bible, Church History, Theology, and Pastoral Counseling are taught in such a way that they draw upon the richness of insight and variety of approach of many Christian traditions, and when the concern is made explicit to see every problem in the light of its bearing upon the emergence of new forms of the Church and new decisions looking toward the unity of the Body of Christ, then the true ecumenical impact in theological education will be made.

E. *Pretheological Requirements.* The question of pretheological studies is pertinent to the issues just raised. Some of the pressure on the theological curriculum arises from the fact that faculties cannot presuppose that college studies will have provided an adequate and standard preparation for each student. Here the splintering of our culture is manifest, for no necessary congruence between liberal arts training and theological study can be assumed. Further, there are many students who come to seminary from engineering schools, premedical courses, or other specialized programs and have little or no general arts training. These indeed may bring resources of disciplined thinking which some arts students may lack, but the variety of backgrounds still creates problems.

The statement of recommendations for pretheological college study which has been for many years in use among the schools of the American Association of Theological Schools was revised in 1956. It begins by stating some general goals: that the student should be able to use the English language, to think clearly, and to have begun his preparation in one of the biblical languages and in a modern foreign language. He should know the world of men and ideas, of nature and human affairs, and his sense of mastery over intellectual materials is deemed important.

The critical problem for theological study, which has been more adequately dealt with we believe in the new form of the Association statement adopted in 1956, concerns not only the scope and number of fields to be included in the college courses and the amount of time devoted to each but the question as to the *kind* of understanding of the sciences and humanities which is sought.

The important point is that the student not only know something about his world and human life as described by the sciences and humanities but that he begin to discern the issues of truth, values, and faith as they arise in human experience. His study of ethics should raise questions as to the relation of values to nature and deal with the presuppositions of ethical systems and the religious questions involved. The method and content of modern science raise many questions for the interpretation of Christian faith in God as creator and man as his creature. What is desired is not that every subject should be taught from a Christian point of view but that the student should see the bearing of his studies upon ultimate issues concerning the meaning of life. He should discover how and where personal commitment is an issue for the scientist, politician, worker, and businessman. He should have such a knowledge of human history and our cultural heritage as to be at home in the dialogue between Christianity and modern thought, and he should not have been protected either by a secularist exclusion of religious questions or a restrictive pietism from seeing the issues in that dialogue.

It is only fair to point out that when theological educators find college graduates wanting in these respects, the college teachers point to the secondary schools and urge that only attention to that level can provide the colleges with opportunity to do their proper work. A recent group of writers on general education point out that "without familiarity in the Bible, classical mythology, and great epic and legendary material, intelligent reading at the college level is exceedingly difficult; and colleges have a right to count on such knowledge in their entering students." [2] The over-all problem of the gulf between Christianity and our cultural mind-set is underlined as these researchers report how few of the students from Andover, Exeter, and Lawrenceville elect courses which have to do with the systematic study of values. From the eleventh grade through college 40 per cent of a group studied took no philosophy, 60 per cent no courses in religion, and 94 per cent no formal work in ethics. [3]

[2] *General Education in School and College,* Cambridge, Harvard University Press, 1952, 84–85, 95 n.

[3] *Ibid.,* 95 n.

The issues involved are sharply raised by the discussion of courses in Bible and in religion in colleges, especially as pretheological courses. The thesis of the Bible Schools is pertinent here. It is argued that whereas liberal education has largely by-passed the biblical heritage and tradition, a Christian liberal education can be developed which places knowledge and interpretation of the Bible at its core. Many Bible institutes and Bible colleges give courses leading to liberal arts degrees with a heavy concentration in biblical studies. The present emphasis of the Bible Schools Accrediting Association is to ensure that this biblical core is related to liberal arts training in science and the humanistic studies. They are developing a distinctive pattern of Christian liberal education guided by a conservative evangelical view of the nature and authority of the biblical revelation. It should be added that the requirement of a certain number of courses in Bible will not by itself secure the dialogue between the meaning of the Bible and the thought world of contemporary man which is required if the Christian faith is to have its full power in a world largely shaped by modern science and technology.

The problem of college religious studies here is met in another context in relation to the departments of religion which offer "majors." There appears to be a turn in the discussion as to whether a college major in religion is desirable for the preseminary student. The usual advice given by seminaries has been against it on the ground that seminary courses will concentrate on such studies and that a religion major will detract from the general liberal education which the student needs. Some critical judgments on this view have lately arisen.[4]

It appears to us that the issues here cannot be resolved by any "yes" or "no" answer. The crucial matter is the content of the college work in religion and more especially the way in which religious and biblical studies are interpreted in relation to other liberal disciplines. There is excellent teaching of religion in many colleges today. Where it seems most effective it lays a foundation for the dialogue between Christian thought with other human knowledge. Such an education may be said to be more truly liberal than one which only adds a bit of religion to the general collection of studies. At the same time, the warning against a narrow concentration on religious studies in college is valid.

We have been speaking of a goal. When we ask how the theological schools deal with students who have not had even a minimal preparation the picture is not encouraging. Very few schools make a detailed assessment of the student's college record and require further college work in areas where he is deficient. The surveyors discovered that often when schools officially have the policy of making such an assessment

---

[4] J. Paul Williams, "But Don't Major in Religion," *The Christian Century,* 71, June 16, 1954.

in practice, little is done to carry it out. This is true even in the elementary matter of ability to read and write good English. Some schools propose to send students for remedial work, but this may have been done in only one or two cases a year. In view of the general chorus of complaint by faculties about English composition it is clear that little of the needed remedial work is being required.

The salient fact which emerges from this survey is that the general tendency among the schools to accept "an A.B. from an accredited college" as sufficient credential for entrance on the seminary course needs correction. It is true that we are dealing here with practical circumstances. More college work means more time and expense for the school and the student. It means perhaps fewer ministers per year graduated for the churches. But it seems to us that considerably more rigor should be exercised. A better prepared group of entering students would help the development of a more nearly adequate seminary curriculum.

II.   *The Fields of Study*

We turn now to an examination of the various fields of theological study to inquire how the principles we have been stating may bear upon answers to the many specific questions which arise. The discussion may conveniently follow the following order: Bible, Church History, Theology, Ethics, Religious Education, Homiletics, Church Administration, Liturgy and Music, the Specialized Ministries. An obvious omission here is Pastoral Theology and Counseling, but it is expedient to discuss this field in the next chapter.

A. *Bible.* The Bible can be studied in many ways and its authority can be variously conceived. It can be read as bearing in itself a complete revelation of God, or it can be regarded as giving its witness to God's word only when it is read in relation to man's critical reflection on all his experience. It can be studied as an object of purely linguistic and historical research, or as a theological source book, or as a devotional guide. The Christian minister needs to be clear in his own view of the nature of the Bible and its authority. He needs to master the biblical content and to develop his powers of interpretation. Two aspects of the problems involved are being given special attention today: the study of the biblical languages, and the emphasis on biblical theology. We shall examine both.

The Biblical Languages. What has happened to the study of biblical languages in the past few generations has been reviewed in the study of trends reported in Chapter One.

Even in those schools where the languages are still required, the amount of requirement has frequently been reduced from what used to obtain when theological and classical learning were so closely held together.

In the discussions of language requirements one hears familiar arguments. Some remind us that not only do the biblical languages have their distinctive meaning so that the key words cannot be translated but that there is a certain outlook and way of conceiving the world which finds expression in these languages. "Without an understanding of the Hebrew mind and of the Semitic background of the New Testament the student cannot know accurately what the Bible means," the argument runs. In rebuttal some teachers of biblical interpretation point out that the explanation to the modern student of these ancient meanings and these "untranslatable words" are always given in English or other modern language which shows that the meanings can be thus communicated.

It seems to us that this discussion admirably illustrates the way in which critical educational questions can become obscured in a dispute over particular requirements. It is argued that the languages constitute a "good discipline." But other subjects such as philosophy or the scientific study of human behavior can make an equally good case as "disciplines." When the values of knowledge of the biblical languages are stressed, the critical question is, "Are these values necessary for all theological students?" Instead of asking whether Hebrew and Greek should be required it seems more to the point to ask whether they should be required of all. If they are not, then which students will benefit most from them? When we see that the churches must develop in each generation a group of biblical scholars, the question remains as to how this is to be done. Is this most efficiently done by requiring a minimal amount of Hebrew and Greek from every theological student?

In the considerable heat of this controversy these conclusions begin to emerge:

First, many who are themselves teachers of Bible say that to require every seminary student to take a minimum of Hebrew and Greek (usually one year of each) is not justified by the results. This holds especially for those students who have no language preparation, and those who have little aptitude for languages. Such students would far better spend their time mastering the English Bible. One professor of Old Testament says: "I can bring my students by the end of the third year to think in terms of God's free sovereignty and of Covenant but I could not do so if I had to take a part of the time available to instruct them in Hebrew." There is also some evidence, though it is not decisive, that schools not requiring Greek and Hebrew require the students to give more time to biblical studies than do those schools which enforce the language requirement.

Second, some experiments are under way which promise help in

Bible study to the student who cannot major in the biblical languages, or even acquire sufficient knowledge to depend on his own scholarship in any degree. Short courses are being designed to acquaint the student with the languages. These courses are of two types with somewhat different aims.

Some brief courses are given to provide a minimal acquaintance with the alphabet, grammar, syntax, and paradigms so that the student can use a lexicon and read a commentary intelligently. In one course described to us this kind of introduction to Hebrew is given in a single quarter after which the student can follow the discussion of the exegesis of an Old Testament passage.

The other type stresses somewhat less the aim of use of the commentaries but approaches a similar goal through acquainting the student with the mode of thought of the biblical writers as this is reflected and dramatized in the character of the languages. The important discussions today of the Semitic caste of mind as it determines not only the Old Testament but gives the structural foundation for the New Testament can be stressed through linguistic analysis to which students can be introduced even though they do not make an extensive study of the language. One Old Testament professor is making use of audiovisual aids in introducing the students quickly to Hebrew words and syntax as these display the characteristics of the culture and mentality out of which the Old Testament came.

The matter of critical importance seems to be that students should discover the central themes which determine the biblical thought of God and his creative and redemptive working. This point is made judiciously in relation to language study by one professor of Old Testament:

> The aim of a B.D. student's training in Old Testament (also in New Testament) is to introduce him to the spirit of biblical religion. He should begin to grasp the perspective on life in terms of which the writers of scripture offered their testimony. In particular, in contrast to the typical Western way of looking at life, the theocentric quality of the biblical perspective should begin to permeate the student's consciousness. The dynamic character of God—the living God—who stands at the center of this perspective, and who is active as Creator and Redeemer, is the focus of attention and should make the deepest impact upon the student. Since the Old Testament is the outcome of a long history and a particular cultural process, this involves becoming acquainted with the ethos of a religious culture.
>
> I am persuaded that it is possible for a student to enter into the spirit and meaning of Israel's religion and culture in this manner, to an appreciable extent, without a knowledge of the Hebrew language. I feel that in the case of the Greek tradition the study of the Greek classics in trans-

lation and with the aid of skilled interpreters who do know Greek, the ethos and meaning of Greek culture has been communicated in significant degree in such experimental institutions as St. John's College and the College of the University of Chicago, (possibly also in the "Great Books" projects). So, I believe, a skilled professor of Old Testament, who knows Hebrew and is deeply informed by the Hebraic spirit, can, by means of the English Bible, communicate the Hebrew ethos fairly adequately. It must be admitted that no person is likely to grasp the Hebraic spirit, on its deepest level, unless he learns to read and, in some sense, think in the Hebrew language. However, for a person to know the Hebrew language well enough so that it enables him thus more deeply to enter into the Hebrew spirit, requires an attitude of mind and a long period of training such as is simply unavailable in the graduate curriculum of three or four years provided for the typical B.D. student.

The teaching of biblical languages and content with emphasis on the spirit of Hebrew religion seems the surest means of securing a lively interest and recognition of the significance of such study. The good teaching being done as well as the movement today toward biblical theology explains the increasing election of Hebrew and Greek by students in some schools where they are not required.

A third observation concerns the supply of students who will be able to develop real scholarship in these languages. Sometimes the argument is made that unless all B.D. students are required to take Hebrew the supply of Old Testament teachers cannot be maintained. Similar statements are made about the New Testament and Greek. One professor described for us a group of eight men all working for Ph.D.'s under a well-known Old Testament scholar. Every man declared that he would not be working in that field had it not been for the requirement of Hebrew. On the other hand, of the teachers of Old Testament who are members of the National Council on Religion in Higher Education, few attended seminaries where Hebrew was required.

It still appears to us that universal requirement is not the answer. Every field can claim that it should be universally required so that its supply of scholars will continue. But there are some things to be done about this situation.

Part of the present difficulty has to do with the rigidity of the B.D. curriculum which we have described. The student who has had no college Hebrew or Greek cannot get enough time in most seminary courses today to develop scholarly foundations in these languages. He has to take too many other things. The answer seems to be that the B.D. curriculum should be left sufficiently open so that students who want to stress the languages can devote adequate time to them. They should be able to concentrate more upon biblical theology and ethics and upon historical studies which allow them to develop their linguistic skill. Schools ought to devise more concentrated reading courses so that such students can be given at least an introduction to other fields. Some things will be sacrificed in such a program but this is the case in any seminary course. No student should receive a B.D. degree on the basis of linguistic skill alone, but students who have the ability and concern to do it should be able to make intensive biblical scholarship the base of their seminary training. This is not the only scholarship the church needs; but it is indispensable, and a man may develop an effective ministry on the basis of a specialized B.D. course in biblical subjects.

A further possibility lies in the development of intensive summer courses in Hebrew and Greek such as are now offered by Princeton Seminary. Languages, it appears, can best be taught in such concentrated programs. Another need is for more adequate counseling of students in college and upon entrance into seminary with respect to languages. It is true that where the biblical languages are required the prestige of tradition and the entrenched power of biblical departments are forces which other fields may have to counteract. But where the languages are not required it is often the case that the worth of this study is not given adequate presentation in the counseling of students.

What the Church needs is for its scholars, ministers, and laity to form a community of shared experience and mutual correction in interpreting the Bible. Knowledge of the biblical languages and specialized scholarship in the biblical backgrounds is one requirement for this conversation, but there is also need for the discussion which comes from philosophical, psychological, and sociological disciplines. Those who have scant acquaintance with biblical languages must depend upon those who have mastered them, but the linguistic scholars must in turn depend on the labors of other scientific and humanistic disciplines. Such a community of diverse but mutually dependent approaches to the meaning of the Bible promises a fuller use of the church's resources and a more adequate maintenance of the necessary linguistic scholarship than does the enforcement of a mechanical and minimal requirement of a year's work in each biblical language for every theological student.

Biblical Theology. One of the striking features of biblical teaching today is the attention given to theological interpretation. This teaching stands in contrast to use of the Bible simply to illustrate one dogmatic standpoint, and to that approach in which literary and historical criticism tend to become not only the prolegomenon but the entire substance of biblical interpretation. The question of the meaning of the Bible for those who wrote it and for us who stand within the Christian community is surely the critical question for faith and for the minister as he preaches and teaches. This meaning cannot be simply read off the Bible by arranging its contents according to a chronological or doctrinal pattern. It must be discovered through a continual interplay between the biblical contents and the issues of life as they arise in our experience. Regarded in this way the problem of teaching becomes more complex but also more exciting. As one biblical scholar says:

> The instructor, dealing with the dramatic movement of Israel's life-story, will have to blend archeological historical form and literary critical and theological considerations in a kind of teaching counterpoint. His aim should not be to teach history by itself, or literary and form criticism for its own sake, or theology abstracted from history; but rather to combine these interests—even as they are combined in the Bible which we study. From this approach the student may come to understand the real life situations of the people, the movement of the drama of which God is protagonist, and the hopes and fears, the tensions and insights, the faith and the doubts which these people experienced along the way.[5]

While the development of this conception is bringing about changes in teaching and courses, its full significance is not yet recognized in many schools. As one professor of Bible put it to the survey: "There are still too many courses called introductions to the Old and New Testaments which are purely histories of the documents, designed for a generation of students that had intimate acquaintance with biblical ideas but no critical understanding of biblical history. Some few students still come to our schools with such a preparation, but not many."

What is needed is the establishment of the character of the biblical outlook coupled with a sound critical method, and an understanding of the relevance of biblical perspectives to contemporary issues.

These points made in connection with the Old Testament bear equally upon the teaching of the New Testament. Here many signs point to an increasing election by students of Greek. While it is not unknown for the two departments of Old Testament and New Testament to have little to do with one another, there is increasing emphasis upon the interdependence of all biblical studies. Just at this time when important new perspectives have been developing, the discovery of the Scrolls of the Qumram community has added exciting new dimensions to both Old and New Testament studies.

B. *Church History.* While biblical scholars raise issues of the nature of theological interpretation of the texts, church historians are absorbed in analogous problems. Among the important questions to the fore are those of the meaning of history when viewed from a Christian perspective, the relation of the biblical view of time to other views of man's historical existence, the relation of positivistic views of historical

---

[5] Bernhard Anderson, "Changing Emphases in Biblical Scholarship," *Journal of Bible and Religion,* Vol. XXIII, April, 1955.

data to theological interpretation, and the importance of examining church history with full recognition of the distinctive character of the Christian community in history with its unity and diversity, its ecumenical dimensions, and its witness as a Church among the many peoples of the world. The teaching of church history succeeds in capturing the imagination of students when these issues are pressed. It is important that the student survey the past as a record of the Church's experience and that he see the ultimate questions about the direction and outcome of human history and the history of the Church within world history.

The practical difficulties in teaching church history today seem to fall into three groups: 1) finding time enough to "cover the ground"; 2) overcoming the resistance of many students, especially American students, who are sometimes said to be allergic to historical study; and 3) the place of the history of Christian thought in relation to church history.

The first problem, that of time, is universal in theological education, but it has some special aspects for the historian. It is hard to find a logical reason for leaving out any portion of the historical development, yet to cover it all is impossible. The special histories of denominations must be covered in many schools. A course in American church history is more and more frequently being required.

The surveyors have raised the question with church historians as to whether a partial solution may not lie in leaving the over-all coverage of many historical periods to reading assignments checked by examination. In this way the teacher would not feel the necessity of lecturing on every topic. To be sure, church historians like all other professors have a variety of teaching methods, but this would appear to be one area where students could be required to cover much of the extensive material by reading and to concentrate in their courses on particular periods and on basic issues where they can plunge deeply enough to achieve some real sense of historical method and movements.

A serious problem confronts the historians in the matter of the history of Christian doctrine. Church history obviously cannot be taught apart from doctrine; yet if general church history is to be covered, history of doctrine cannot receive concentrated attention in that course. A great many schools require general courses in church history for the B. D. students but require no courses in history of doctrine, and in many cases very little is offered in this field anywhere in the curriculum. In view of the intrinsic importance of the history of Christian thought as well as the increasing interest in ecumenical discussion this seems an anomalous situation.

One of the conferences held in connection with the survey devoted some time to discussing the teaching of church history. The question was asked whether American theological students do not tend to be deficient in the sense for historical study. The faculties present agreed that the American student probably finds less initial stimulus in his cultural surrounding to historical curiosity. The monuments of the past are not so numerous or symbolic of so long a history as in Europe. The American ethos tends to focus attention on the future. Yet it was agreed that these are relative judgments and that successful teaching of church history is not such a great rarity. It was pointed out that good historical teaching comes from the teacher's capacity for imaginative projection into the past so that the student is not only helped to realize what life was at another time, but that he discovers through the historical experience the universality of human problems and the special ideals and circumstances which have shaped his own being. Whether the gift for imaginative historical teaching can be cultivated or not remained something of an unanswered question in this discussion, but it seems clear that the difference between success and failure in quickening the students' interest depends more on the teacher in historical studies than in most other fields.

C. *Theology.* At least one basic course in systematic theology will be found in nearly every theological curriculum. Frequently it is given in the second year, and often consists of an entire year's course. The problem of introduction to theology in the first year is dealt with variously. The surveyors found many schools in which one course is given in the first year to introduce the student to theological thinking. This course may be an introductory discussion of Christian concepts of God, Christ, and Salvation. Sometimes it offers an interpretation of the rise of Christian doctrine with special attention to Greek philosophy and to other philosophical movements and in this way serves to fill in some of the background in history of Western thought which students often lack. The surveyors found no schools offering in the first year an introduction to Christian thinking which were not convinced of its usefulness.

Two topics in connection with theology can be given attention here. The first is the vexing question of the relation of theology to philosophical studies and the variety of training in philosophy which students have. Not many schools are in a position to require students to take additional work in philosophy before they begin theological studies. Some try to meet this deficiency by the introductory course just mentioned, or with a general course in philosophy of religion. Neither method can make up for a student's ignorance of the history of Western thought. It should be pointed out that what is involved here is not only technical philosophical studies in epistemology and metaphysics but the entire tradition of Western philosophical, ethical, and political thought, the interpretation of scientific knowledge and method, and the history of rational, artistic, and moral values in civilization.

A more vigorous attempt should be made to see that students acquire the background necessary to an appreciation of the history of Christian thought as it has been affected by and has shaped our intellectual history. Neither understanding of the history of Christian doctrine nor the formulation of contemporary problems of Christian thought is possible without some grasp of these presuppositions of Western culture which have been largely formulated in philosophical terms.

Theologians take different views of the significance of philosophical categories and methods for the statement of Christian faith, but in any view the question of "apologetics" must be faced. How is the Christian witness to be given intelligibly and persuasively to those who stand outside the faith, or who think they stand outside it or who profess another faith? Too many schools give the student an acquaintance with Christian faith as formulated in some theological tradition but do very little with the analysis of the communication of Christian ideas in relation with or opposition to the categories and spirit of contemporary culture. Reflection on such issues as the relation of biblical ideas of time to modern conceptions of time, history, and human destiny, or the critical issues between Christian and the progressive or cyclical or Marxist views of history are fundamental for the preacher who would bring the Gospel to bear on life today. This requires courses in apologetics taught by faculty members who are versed in the dominant modes of thought of our time, and who can interpret the truth as we know it in Christ through insight into the human situation for which that truth is the saving word.

Non-Christian Religions. The study of religions other than Christianity can be properly related to the historical field as well as the theological but we shall discuss it here. A few schools offer and require of B.D. students at least one course in non-Christian religions. A very few have major departments in this area but unquestionably it is badly neglected. The majority of theological schools offer no work in non-Christian religions. For many years the accepted statement on pre-theological training for example had nothing to say about work in this field.

One of the professors who has made such studies an integral part of the theological program in his school was asked to state their significance in preparing the Christian pastor of an American congregation. He replied that if we consider political education as an analogous study we see that our problem is so to educate ourselves that we see our local political decisions in the context of the world issues which bear upon them. So also as we attempt to develop a more competent Christian judgment, we need to know the actual religious world in which we live, and that world contains many faiths other than our own. To neglect study of other religions is a provincialism which our Christian faith itself in its claim for universal significance cannot tolerate.

This reply suggests a new phase into which this study of non-Christian religions has moved. It is no longer an attempt to portray the benightedness of non-Christian faith; nor is it a detached comparative analysis of other religions as interesting cultural objects. It is rather the effort of the Christian community to discover the religious situation of mankind, to be both appreciative and critical of all religious experience and traditions, and to prepare more adequately for the serious discussion between Christianity and other religious faiths which seems certain to increase. Except in those schools which have faculty and other resources to do advanced work in this field, the most that can be hoped for is more emphasis on this study in the pretheological course, provision for some work in world religions in seminaries, and the use in courses in church history, theology, and apologetics of materials relevant to the great religions and their significance for the Christian faith.

D. *Ethics and Social Studies.* At the outset of this study the surveyors tacitly assumed that because of the critical issues of war and world revolution, as well as through the influence of the social gospel movement, seminary curricula would show a marked emphasis upon studies in Christian ethics. This assumption now appears erroneous. Ethics is rarely completely ignored, but it receives only minimal attention in a large number of schools. It should be said further that too often the one required course in ethics gives a general approach to basic principles, quite necessary in itself but rarely probing concrete personal and social issues in the common life except for some attention to problems of pastoral ethics.

There are to be sure some schools which make ethics a major study. Usually they are schools with large faculties. In most schools ethics is assigned to the professor of theology, or of some other subject, who must give one required course which covers biblical, historical, and contemporary ethics.

The sociological studies which are indispensable to interpretation of Christian ethical doctrines are even less frequently represented. Action without regard for what human beings are and how they behave in their various groupings can be futile or destructive. The growing concern for the introduction of theological students to sociological concepts stems from the desire to relate Christian ethics, and indeed all understanding of Christian faith, to those aspects of human life with which sociologists are concerned. Studies of group power and conflict, of caste and class, of ideology and social strata, authoritarian and democratic social structures, the relation of freedom and order, and such studies of sociological determinants of the American spirit as Riesman's *The Lonely Crowd* or Mills's *White Collar,* describe forces which shape the common life and spirit. The Church is itself a social group, acting in human society. The meaning of Christian community in the Body of Christ cannot be absorbed into sociology, but it cannot be understood apart from its sociological aspects.

It is impossible to prescribe how the sciences and other studies of man should be represented in every theological faculty and curriculum. The introduction of a body of scientific method and data in one area can demonstrate the significance of such study for Christian faith, and can provide the student with a point of view for the relating of theological understanding to other fields. The student who discovers the way in which psychology or sociology or literary criticism can function as a mediating discipline between the Gospel and contemporary man's search for faith has one of the prime requisites for a lifetime of fruitful reflection. Even where the Christian rejects as idolatrous or irrelevant certain secular ways of thinking, he needs to know whereof he speaks.

E. *The Work of the Pastor and Teacher.* When we turn to the fields of homiletics, religious education, and church administration, as well as to liturgy and church music, we come to studies which are often designated "practical" in contrast to "theoretical." No one is happy about this designation. The suggestion that theology and Bible are not "practical" is as odious as the implication that religious education and preaching have no body of theory. What distinguishes these fields is that they have to do with the meaning of Christian faith as it bears upon specific functions of the minister or other religious worker so that work in these fields involves practice as well as instruction. Many aspects of these studies will be discussed in the next chapter, but basic principles must be discussed here. There is a deep concern to consider these studies within the organic unity of Christian understanding and ministry rather than to treat them merely as "skills" or to allow them to develop autonomous self-interpretations apart from encounter with the central themes of Christian thought. This is not to say that no theological insight can arise out of preaching and pastoral experience. It is only to say that an adequate theology must involve the continued exploration of both tradition and experience. Therefore no one field in theological studies can claim to possess the final word of judgment over the others.

Homiletics. It is difficult to describe recent developments in homiletics because they are in experimental stages amidst groping for new directions. The heart of the matter is the emphasis on Christian preaching as growing out of the preacher's response to the Gospel and his bringing to bear on the communication of the Gospel all the resources which his Christian experience and theological training provide. Specifically this means in many schools an increase of courses in the *content* of preaching. Preaching focuses attention not only on doctrine but upon the event of the meeting of preacher and congregation in response to the Word of God which is the source of doctrine. Recent emphases in biblical interpretation have reinforced this conception. The Gospel was preached and heard before it was written, and preaching is a continuing action in the Church through which the Holy Spirit renews the substance of faith in the lives of believers.

One implication of this view for the curriculum is that the entire theological faculty has responsibility for instruction relevant to preaching. Courses in various fields are taught so as to bear upon the preacher's task. Faculty members from all fields are often made responsible for criticism of student sermons. In one school excellent criticism is given by members of the college faculty of arts on the same campus. These reflective laymen bring not only their own critical resources but some of the experience of the typical congregation to their hearing of the sermon.

Such concentration of faculty resources on homiletics has an important demonstration in a Lutheran school (Chicago Lutheran at Maywood, Illinois) in which three professors, one theologian, one biblical scholar, and one teacher of speech share responsibility for the course. The assigned pericope of the United Lutheran Church is used as each week's sermon text. The biblical teacher deals with exegesis, the theologian discusses theological issues and their relation to contemporary problems, and the professor of speech criticizes the student's finished sermon and its delivery. All join in analysis of the sermon. While this program appears suited to a specific situation it typifies the concern for biblical and theological interpretation of the content of preaching.

Of even greater importance than specific courses is the kind of teacher of homiletics for which the schools are looking. One traditional arrangement is to have this instruction given by the president of the school who may have distinguished himself in preaching and pastoral work. Sometimes schools have added to their faculties, for part-time or full-time teaching, men of especial pulpit brilliance.

It is no criticism of these men to say that there are some limitations in this arrangement. It is true that students need self-confidence in preaching. The inspiration of a great preacher has value in addition to all that he may teach of how it should be done; but with notable exceptions this kind of teaching may not provide, and in some cases it may obstruct, collaboration with the other members of the theological faculty. When the need for clarity as to the content of the Christian message is so great, schools are searching for teachers of preaching who are themselves concerned with contemporary theological issues, and who are able to be mediators to the students of the bearing of all their studies upon the preaching task.

When we ask where such men are to be found we raise a real problem. The man who preaches effectively may not always be capable of teaching others. Further, as we have noted, even when the schools find the man who can preach and teach, they discover that in order to match the salary paid by his church in many cases they would have to offer a salary far in excess of that paid to other seminary professors. Some schools are concluding that it may be wiser to assign young men to this department and let them develop some new modes of teaching rather than to take men who are far along in their ministry and who have established reputations. The contributions of such younger men may be less spectacular in the immediate present, but it may produce a result of lasting worth in the church's ministry.

Another approach to preaching is given by the development of "communications" as a field of special study. This reflects not only the influence of mass communications with their attendant effect upon modes of public address but also the conviction that preaching should be seen as one form of communication within the church, and should be related to liturgy, sacrament, teaching, and counseling rather than set apart and dramatized without reference to the rest of the church's life.

Those eager for "plain and simple" presentation of the Gospel often forget that communication in the Christian sense implies sharing in a community of meaning. It is only through personal participation in biblical ways of thought and a grasp of ways of stating the church's faith in relation to contemporary modes of thought that the basis for adequate communication of the Gospel can be laid. Undoubtedly much can be done to increase the clarity of preaching and theological writing, but the deeper problem must not be lost sight of in the midst of concern with techniques. This is to provide that hard-won knowledge of the sources and nature of Christian convictions out of which encounter with the Word of God must come. Students who have been taught their Bible, history, and theology in living commerce with human problems will be better able to communicate the Gospel in congregations.

Religious Education. The surveyors found a fairly widespread feeling among religious educators that ministers do not give enough attention to this part of their church program; some spoke emphatically about ministerial indifference to the church school. One professor in this field has recently written, "I hazard the opinion, based on some years of observing youth leaders who are seminary students, that 50 to 75 per cent of our future pastors are headed for maintaining the existing void between youth and ministers." [6] While taking note of this judgment we have also been struck by the number of capable ministers we have interviewed who are building strong congregations and who show a special interest in the educational responsibility of the church. A number of these very busy ministers take time to do some teaching in their church schools. Perhaps one mark of effective ministry is the taking of responsibility for Christian nurture of all ages.

Everything in the life of the church and work of the pastor may involve teaching, and have an educational aspect. One important thesis of the religious education movement has been the necessity of taking an educational point of view toward the whole of the church's work. When this field has been strongly under the influence of progressive education theory, as in the second and third decades of this century, it has sometimes appeared to develop a theology of its own, and to threaten to create a rival curriculum within the theological school.

It can be reported that the extreme division which sometimes resulted from the clash of educational and theological theory has been considerably lessened. One factor has been the attention given by both educators and theologians to the psychological understanding of human personality. The recognition of self-centeredness and guilt, with the resultant need for the message of redemption and the community which witnesses to it, have been reinforced by explorations in depth psychology, group dynamics, and sociological studies, as well as by contemporary theological interpretations of the nature and depth of sin. Such a conversation between those dealing primarily with educational processes and those concerned with theological meanings is far preferable to the setting up of autonomous realms which merely pass judgment upon the other's meanings and values. The biblical theme of "growth in grace" binds the Christian faith and the educational problem together.

It is our judgment, which is shared by many in the field, that the establishment of the concept of the teaching function of church and of the pastor is of basic importance and has been largely accomplished with the help of religious educators. The minister needs to relate the content of Christian faith to the processes of human growth, and to see his church as a teaching community.

This viewpoint obviously affects the whole of the theological curriculum, and ought to be encouraged by what is done in every field. It therefore should not be left to the department of religious education to carry the whole responsibility for the teaching function of the church. Basic educational theory should be provided, as well as attention to some of the special responsibilities of the church such as those involving

[6] Wesner Fallaw, "Where Are the Pastors of Youth?", *The Christian Century*, Oct. 6, 1954, 1201.

children and youth. But here again the specialized training which religious education departments offer for men and women who are to become directors of religious education, as in the case of other specialized ministries, should not become a source of fragmentation of the basic curriculum for the training of the pastor.

It is true that the large majority of Christian pastors must be their own directors of religious education in their churches; but it appears to us that some of the specialized training required can be most effectively given through post-B.D. institutes. If everything needed in this field is crowded into the three-year course, the problem of the curriculum becomes insoluble.

Church Administration. The surveyors received a remarkably consistent testimony from ministers as to the need for some imaginative new approaches to church administration. The American church depends in part upon skillful organization to maintain its effectiveness as a Christian community. Many of the conspicuous examples of ministerial failure which were reported to us had to do with ineptness in handling organizational problems. The difficulties lie not only in ignorance of organizational techniques but also in failures in personal relationships. Good administration depends on moral insight and loyalty, the keeping of promises, respect for principles of democratic discussion, and refusal to by-pass constituted authority. Devotion to the common enterprise above personal feelings can mark the difference between effective ministry and catastrophe.

As in all Christian experience, behind these moral imperatives there lie the convictions of faith. The prime question of church administration is the clarification of the nature and goals of the Church. Ministers said to us frequently, "We need to see more clearly what we are aiming at in our church activities, and we need specific knowledge of how things can be done in order to go in the right direction."

When we look at curricular offerings in this light there appears to be need for considerably more attention to this field. There are many courses in the doctrine of the Church, courses in church polity which are mainly reviews of the polity of a particular denomination or courses in comparative polity, and courses in church administration which deal with practical details and skills; but rarely are all these brought together so that the student is helped to see church organization and his responsibilities in relation to a clear conception of the Church's nature and task. Once we grant that church administration requires theological and psychological as well as organizational perspectives, the way may be opened for new developments. Ministers have often said to us that association with an experienced minister in their field work was of the greatest help in this area. Unquestionably there are severe limits to what any classroom course can accomplish, yet the need has emerged from our study for a greater attention in the schools to the way in which the organizational and administrative activity which bulks so large in the life of the American minister today can be placed upon a foundation of Christian churchmanship and effective method.

Liturgy and Church Music. We confess we were able to devote far too little time to this important field. With respect to liturgy, adequate discussion of what ought to be done would involve nothing less than a review of the entire liturgical problem in its ecumenical setting. In those churches with well-defined liturgical traditions such as the Episcopal the courses given in this field have at least some clear directives as to content and aims. In Episcopal schools, moreover, instruction in church music is determined by its close relationship to liturgy and by the fact that the Episcopal priest is by canon law responsible for the church music in his parish. In schools of a freer liturgical tradition, courses in "worship" tend of necessity to become collections of historical, practical, and devotional materials with attention to the "Sunday morning service." But the conviction that the spirit is more important than the form, along with the existing variety of church practice, makes it difficult to achieve an orderly and consistent approach to the problem. That there is growing attention to worship in all denominations is clear from curricular offerings as well as in the general influence of the liturgical movement. One indication is the determination in many schools to teach preaching in relation to its setting in worship. We discuss elsewhere the liturgical and worship life in the schools themselves and turn here to a brief comment about church music.

When we consider the large part which music plays in nearly all our church life, the extent to which we worship through hymns and anthems, the heavy expenditures for instruments, choir music, and robes, we must admit that the extent to which we allow our musical standards in the churches to be determined by haphazard training and expediency appears puzzling. There are good schools of church music doing heroic work as they seek to give adequate musical training and such theological understanding of church music as will serve the high purpose of Christian worship. There are some churches which through economic affluence can command especially able and trained musicians. But as we examine the general situation two facts must be faced. The first is that far too few ministers have an adequate introduction to the meaning of music in the Church, its tradition of hymnology, its ways of "singing unto the Lord." Granted there is a continual tension between popular taste in hymns and a cultivated standard of genuine religious music, the real task of the Church is to raise the standards and to achieve a stronger and less sentimental Christian worship. One minister remarked that in his city the chorus in the public high school was doing more to bring good church music to the community than any of the churches. Ministers need to be helped to develop a theory of church music and appreciation of musical standards.

The second fact is that much responsibility falls upon or is left to organists and choir directors, and that too few ministers or churches have any idea of what kind of training should be insisted upon for these offices. Excellence of musical taste itself is of course a first requirement and will guide many decisions in the right direction. But we are speaking of Christian worship and here theological understanding of the nature of the Church and the meaning of the Christian service is necessary. Bad theology in hymns reinforced by trivial music can undo much honest preaching and teaching. The greatest problem for the schools then appears to be to promote among the churches such wide understanding of what is involved that good theological training will be demanded as the necessary foundation for church musicianship. Too often schools which have developed programs for such training find that they must compete with far less adequate programs offered by schools of music and college departments which are in no position to provide the necessary theological elements.

F. *The Specialized Ministries.* We have already discussed the increasing need for training in such specialized ministries as chaplaincies and administrative positions, as well as for churches which are presumed to have distinctive problems because of their location in a rural area or inner city. We propose in our recommendations that most of such training should be given through in-service institutes after the B.D. course. Some additional support for our proposal comes from an examination of two special fields, the armed forces chaplaincy, and the ministry of town and country churches.

Armed Services Chaplaincy. Several arguments support the view that the most important thing for the seminary to give the future chaplain is a broad theological education, while leaving training in military protocol and detail of the chaplain's work to the armed services, schools. The chaplain today has most of the responsibilities he would have in any parish. He is in charge of a full religious education program for military personnel and their families. He may be involved in as many church activities as in a good-sized church. He leads worship for congregations of very different backgrounds and needs to be flexible enough in his thinking and practice to make adjustments for a varied group. He spends much time in counseling. If he is stationed in a foreign country he needs to know and work with missionaries. He especially needs a mature Christian outlook on the relationship of Christians and non-Christians and on the attitudes involved in relationships of Americans to people of other countries.

There are other circumstances which imply the need for general theological work as the basis for an effective ministry which begins in the chaplaincy. Most men will someday leave the chaplaincy to become pastors of churches. They need, therefore, to be prepared for whatever responsibilities may fall upon them in or beyond this special ministry. The demands which are found in the chaplaincy are of a kind which reinforce the need for those experiences and qualities which are basic to all theological education. The chaplain needs to have as broad an experience of human life as possible. He deals with a cross section of the American community, not with a particular social stratum or class. He works without some of the protections which sometimes surround the minister in civilian life. The need both for broad human understanding and for personal moral character is, if possible, even greater here than elsewhere.

The military chaplain often lives an isolated and lonely life so far as relationships to the churches are concerned. There is value in providing schools and institutes in which chaplains can be with their fellow ministers, missionaries, and religious educators, and know that they are part of the church's life. It is also good for civilian ministers to know the problems of the religious life in the armed services. They counsel service men and are pastors of parents whose sons and daughters go into the services.

A seminary curriculum which will best prepare chaplains will be a general theological curriculum in which attention is given in many courses to experiences in military life. Courses in counseling, religious education, worship, and theology, can turn for some concrete situations to the problems chaplains face. One school designates a certain number of courses in its curriculum, especially courses in religious education, missions, and counseling as of special interest to students thinking of the chaplaincy. Through faculty consultation ways are found to introduce relevant material into the courses, but no courses are set apart and designated for chaplains only.

We have here a clear case of how a special ministry becomes most effective when it represents and draws upon the whole church, and in turn brings to the attention of churches and schools the experience of an important form of church work.

Town and Country Church. "Town and country" is the official designation for departments dealing with the church in rural areas. A population of 2,500 or less is often taken as the definition of the "town" though some denominational departments set the figure at 10,000. Some towns of 10,000 more obviously come under the "rural" category than others. For brevity we shall use the term "rural church" in our discussion. Rapid changes in the American rural scene cause this term to cover a wide variety of situations.

How specialized then can training for the rural parish be? Some contrasts with the chaplaincy training are instructive. Seminary students are not chaplains while they are in course; but many seminary students are pastors of rural churches during their seminary course. The problem of financial support for these churches looms especially large. The student pastor may have to give special attention to the ways of financing a rural parish in order to sustain the church's ability to support even a part-time pastor. This may involve plans for the minister and his wife's partial self-support by farming or gardening. Such practical necessities may require the seminary to provide interpretation and practical guidance for students who face these problems.

Those acquainted with this field believe that the pastor of a rural church finds elements in the ways of life and thought of his congregation which may differ in important respects from other churches. Habits of giving to the church have been conditioned by the farmer's way of life. The planning of church programs and enlistment of lay leadership requires special methods. The Gospel is one, but its communication always requires sensitivity to the experience and mind-set of the hearer. Those close to the rural church believe that attention should be given to the opportunities and requirements of preaching in this setting. Often a deeply rooted religious faith must be given a broader and less sectarian theological interpretation. The problem of the community which has too many small churches is often encountered.

While we grant that every specific situation in which the church serves makes its special demands upon the ministry, there is real danger that exclusive emphasis on preparation for one type of ministry may fail to provide the foundation which in the long run every minister needs whatever the particular circumstances of his work. If it is desirable that a theological student be introduced to the needs of the town and country church it is equally desirable that he have as broad an experience as possible in other types of churches. In one rural church course the surveyors heard a number of pastors describe their local situation. Many of the problems had to do with the fact that the open country churches they had been serving now were being surrounded by communities which had become suburbs or housing developments adjacent to new factories. These "rural" churches were experiencing the stresses of growth and adjustment to a totally new situation.

Such experience in part underlies the insistence by professors in this field that when they introduce, as they have in many instances, sociological studies into the schools, these are not to become merely auxiliary support for the study of rural peculiarities. Rather the rural experience offers one concrete body of data which can contribute to, and be interpreted by, the sociological theory which is relevant to understanding every society.

What is essential to the preparation of any Christian minister is his grasp of the Christian faith in its promise and relevance for every human situation. The schools should seek such an encounter with a variety of concrete experience in many types of churches which will extend the student's understanding of the Christian faith, of himself and his vocation, and of human needs. It should not be a concentration on the needs and skills required in dealing with but one type of church problem; and it should not substitute "vocational training" for mastery of the Christian heritage.

The establishing of a theological curriculum is an act of faith. It seeks to give order and substance to the acquiring of a deeper knowledge of the meaning of the Word of God for man. It expresses faith in the community of worship and scholarship as the nurturing body for a continuing ministry. And it depends upon faith that knowledge and insight can be wedded to growth in practical adequacy for the church's ministry. These goals of theological study require more than the already crowded three years of the course if they are to be realized; and they can only be fulfilled as students grow in maturity through experience in the church as well as in academic understanding. We turn then in the next chapter to the question of field work and other in-service training within the present curricular pattern and in the final chapter to a proposal for the extension of theological study into the years of the minister's active service when alone many matters fundamental to understanding the Gospel, Church, and Ministry can be seen in their true dimensions.

CHAPTER SIX

Theological Teaching in Classroom, Field, and Library

A theological school, like a church, is a community of Christian living and worship, but the axis on which the school turns is the relationship of teaching and learning. The elements in the encounter of teacher and student in theological study are for the most part those found in all educational endeavors. Subject matter has to be mastered; the student should discover his powers and limitations; and, as in all professional education, his knowledge and skills must be developed to make him adequate for the tasks he will face. But theological study has a dimension requiring special educational methods, yet transcending all method since it touches the realm of grace. Growth in Christian self-understanding and commitment cannot be bound to the formal categories of teaching and learning. The work of reading, classroom discussion, and lecturing must go on, yet the ultimate presupposition of all theological learning is that God's initiative and redemptive power are the ultimate resource.

The teacher of theology is acutely aware of the truth in the familiar remark that his students as persons are more important than the subject matter. The decisive issues of the student's preparation to be a good minister have to do with his relation to that realm of grace which his preaching and pastoral service are to serve. Such personal faith is set in the context of the ongoing life of the Christian community which both depends upon and supports each individual life. Therefore amid all the human circumstances of school, classes, assignments, papers, and field work, the dominant theme of life standing in need before God and finding its fulfillment in him is to be clearly heard.

Our discussion begins with a consideration of that part of the teaching and learning process which goes beyond the classroom, that is, the student's experience in churches and other institutions in the field. We then consider the resources and functions of the library, and finally analyze the heart of the process, the association of older and younger scholars in the teaching situation.

I. *Field Work*

Nearly all theological students are engaged for at least part of their course in some work in churches and other institutions which provide practical experience through which ideally the student's academic preparation is sharpened in its relevance to human needs, and in which his maturity is furthered through his bearing responsibility for religious ministry. Such work in the churches reminds the student and the school that Christian learning finds its justification ultimately in the service of God and his people.

While we affirm this high view of field work as church work we must acknowledge that there is no other aspect of theological education in which economic necessities play so large a role in determining the form and scope of what is actually done. In nearly all seminaries field work arrangements represent attempts to combine the educational value of practical experience with the need of students for income, and the need of churches for ministers. We ask, therefore, how far the field work programs serve and how far they may frustrate the most adequate preparation for Christian ministry.

As used today the term "field work" covers a wide variety of plans. In some schools it simply means whatever work the students do outside the school, usually in a church or social service institution, but not always so. In such schools the field work director, if there is one, is responsible solely for helping students to make contacts and find positions. He may be a faculty member with responsibility for teaching in a department and may give some advisory counsel to students as he has time. Here the field work involves a minimum of explicit educational direction. In contrast there are schools which maintain close supervision over the placement of students and which provide a staff of supervisors and courses which aim at securing the maximum educational value. Most seminaries today have field work programs which lie somewhere in between these two. Nearly all seek some integration and supervision over students' field work, but in the best cases the amount of supervision actually given remains limited. Staffs adequate for thorough observation and counseling of students remain beyond the financial reach of the best-supported schools and persons who combine the requisite theological, advisory, and administrative skills are hard to find.

The three central problems of field work are first, the finding of the number and kinds of opportunities that students need in their developing experience; second, the provision of adequate supervision both by the school and by those under whom students work on the field; and third, the achievement of a working relationship between curriculum and field experience so that the student finds each aspect of his study enriching the other. Generally the schools are fully aware of these problems. What is actually done and not done about them is explicable in part by the limits of available resources, of money, and of staff personnel. The plan at Duke University which allows students a certain subsidy during the school year in exchange for summer service on the field is most unusual. Few schools have such an extensive scholarship aid program.

In connection with the problem of the types of field work the widely accepted principle is that the student should from year to year be placed in situations geared to his developing understanding and powers. Many crises in the student's understanding of himself and of the Christian faith occur in connection with his field work. A situation which presents him with difficulties he is not ready to cope with can break his morale, yet the needs to encounter the real problems in the life of the church. Most faculty and field work directors agree that some variety of field work experiences during the student's course is desirable. The persons with whom he works should be of different ages and types of experience. Those who supervise him on the field should know how to help him learn through his experience. Perferably in every situation the student should be able to give some personal and useful service to people. He should encounter human needs and begin to discover the meaning of ministry to them.

In practice most schools can locate their studies in situations offering some remuneration and significant experience, but the principle of placing each student in work that fits his educational program and personal needs is exceedingly hard to follow. The churches and students often wish to preserve a working relationship for more than one year so that some of the variety of experience is sacrificed. In some schools students must commute long distances to the field each week. A further important exception to the statement that some position will be open to the students is to be made in the cases of many Negro schools and of Negro students in integrated schools. The community and its churches may not be open to Negro students. The instances in which they find positions as assistants in predominantly white churches are increasing but the limited number of these opportunities is a serious problem. The churches which are open to them in some cases offer little by way of educationally significant experience.

Ideally the student should find reinforcement of his academic interests and energies in his field work and it is not uncommon to hear testimonies of the exhilaration experienced in seeing the mutual significance of theological study and the church's task. But alongside this must be placed the common report of the divided mind and spirit which the heavy burden of work places upon the student. He often finds it difficult to give himself wholeheartedly to either his studies or his church work since the responsibility of both weigh so heavily upon him.

The Student Pastorate. The large number of theological students who serve as pastors of churches while they work toward their degrees is one of the important facts in the American scene. No law or medical student practices his profession while he is attending his professional school. The doctor does not serve as intern until much of the basic course has been covered. But many a seminary student serves as pastor and carries full responsibility for preaching and pastoral care throughout the entire three years of his course. In some denominations he may already be ordained to the ministry before he begins his theological study. In some he may receive a license to preach and perform certain other pastoral duties while he completes his ministerial degree. In others such as the Episcopal, Presbyterian, and Reformed, graduation from seminary is usually prerequisite to preaching and parish responsibilities.

A large section of American Protestantism, including Methodists, Congregationalists, Baptists, and Disciples, depends for its ministry in part upon men who are getting their formal training while serving as pastors. Some schools in this group do not in principle allow the first-year student to have a pastorate; but many exceptions are made when it is necessary in order that the student make his way financially. The parsonage supplied to his family by the church may be the key item. In a large number of schools over half the students are pastors of churches; and in not a few the figure is as high as 80 per cent.

In an increasing number of seminaries the rule is enforced that when students spend more than a prescribed minimum (usually about twenty hours) on the field during the week (and this includes most student pastors) four years must be taken to complete the course.

There is little point in arguing whether the student pastorate is or is not an ideal arrangement for theological education. Probably no categorical statement for or against could be proved. What needs to be faced is that in those churches where the polity permits it and where students are needed as pastors the ministry is not being supplied and theological courses are not completed apart from this plan. What the effects are upon the student's work and upon his preparation for his later ministry is the subject of much debate among faculties and field work directors. Those who believe in the positive value of the student pastorate argue that the student is learning about the church in bearing prime responsibility for a parish. The alternation between academic study and parish responsibility is recreative and wholesome, it is said. Good students can carry their school work and maintain a high standard of pastoral service. This is proved by the fact that often the student with high academic rating will be found to be doing good to superior work in the field.

Many faculty members do not agree. They believe that students are not able to concentrate adequately on their class work and bear responsibility for a church at the same time. Students who must prepare a sermon for every Sunday easily fall into slipshod habits of preparation. They must get by with a minimum of thoughtful attention to the needs of their hearers, and to the fundamental study which ought to lie back of the preaching. Further, it is maintained that the laxity with which academic requirements are enforced in many seminaries is due to the consideration by their faculties that they must not require too much of men so heavily burdened with church work. Finally, the tendency in American education in general to attempt to define standards and performances quantitatively, by the amassing of a sufficient number of credits and grade points, is exaggerated in the schools and denominations that permit men to enter the ministry prior to their theological preparation. Some schools serve a kind of floating population of students, who take a few courses now and then when church work is not too demanding and so ultimately satisfy the catalogue requirements for graduation.

It is clear that the points on both sides have weight and that each may be applicable to specific instances depending upon the maturity of the student, his habits of study, and his resources of energy. When the arguments are all in it is hard to escape the conclusion that too many schools do not take the problems involved in the student pastorate seriously enough. Granted the practical circumstances make this plan inevitable, it is all the more urgent that the difficulties be faced. While some student pastors of exceptional ability can do the extensive reading, develop the scholarly expertness through writing, and find opportunity for the self-searching and attention to a wide variety of human experiences which ought to go into a theological course, it is doubtful that this is so for a great many. One must also raise the question of the effect upon churches of leadership which is often immature. We would not think of receiving medical treatment from a student who had not been given a thorough introduction to fundamental principles of medicine. We take too lightly the harm that unclear thinking and immature emotions on the part of a minister may do.

When it is said that the student pastorate does not prevent adequate theological education, much depends on the standards which are held for the schools and for the students. If the emphasis is upon the completion of a prescribed number of courses, with the meeting of many specific requirements for readings, papers, and examinations, then this can be fulfilled in a routine or even better-than-average manner while a heavy load is carried outside. But theological education requires long periods of vigorous exploration of new ideas and mastery of some portions of the immense body of Christian tradition. The student needs to "go into himself" in periods when he concentrates his full intellectual and spiritual powers on ultimate questions of faith. It must be seriously questioned whether this can be done while the student is acting as pastor.

To raise this question does not lead to the suggestion that the student pastorate should be prohibited. This would be unrealistic. But it does mean that schools should seek in every way to lessen the loads such students carry. Scholarship aid which would give at least one year relatively free from outside responsibilities would help. Student pastors should be required to reduce their academic schedule and spread their theological courses over at least four years. Care should be exercised in counseling the student pastor so that he is not permitted to adopt a minimal standard of performance and remain satisfied with it. Churches can sometimes help by relieving pastors of some extra responsibilities.

The Problem of Supervision. All students, whether they are pastors or not, need supervision on the field. Most schools agree that the crux of the field work problem lies here. Supervision does not mean standing over the student and giving directions. It means offering opportunity for reflective criticism and counsel, so that the student is helped to recognize real problems and his capacity for dealing with them. In one large school a field work supervisor said that it would take between fifty and a hundred faculty people to do adequately the work of observation, counsel, and direction which is needed. Allowing for exaggeration, it is still true that nearly every school could profitably triple the number of its faculty assigned to field work.

Group supervision offers a partial answer to this problem. Field work courses or colloquia can be arranged for several students. Such courses range from a clinic in which problems being faced by the students are discussed, to formal courses in which the instructor deals with the theory and practice of the church in modern society and lays a foundation for the student's grasp of the particular problems he encounters. Most field work courses combine these two types. Students may be divided into groups according to the types of work they are doing, though this lessens the opportunity for sharing a variety of experiences.

Certainly the economic problem weighs heavily in achieving adequate field work supervision. There are, however, some things which could be done to inject more educational nourishment into field work while adding little to its cost. Each of these plans is being used somewhere, through none very widely. First, many schools could exercise greater control over the arrangements made between students and the institutions they serve. Granted there are values in a student's taking responsibility for finding his work and making arrangements about it; there is a stronger argument for having all student positions approved

by the school. Stipulations should be made which are clearly understood by both student and the institution he serves as to the amount
of time he is to give; and there should be periodic checks on this. A
surprising number of schools claim no function of approval over the
student's field assignment. This is an abdication of the school's right to
direct the student's educational experience.

Second, schools can develop the practice of holding conferences for
those who will be the supervisors on the field. The aims and potentialities of the field work experience can be explored in such meetings. Mis-
understandings can be faced. Ministers can be made more aware than
frequently they are of the educational value of their work with students.
Some of the common problems which students encounter can be out-
lined and suggestions for meeting them discussed. Further, and by no
means unimportant, some of the unintentional mistakes which supervisors make can be pointed out and corrected. The holding of such
conferences need not be expensive. The technique has been used
effectively by schools of social work.

Third, there would be value in acquainting congregations with the
aims of the field training. The lay workers in a church can either help
or obstruct the realization of a significant experience for the student.
Not infrequently they need to exercise Christian patience and charity
with the immature. Some boards of trustees need to consider more
carefully and from an educational point of view the conditions set for
students' employment. When difficulties arise school and church need
to co-operate in taking constructive measures.

While use of the general faculty for field supervision is rarely desirable it is possible to have some faculty consultation with students on
problems arising in the field. Such meetings take faculty time, but they
may save hours which would otherwise be spent in individual counseling. An occasional colloquium in which a group of faculty and students
take up typical situations may help students with urgent problems.
Such opportunity for the student to bring to the faculty in a more
informal setting problems discovered on the field offers a relatively
simple device for interpreting the relations between experience and
theology.

Before we move to the discussion of clinical training programs, there
is one church work plan which must be discussed further, the intern
year.

II. *The Intern Year*

Internship programs which require a year of work in a church
either between the middle and senior years or as a fourth year have developed during the past twenty years. Three Lutheran denominations,
the Augustana Synod, the American Lutheran Church, and the Evan-

gelical Lutheran Church, have had extensive experience with the plan. Other denominations and seminaries are putting it into operation. Noteworthy among recent ventures is that of Andover-Newton Theological School whose program has certain distinctive features. In this latter situation there is a heterogeneous church constituency over against the high degree of homogeneity and cohesiveness of the Lutheran groups.

In the three Lutheran programs there is a general consensus of judgment on the values and problems of the internship. These schools send students into church positions between the middle and senior years. At Augustana and Wartburg (the American Lutheran Seminary whose internship program was studied), the placement of interns rests largely in the hands of the seminary administration. Both, it is said, have more applications for interns from churches and conference presidents than available students. Thus both schools can select the pastors and the church situations into which students go. After twenty years of experience, Augustana, for example, has been able, it is said, to weed out situations that have not been educationally beneficial. The same statement is made at Wartburg. Because of the personal acquaintance of the faculty with most of the pastors, students can be sent to men who will particularly meet their needs. In both schools it is the policy to send a student to another part of the country than the one in which he grew up. An effort may also be made to send rural men to urban churches, and urban men to rural churches, lazy men to hard-working pastors, men who are excessively narrow in their point of view on churchmanship or piety to pastors who can sympathetically enlarge their vision.

In all three denominations an effort is made to give the intern a wide experience. Although some of the men serve missions in which they are the only professional leaders, an effort is made to put them under helpful supervision. Most are placed as assistants to pastors. Wartburg requires that such an assistant be given opportunity to preach once a month, and asks that he be admitted to the meetings of all official boards and committees. Pastors who abuse the privilege of an intern by making an errand boy of him may find it difficult to get a student a second year. Augustana provides interns with a reading list to encourage the integration of field and academic experience.

The plan requires that a student's transportation from the seminary to the field and back be paid by the church. The minimum remuneration varies; for one school it is $75 per month plus room and board, with the church assuming no responsibility for the student's wife. In another the minimum salary is $150 for single, $175 for married men, with an additional $25 car allowance in both cases. Most men, it is said, are offered $2400 plus car allowance. In a third instance the school requires a $90 a month minimum, plus room and board.

The student must make periodic reports to his school. When he returns from his internship, he is given an extended interview with the staff member responsible for the program. At this session an effort is made to go beyond the data of number of calls and sermons to the student's new self-understanding that may have emerged.

Some problems are common to these schools. All agree that the student who manifests an unco-operative attitude or laziness on the field has usually been a problem student in the seminary. The president of one of the seminaries believes that there is a "high correspondence between internship performance and expectations based on the psychological testing program." Sometimes personality clashes occur between a pastor and his intern, and this is more often the case when the appointment is made by the school than when the student makes his own arrangements. Men may learn bad habits during the internship. This is less true where schools can eliminate faulty supervisors. The elimination process, however, may lead to tension between the school and pastors or congregations that are left out. The crucial factor in the value to a student remains the pastor to whom he is assigned. President Mattson succinctly states what lies at the heart of many particular problems: "The parish looks at internship from the point of view of service and the school looks at it from the point of view of education."

All the schools agree on the positive values that accrue. The year, like clinical training for some students, is often a period of intense personal growth, of new understanding of self, the ministry, and the church. The new level of maturity has an impact on the final year of academic work. Practical courses have a new relevance. The student brings existential questions to his studies of theology and Bible.

Some factors that make internship work well in these Lutheran schools do not exist for many others. The Lutheran seminaries are denominational, and in most instances of effective internship programs they are the only seminary for their group, or are one of two. Most of the ministers are alumni and are known by members of the faculty. The school is closely integrated with the program of the church and the head of the seminary is one of the denominational leaders. There is much greater homogeneity among students, ministers, and churches than exists in many seminaries.

Andover-Newton's program differs considerably from those just described. The intern year is the fourth year, after which the student receives his degree. Most students have sole responsibility for a congregation, though an effort has been made to find interested senior ministers to advise them. The interns return to Newton Centre every two weeks for a day of discussion, counseling, and library work. The effort is to help "the student integrate the academic courses he has taken during his first three years and the practical tasks of the ministry." The faculty has given much time to the development of the program and demonstrates capacities for strenuous self-criticism while continuing to believe in its ultimate effectiveness.

Many problems are acknowledged in this program. Students have to go as far as three hundred miles to find a satisfactory church, making the return visits time-consuming and costly. Interns are often such effective ministers that they retain their assignment as full pastors, thus diminishing the supply of churches available for interns. Distance and expense limit field supervision by the faculty and most neighboring pastors are unable to give time to such work. Students become engrossed in their church work, and do not find time to carry out assignments made during the visits to the school. Several reported that the most effective session during the year was an analysis of case studies of problem persons or groups in the congregations. Yet several confessed that their preparation of these studies was hurried and superficial. Some revisions of the program to meet such problems are now under way.

The strengths of the Andover-Newton idea are many. It was conceived by the faculty as a whole, not by the field work department alone. The entire faculty has continued to take responsibility for it. Discussions between a biblical theologian and the religious educator on the church school and its purpose were a highlight of a recent year. The students meet with theologians, psychologists, educators, and other members of the staff during various sessions. The integration of academic work and ministerial practice has a greater possibility of fruition under these circumstances.

The conditions of an effective internship program are not easily produced by all churches and schools. For this reason it cannot be suggested as a panacea to the in-service problem. Effective working relations between school and churches and pastors must be developed. Cultural and religious homogeneity is helpful. Authority to make or strongly suggest appointments has been crucial in some programs. The development of the program by the whole faculty, and not in an *ad hoc* fashion by one person or department is essential. It appears that schools serving particular regions have a better chance to develop the program than national schools, denominational schools better than nondenominational schools. New programs such as that in the Federated Theological Faculty at the University of Chicago may open up new possibilities.

III. *Pastoral Theology and Clinical Training*

In the previous chapter we deferred discussion of the field of pastoral care until we could relate it to the development of clinical training, because the close connection between the traditional discipline of "pastoral theology" or "care of souls" and the psychological approach to human personality through firsthand experience of human problems is widely recognized today, and has given rise to one of the most influential movements in theological education, the emphasis on the preparation of the Christian pastor as counselor. The considerable growth of interest in this field is related not only to the increasing demands upon ministers for such preparation but also to the emphasis in the schools upon the importance of the student's discovery of his psychological motivations, his insight into the emotional aspects of his experience, and his achievement of the kind of understanding of people and the problems of mental health which will enable him to serve skillfully at one of the critical points in contemporary man's life.

Firsthand experience with persons in trouble is the basic material out of which Christian skill in care of souls must come. The disciplines of psychology and sociology must be brought into the interpretation both of the data and the strategies of dealing with the problems. Yet in spite of the ease with which this field can lead out and away from its theological center there is a strong determination in the schools to keep the psychological approach to personality in close relation to the Church and its faith. There is indeed considerable tension within some schools on the place of this field in the curriculum. Its popularity at the present time tends to create a situation in which this interest might develop its own force and direction, even its own "theology," and pull away from the rest of the school. We discover some apprehension on this score, but the apprehension is usually shared by the men in the pastoral field which is a healthy state of affairs.

In considering clinical training in relation to the course offerings in pastoral theology it will be desirable to speak first of the former since the courses tend to be effective in the measure in which they use case material. Certain problems come with this emphasis. An adequate course must communicate a structural interpretation of the field and the principles of pastoral ministry, and it must be related to the rest of the theological curriculum. Further, there are many students who never enter a clinical training program, and they must have adequate work in pastoral theology.

Granting that the development of pastoral theology as a theological discipline is still in process, it is clear that the center of interest in this field today is in the area of "counseling" which includes ministry to people at the point of their anxieties, frustrations, and threats of mental illness, with exploration of the emotional dynamics of human behavior in the individual and in the group. The increased emphasis on psychological testing of the students and various procedures designed to bring out their psychological needs are symptomatic of this concern. Much of the emotional conflict, guilt, and unease of spirit which in other times has found release and healing through the confessional, revival meeting, or, in many instances, was never understood at all has in our day found a mode of expression and resources for therapy through the development of psychological knowledge and new therapeutic methods. While some of this new approach has developed outside of, and even in conscious opposition to, established religious forms, the problems are those which religion has in part at least traditionally recognized. In dealing with them the co-operation of psychologists, doctors, and ministers is required. It is encouraging to see in many quarters the breaking down of earlier rigid dogmatisms and the search for more fruitful co-operation as new ways are sought to penetrate the mystery of the human spirit and unravel some of its ills.

One type of situation in which the theological student can be led to a deeper understanding of his ministry and can acquire skill in dealing with human problems is that in which he encounters specific human needs with the help of supervisors who bring experience and technical knowledge to bear upon the kinds of problems under consideration. Such a situation is broadly what is meant by "clinical training." The word suggests the hospital, and much of this work is done in hospitals and kindred institutions. The term, however, includes prisons, courts, and social service institutions in which the conditions of technical supervision and controlled observation are present. The training can be called "theological" only if the work involves a ministry in which the special responsibilities of the Church are explicitly or implicitly involved. The aim is the fusion of scientific understanding with Christian wisdom and concern. Our definition of clinical training is somewhat different than that proposed by Professor Rollin Fairbanks; "Clinical training is the performance of pastoral work under competent supervision, such work being recorded and submitted for evaluation and criticism," but the intent of the two descriptions is similar.[1]

The situation of clinical training today can be understood only if we remember that the modern emphasis on this approach to pastoral work developed outside the seminaries before it was brought within them. A few men including Anton Boisen and Richard Cabot who were giving special attention to problems of mental health established The Council for Clinical Pastoral Training in 1930. The Institute for Pastoral Care was established by another independent group in 1944. These two programs have between them initiated and been responsible for a considerable part of the clinical training of pastors for twenty-five years. Many schools have made use of these programs or developed similar ones. The Council for Clinical Training takes groups of students

[1] Seward Hiltner, Ed., *Clinical Pastoral Training*, New York, 1945, 38.

for a twelve-weeks' course. The Institute for Pastoral Care has a six-weeks' program. A very few schools, Virginia Theological Seminary for example, require the clinical training course of all seminary students. Many schools make it optional for students as one unit of the field work requirement. Any course credit is given by the schools, not by the Council or Institute.

Some clinical training programs in the schools are directly connected with courses offered by the school and the direction is shared by a member of the faculty. The course in group therapy at the University of Southern California, for example, includes formal course work, the organization of the students in a group therapy program, and work in group therapy in a hospital under the direction of a psychiatrist.

The growth of this program is shown by the following data. In 1943 thirteen seminaries were related to some kind of clinical training program. Nine years later in 1952 there were forty-three schools. Reports made to the present study indicate that about three-fourths of the accredited seminaries, one-third of the others, had either developed clinical training programs of their own by 1955 or sent students to the Council or Institute for such training. In many cases, however, it was apparent that the school's relation to the latter programs was very tenuous and that few students availed themselves of the opportunities. Some of the independent programs were highly developed; others were rather sketchy in character and content.

The Council, the Institute, and the theological schools whose students have had training under these or other auspices have encountered three problems from the beginning. One is financial. While in most cases the hospitals provide maintenance, and the seminaries contribute a small amount per student for those who elect the program, the organization and direction of the program requires much more substantial financial support.

The second problem is the securing of adequate staff supervision. In many cases it is difficult to find enough institutions accessible to students, and it is agreed on all sides that supervisors vary considerably in their teaching skill.

The third problem is the relationship of the seminaries to these independent institutes. On this point a searching discussion is going on at the present time. The two agencies we have been describing have had from the beginning somewhat different philosophies and concerns. Further, when the schools examine these programs from the standpoint of theological study they often desire to introduce specific requirements for integration in the academic courses, and they may prefer courses in psychology or other courses in pastoral theology without a requirement of clinical training *per se* for all students.

There are strong arguments for preserving a measure of independent action for the clinical training programs. Domination by a school or by a particular theological point of view may take away from the student's experience some of its most important ingredients. Further, one of the significant aspects of the program has been that it has brought together students from many seminaries and denominations in a situation in which each has had to look afresh at human needs without relying exclusively on his confessional heritage.

While these values must be preserved, there is also a strong case for a closer relationship to the seminaries and divinity schools. If the schools wish to make extensive use of this kind of education they must take more responsibility for supporting it and play a co-operative role in helping to criticize and shape its future course. From the side of those offering the training it must be recognized that its mission is to further the preparation of Christian ministers and to achieve better understanding between the ministry and medical professions. Clinical training programs need the schools not only for students and financial support but also as a source of constructive criticism.

Recommendations for specific organizations are hazardous and it is not possible for our survey to draw any detailed plan in relation to the clinical training institutes. This is an area in which the schools need to develop the widest possible co-operation among themselves. The expense, limited facilities, and technical requirements make such co-operation not only fruitful but absolutely necessary. Further, it would appear that whatever value there may be in the semi-independent work of the Council and Institute, the two of them might well co-operate on further projects (they now jointly sponsor the journal, *Pastoral Counselling*), and some way be found to bring the schools more fully into the support, criticism, and shaping of the policies of these institutes.

What promises to be an outstanding example of joint effort in this field is the establishment in 1954 of the Institute of Religion at the great Texas Medical Center in Houston which unites the resources of the Baylor University School of Medicine with those of the five Texas seminaries which co-operate in the program. These are: Austin Presbyterian, Brite College of the Bible, Episcopal Theological Seminary of the Southwest, Perkins School of Theology, and Southwestern Baptist. The work of the Institute of Religion is to be an integral part of the pastoral care department of each of these five seminaries and to be related to the Baylor Medical School. Students from each seminary are to receive their "clinical pastoral education" in Houston, but are to receive credit in their own seminaries for the courses taken in the Institute. Provision is made for obtaining B.D., Th.M., S.T.M., and Th.D. degrees. Members of the Institute faculty are chosen by mutual selection and become members of the faculties of each of the five seminaries. The training programs not only for ministers but also for medical students, nurses, and doctors offer a splendid opportunity for developing working understanding among all the professions concerned with persons in need of healing and religious ministry.

There are schools so situated that they can develop types of clinical training within their own curriculum. The favorable situation includes location near hospitals and other institutions, interested persons in these institutions, and members of the theological faculty who can give direction. Cases in point are the University of Chicago where a professor of pastoral theology is a member of both the divinity and medical faculties and the group therapy program in the School of Religion at the University of Southern California.

The development of the field of pastoral theology at Southern Baptist Seminary in Louisville, Kentucky, illustrates the variety of possibilities which are open and some methods of relating this work to the theological curriculum.

In this school the work in pastoral theology which includes field training in clinical situations is given for the most part at the Th.M. level, after the completion of the B.D. course. The degree is given in theology, not in pastoral counseling. The course is designed to make explicit the relationship between pastoral work and the "body of divinity." Further, the program is kept under the full supervision of the seminary. This means that the institutions in which students work are located in the surrounding geographical area. The relationships built up over many years between the seminary professor of pastoral theology and the institutional directors are an important factor. The seminary staff includes one full-time professor, one full-time instructor, and one graduate fellow.

Several features of this program require comment. In the first place, by giving the work at the Th.M. level the B.D. course is freed from much of the pressure which arises from the introduction of new courses. For students who do not go beyond the B.D. a basic course in pastoral theology is provided. The emphasis at the B.D. level is put upon problems of the family and marriage relationship. It is here that the pastor in a rural community is least likely to have other professional help available, and the problems are those which every pastor is certain to encounter.

The seminary is located in Louisville where several types of work are open to the students, including mental hospitals, general hospitals, juvenile court, and correctional institutions; and each situation is one in which the requirements for scientific study and teaching can be met.

The stress placed here upon the relating of studies in pastoral theology to the remainder of the curriculum is characteristic of most of the advanced work being done in this field. The theological perspective is emphasized, and the insights derived from clinical study play their part in the interpretation of the Bible, church history, and theology.

There is no claim that the department just described has solved all problems in its own situation let alone whether it is applicable to others, but it represents a forthright attempt to find the proper and effective place for such studies within the traditional theological curriculum. There are many seminaries in locations where institutional opportunities are abundantly available if faculty staff time can be found to develop them.

Some Critical Issues in Pastoral Theology. The student needs three contributions from his work in pastoral theology; first, an interpretation of the care of souls within the church and his pastoral office; second, an interpretation of the meaning of the data and scientific understanding in this field for Christian faith and theology, and third, growth in self-knowledge both as a person and as one who is to be a channel for the healing promised in the Gospel.

There are a variety of views in Christian history on the role of the Christian pastor. The doctrine of the Church, of the authority of the pastor, of the structure of repentance, penitence, and forgiveness, all have an influence. But always the Christian minister works within the form and spirit of the Christian community. As pastor and as priest he is not only to counsel, but to give witness, to admonish, to instruct, to preach, and to share the common life. He deals with a congregation of people in all stages of Christian maturity and seeks to help them and himself to grow in grace. The role of the counselor can be significant in all these relationships. Undoubtedly the emphasis on understanding and on the nonjudgmental approach to the release of human anxieties has brought a needed corrective of traditional authoritarianism, yet in the end this perspective must take its place within a larger setting. One specific example is the necessity in Christian faith for defining responsibility in social as well as in individual terms. The person who has learned to handle his own inner emotional life still must be pointed toward the meaning of Christian love as bearing the burden of his neighbor.

Second, the student can learn in pastoral theology how knowledge derived from human experience can enrich and be illuminated by other theological studies. The pitfall is that he may begin to "psychologize" everything and try to solve every problem of faith through psychological analysis. Wise instruction can preserve balance here and allow for the valid insight which psychology brings to the understanding of Christian experience. For example, insight into the meaning of self-acceptance and forgiveness in human relations is not irrelevant to the understanding of God's forgiveness.

Finally, the student needs to come to fuller self-knowledge. This may happen as he encounters people who are suffering, perhaps in extreme ways, from their anxieties and frustrations. The crisis of feeling one's inadequacy to meet these problems; the discovery of some of the structures of human ills; and the experience of sharing with fellow students in a search for answers all may contribute to the deepening of self-understanding.

One of the reasons why expert supervision and counsel for the student in this training is so important is that the crisis in his own experience may be very deep. His own commitment, the form of his own religious heritage and traditions, may all appear for a time to be inadequate supports as he begins to discover the Christian faith at a profounder level. Those who are most successful in giving personal guidance may not necessarily be theologically trained; but they are aware of what is involved and they are themselves far from the simple-minded view that all psychological understanding represents maturity or that every religious view of life is immature.

We must add the warning that the student needs to learn the kinds of problems which require medical attention and which as pastor he should not try to handle. His ministry is to the person in his religious need.

We have been speaking of goals for theological education in the field of pastoral care. The question remains whether their achievement always requires the clinical training experience. We have asked a good many about this who are in a position to know, and the answer given is that this kind of understanding does not necessarily have to come through clinical training nor does it always result from such training. Even those who describe their experience in such a program as a reorientation akin to conversion say that for some students other types of experience may be more appropriate. Self-knowledge may come through any profound human experience, and the discovery of the meaning of the pastoral office may develop in a variety of ways.

When one considers the revitalization of much in the theological curriculum today through new emphases in psychology and pastoral counseling, it must be concluded that a significant new turn in the education of the ministry has been taken. Powerful new resources are available throughout the curriculum because of work in this field. It is of first importance, therefore, that the field of pastoral care be accepted as the responsibility of the entire school and not isolated as a subordinate department concerned with practical skills alone. Theological, historical, and other fields need to be conscious of the understanding which students are securing through pastoral care and be alert to its significance for all theological reflection, just as those dealing with the psychological and clinical data need to develop their understanding in the context of the Christian faith.

IV. *Teaching and Libraries*

We begin our comment on the present situation regarding libraries in theological schools with some observations on the relationship of librarians to the teaching and learning process. It is not always recognized that the librarian is in a strategic teaching position in the school. Often the librarian knows more about the operation of the school as a teaching institution and the study habits of students than do other members of the faculty and administrative officers. Many librarians have analyzed perceptively the way students respond to various types of assignments, their problems in developing bibliography for research projects, and their writing of papers. Librarians sometimes serve as informal listening posts for student opinion and as academic and personal counselors. The librarians' testimony has supported our criticism of the too rigid assignments in many courses. The student goes to the required book, usually finding it on a reserve shelf. He reads what is necessary in order to prepare a paper on the assigned topic. In too many cases he never reads the whole book, nor looks beyond the particular assignment for new insights and problems. In many schools the librarian is the one person who can supply even a rough estimate of the extent of the students' reading and their general literary culture. Circulation figures, for example, supply one index of the intellectual tone in the school.

This function of critical observation of study habits is only one aspect of the relationship between the librarian, the library, and the teaching process. The lecture, discussion, assignment, and reading of the books form an interdependent whole. The student's learning to find his way in pursuit of knowledge on a problem is fundamental to the habit of scholarly discipline which should bear fruit in all the years of his ministry. This involves far more than use of the card catalogue. It requires familiarity with research materials, habits of practiced browsing, and the curiosity to explore unusual resources.

Most schools provide an orientation session in the library at the beginning of the course, and this has value, but it hardly touches the need to discover the working relationship between classroom and library, and the development of the kinds of assignments which lead to growth in independent scholarship. Librarians can be of great assistance in advising on assignments and observing their results, and this matter goes to the roots of the educational process.

Many students need help with their emotional attitudes toward reading. Many have never learned how to read, or to work out a bibliography, or to discriminate between what is important and what is not in pursuing a subject. Too few discussions are held between librarians and faculties on these points. In instances in which the librarian is also a faculty member this may take place more often; but in many schools the librarian does not have faculty status.

The statements just made do not lead us to a categorical position as to faculty status for the librarian. They do emphasize two critical points: first, good communication between the librarian and those who teach and counsel the students may well be enhanced by faculty status; second, such character, ability, and training in the librarian that he or she merits the responsibility of full relation to the teaching function.

If the theological libraries are to serve their proper function, eternal vigilance is required on the basic matters of adequately trained persons who know the full dimensions of their task, adequate book collections both for teaching and for research, and adequate physical plant. While we found it impractical in the survey to give sufficient time to a detailed study of the libraries and their problems, we note with especial appreciation the work being done by the American Theological Library Association. This has been an excellent example of what can be accomplished through co-operation among the schools. Standards have been established and many improvements have been made through the work of the Association. Yet those who are most encouraged by the result are acutely conscious of the great needs and of the present danger signals concerning adequate personnel and financial support to maintain and improve the libraries.

We call attention to some important factors in the present situation which are clearly recognized in the studies of the Theological Library Association.

There has been steady improvement in the general situation of theological libraries over the past ten years. But of the schools belonging to the American Association of Theological Schools, nineteen reported in 1955 that their libraries were badly housed; ten more their need of some new space or building. (Cf. also Ch. Two Secs. I, II.) In many libraries space for periodicals is lacking, and there are no study carrells. Several could use more reading space. Many libraries were built to take care of the books but with inadequate provision for the librarian's office, and for cataloguing and work rooms. Sometimes when the librarian himself reported adequate office space the surveyors' personal observations forced them to conclude that the librarian had developed a stoic attitude through many years in cramped quarters.

Libraries are expensive and the costs of trained personnel, of books, and of plant are rising. Any figure which purports to state a minimal budget for a theological library is apt to be misleading. The size of the school, its degree programs, the extent of its present collection, the needs of its faculty for books related to their research and writing, all have to be brought into a significant judgment on budgetary needs. As the schools try to provide salaries to attract those who not only have training in librarianship but special competence in theology, the budgetary standards require continual reappraisal and effort. Keeping in mind the impossibility of applying a general rule, we can say that the data gathered in our survey show that a large number of libraries are barely managing to keep a minimal standard for staff and book collection, and that the maintenance of genuinely adequate libraries is becoming an increasingly acute problem for nearly all the schools.

Standards for adequacy in book collections are also hard to determine with precision. It is doubtful whether a basic list of requirements even at the B.D. level would be applicable to all in view of differences of emphasis in the various traditions. At the graduate level "adequacy" involves many special factors. One is the aims held for the degree programs for masters and doctoral candidates. As discussed elsewhere in this volume, these aims vary considerably from school to school. Only five schools reporting to us stated that their libraries were inadequate for the graduate programs they offer. When we note that one of the schools which acknowledged inadequacy possesses one of the leading theological libraries in the nation, we are forced to question the measure of "adequacy" many schools apply to themselves. It should be further emphasized that libraries exist to serve the faculty in their study and writing. Specialized collections and books in languages other than English are required. In the light of these needs while there can be definite encouragement because of recent progress, there is still much to be done before it can be said that the schools have adequate working collections for faculty and students.

The need for trained and competent librarians is related both to the financial problem of adequate salaries and to the scarcity of people with the requisite background who enter this field. The salaries of librarians tend to be too far below the faculty level, even in those cases where the librarian has good preparation. Further, even a well-trained head of staff is likely to be overburdened with cataloguing and other duties, and his assistants are often completely untrained people. While many students or student wives can be trained for routine duties in a year or two, they soon leave the school and the process must be repeated. Thus librarians are unable to give full attention to the development of the book collection and other activities designed to increase the use of the library. While more adequate salaries would improve the present level of performance and would attract a greater number of librarians with the necessary background, it must also be said that there is a scarcity of available people. Ways must be found to interest more theologically educated people in librarianship. This is one place where more women with theological training could find a meaningful service. Lying back of the problem of enlisting competent people there is the question of how the schools conceive the librarian's task. If this is regarded mainly as the shelving of books, then few able people will be enlisted. A creative conception of the librarian's role as teacher and advisor is called for throughout the schools.

We come then to the long-range problems of theological libraries in the United States and Canada. With rising costs even the large university libraries are finding it hard to maintain standards. The problem for theological schools will become more acute, partly because they all depend in some degree on the great university collections, and partly because their own costs are so high. This fact coupled with the tremendous flood of book publishing today points clearly to the need for more co-operative strategies among the libraries in the future. Much more needs to be done through interlibrary co-operation in the development of special collections and their location in the schools and regions where they can be most conveniently used, thus avoiding the burden of several parallel collections. Co-operation of this kind has had a notable beginning among the schools in the San Francisco area. Schools in a particular denomination should consider a division of labor in developing the historical background and outstanding figures in their tradition, or rely upon denominational historical commissions and societies as is being practiced in some measure by the Disciples of Christ and the Presbyterian Church, U.S.A. Special collections needed for their ecumenical significance and intrinsic importance such as an American library of Eastern Orthodox church history ought to be undertaken as a co-operative project. Co-operative microfilming of important serial publication and the increasingly important use of the microtext for books can be undertaken. Since scholars may usually travel without too great difficulty for special research, there is every reason why the schools should develop the practice of mutual consultation and division of labor. The cost factor alone makes this imperative.

The principles involved in the development of the theological curriculum bear upon the selection of the books. We have taken the view throughout this report that theological studies should develop in close relationship to the mediating disciplines in the sciences and humanities. This requires provision in the theological libraries for the important works in philosophy, sociology, psychology, and kindred studies. The theological school cannot itself develop a complete university library; yet it must not exclude the materials which provide the dialogue between theology and the other studies. The many judgments which a faculty and librarian must make here offer a clear example of the kind of perspective and breadth of outlook required of those responsible for the future of theological libraries.

The point just made raises the question of the working relationship between theological and university libraries. There has been an emphasis in accrediting standards upon the independent status of the theological library and a tendency to look with disfavor upon the merger of the theological school's collection with that of a college or university. Obviously there are reasons for this concern. Theological students must be able to go directly to the books they use. But the need to relate theology to other disciplines puts a great burden on the theological collection. Therefore, in some instances, the integration of the theological library with a university collection offers distinct advantages. The effectiveness of particular working arrangements is a better basis for judgment on this problem than a flat rule against integration in a larger library.

Schools often state in their catalogues that the library is the center of the academic life as the chapel is the center of the worship life in the community. This suggests that schools might well take more seriously the attractiveness of their libraries as places to read and study. Reproductions of good painting and sculpture are now inexpensive and could enhance the interest of many drab rooms. Too many libraries look like morgues. Elemental matters such as good housekeeping, cleanliness, and heat are important. Adequate lighting is absolutely essential. Libraries can become places where students and faculty like to come. With the great increase in married students some schools have made provision for attractive reading and browsing rooms, sometimes with record players and books of general interest, and thus have provided a retreat and quiet center for those who live in crowded quarters. And the library itself should be a place where one can work uninterruptedly and without distraction.

We cannot speak in detail of the many ingenious methods which librarians have devised to call attention to books and journals, and to promote the love of reading. Model personal libraries for theological students, brief reviews of recent books, special displays, are all useful. While the role of the librarian in the school remains in part a silent one it is not passive when rightly conceived. The librarian can be indispensable in creating the intellectual atmosphere in which minds grow.

V. *Teaching and Learning*

We have examined the setting of theological teaching. What of the action itself? Is there ground for the suspicion that theological teaching suffers more than most from the "endemic diseases of education," the unreflective transmission of doctrine, the rote learning, the loss of a personal center in a mass of detail? In our survey we have asked students, teachers, and administrators many questions about teaching. We have observed some teaching, and we have tried to find out where the marks of good teaching are evident and where improvement seems most in order.

Any wholesale condemnation of theological teaching as being slavishly traditional and unimaginative cannot be supported by the facts. To be sure, there is a wide variety of performance, and there is a difference in the goals which teachers and schools set for themselves. Those who bear a major responsibility for transmitting a doctrinal position necessarily give considerable time to making sure the student encounters that tradition. Those who put emphasis on the development of the individual student and his religious thinking may give more attention to providing the stimulus of conflicting points of view. Both may teach effectively.

While we allow for these differences there are points at which questions must be asked about the adequacy of our teaching. After examining certain of these we shall discuss the positive goals of good teaching.

The Didactic Stance. Granted many special circumstances it is our judgment that there is in theological teaching today far too much of the "didactic stance." This is not primarily a question of particular teaching methods. A course of lectures can stimulate thought, pose issues, and examine many sides of questions, setting the student free to pursue his own critical reactions while a discussion course may still be so dominated by the professor and his point of view that it becomes an example of rigid dogmatism. What really counts is the relationship in which teacher, student, and subject matter stand at the beginning of the course and at the end. If this consists in the existence of an inert mass of fact and idea which is handed in small pieces by the teacher to the student then the heart of intellectual inquiry is betrayed. How much teaching of this sort is going on in the seminaries is hard to estimate. Since the present study afforded only occasional opportunities for classroom observation the few glaring instances of bad teaching encountered cannot be regarded as symptomatic. But the "didactic stance" may manifest itself in the atmosphere of a school and in the general theory of education that pervades it. And it is the impression not only of the staff of the present study but of many pastors and theological teachers they consulted that, in common with many other types of education in America, seminary education is deeply affected by the "disease."

One symptom of the "didactic" disease is the great amount of lecturing to the exclusion of discussion. Opportunity for discussion is important to the student, and the lack of time for it is a common cause of complaint. Another symptom is the pressure many teachers admit they feel to "get everything in" their course, as if the student must hear everything from the professor at least once whether he has read it in a book or not and whether he appropriates it or not.

With the already unbearable pressure on the curriculum it would seem a good principle that anything which students can learn by reading or in other ways should not take time in the classroom. Obviously there are qualifications to be made when major points need emphasis, but much of the extensive coverage of historical periods and of theological points of view can be left to the student's reading. This puts a premium on the student's ability to read well and quickly. On this point many need help; but that problem should be met in other ways than to take class hours for a pedestrian review of materials which can be assimilated in one-fourth the time by reading.

Another manifestation of the loss of cutting edge in the teaching situation is the mechanical system of assignments which is encountered more often than one would expect in graduate schools. Students are given certain sections of books to read, or are taken through a textbook chapter by chapter. Sometimes they are given a series of papers to write, each of which requires some reading, but the character of the assignment makes it impossible for the student to take time for an entire book, to reflect upon its argument, and to allow new ideas to take root and grow, or to work on a problem independently finding his own resources in the library.

The goal of critical and reflective reading can be defeated by the assignment of too many books. Students are sometimes put in the position of having to read basic works superficially in order to meet the requirements. Difficulties can also be created by the total load of assignments in a term. It is not unusual to find students who must write as many as six or seven term papers at one time. The concentration which is necessary in theological thinking becomes impossible.

We are not saying that theological students generally are overworked. Many of them carry heavy total loads with their outside work, but if anything the number of hours of study should be increased. The important question is how the study hours are spent. We must underline the fact that in theological education even more than in some other fields the need is for personal maturation, an exploration of complex ideas, and a personal encounter with ultimate problems which cannot be reduced to the memorization of details or to a series of neatly planned lessons. The student's attention should indeed be focused on the subject matter and not upon his own feelings, but the subject matter consists of ideas and symbols in the realm of spirit which must be dealt with in their depth and relatedness.

This means that the "timing" of the student's study is of great importance and differs with the degree of maturity of the student as well as with his native ability. One of the chief evils of a rigid system of assignments is that all are forced to maintain the same pace. It is not an answer to say that students who can do extra work are free to do so. The point is that good theological teaching requires the instructors and schools to give attention to encouraging those who can advance more rapidly.

These points reflect complaints often made about education and seem obvious enough. We need to ask why some theological schools still exhibit to more than a tolerable degree these traits of uninspired teaching.

One cause is traditionally associated with theology, the dogmatic standpoint reinforced by a conception of preaching as "handing down the truth." If a creedal or confessional tradition is accepted as authoritative then the transmission of this tradition becomes a prime responsibility, and the simplest means of perpetuating the perspective is to continue to state it without too much critical examination. We have not found this kind of dogmatism in extreme form in many schools; but what we do find in many confessionally oriented schools is that acceptance of the tradition has created a climate in which the stimulus of tension with other viewpoints is absent.

It is here that the establishment of the ecumenical context for theological education provides one of the conditions for a more vigorous challenge to the student's thinking. Certainly it is not easy to create this context in which many Christian traditions are set in relation to one another and at the same time to achieve the full impact of one tradition. Perhaps in one sense this cannot be done and this fact creates the profound ecumenical tension within the church. How ecumenical shall we be? Still, unwillingness to accept the tensions involved in relating a church tradition to the ecumenical scene would seem to be one of the factors which makes theological education more rigid than it ought to be.

It should be said at once that the "dogmatic stance" in theological education is not confined to those who hold one of the traditional theological positions. Any point of view can be so projected. An individual professor or an entire school can become identified with a single theological outlook located anywhere in the theological spectrum. The problem faced by such a school is how to preserve the significance of this theological thesis and yet to set students free to examine it critically, to appropriate it only after being exposed to alternative standpoints, and to come to conclusions which represent their own free decisions.

The following principles seem applicable concerning the significance of a controlling doctrinal point of view whether it be "traditional" or "antitraditional": First, a theological school which provides only one theological viewpoint in its entire faculty is likely to be preventing the profoundest kind of intellectual inquiry and is not doing the most for the students' development even within the point of view the school is anxious to promote. Second, the preservation in a school of a definite theological perspective which has power and integrity is not incompatible with the emphasis on freedom and critical inquiry. Third, no desire to preserve a doctrinal position can justify the unimaginative treatment of students, with assignments which tend to produce a certain amount of routine work but which do not develop responsibility for exploring ultimate questions and the habit of reflective thinking.

Getting Everything In. Another pressure upon teachers which leads to routine methods is the need to cover quickly all the ground that is expected by the governing board of the school and other ecclesiastical bodies. So long as the conception is prevalent that the student who graduates from the seminary should be prepared for every eventuality, the schools will be under pressure to see that every question which may arise in a minister's life be "covered in a course." The subconscious acceptance by the schools of the impossible goal of preparing the students for everything exerts a constant pressure upon curriculum builders and teachers. The frantic effort is to "get everything in," and the only solution is to treat "everything" superficially.

Canonical and ordination examinations in which churches and ecclesiastical boards test the preparation of candidates for the ministry can be significant educational experiences and can be an important check upon the adequacy of seminary work. At the same time churches need to recognize how the procedures and standards for such examinations exert a potent force upon the teaching that is done in the schools. If examiners show that they are more concerned with theological honesty and maturity than with rote learning the schools will be more free to develop significant courses, and to teach with greater effectiveness.

A third factor which produces the didactic tendency lies in the students themselves. Not all are seeking release of their imaginative powers. The craving for intellectual and spiritual security is one side of the ambivalence in the student mind. Rebellion against authority and the desperate need to be "told" can exist side by side and reinforce each other. Theological students may complain that they are at loose ends through the upset brought about by new theological ideas, and at the same time resist efforts to direct their attention to historic structures of faith which would throw light on their problems.

It is important here, as in other types of anxiety, to see that provision of artificial support may not touch the core of the problem. Students often become excessively dependent upon their professors and upon specific assignments. It is easy to work out a course in which the student feels secure in doing exactly what is expected of him, but this may postpone his facing the questions upon which his personal growth depends.

Teachers as well as students have their anxiety patterns. It is uncommon but still possible to find the teacher who covers his own sense of inadequacy by making excessive and legalistic demands. The teacher may avoid facing the questions which trouble him by confining his course to a well-marked route. Perhaps more common is the professor who feels that his department is slighted in the curricular requirements, or that it is looked down upon, or that his own scholarship is not appreciated, and who makes ruthless demands upon students as a way of asserting the importance of his course.

Lest we lay undue stress on the psychological aspects of these problems let us recognize that attention to individual students, and the development of courses which free them to make their own pace, require time and an adequate faculty. The small faculties in the schools and the heavy work loads many of them carry are a major factor in slowing the pace for everyone down to a walk when most should be running ahead at a variety of speeds.

The consequences of teaching which tries merely to transmit blocks of content have been keenly described for us in a letter by Canon Theodore Wedel whose significant work as Warden of the College of Preachers in Washington puts him in a position to reflect upon the intellectual habits of ministers:

As I see the clergy . . . I am increasingly distressed over one dismal fact. Their seminary education has come to be locked up in a museum of memory, or in a deep freeze. Their life of study is in the past and does not continue into the present. If three years of work in a seminary are to suffice, by way of content equipment, for a lifetime, the seminary is burdened with an impossible task. Are we not still victims of the "content" illusion? Seminary curricula are under the tyrannical ideal of teaching subjects in place of nurturing students to be "students." Equip a man with the habits of study and with mastery over tools and he surely does not need to be spoon-fed in every "subject."

The clergy I deal with are, most of them, still victims of the content illusion. Their theology is that of the seminary professor whose lectures are enshrined in their class room notes. Independent reading and "dialogue with an author" is scarcely known. Whenever a man appears who has been turned into a *now* student he is a joy. . . . If he has missed out on a course in psychology in college or seminary, he will read himself into psychology. In other words, he *is* a student in place of a man who has *been* one. . . .[2]

Methods of Integration. The provision which some schools make for tutors offers one way of moving toward the kind of education Canon Wedel is urging. Not many schools are in a position to provide tutors. There must be competent graduate students or others available. There must be money for tutors' fees or scholarship aid. But where tutors can

[2] From a letter to the director of the Study. Quoted by permission.

be provided they give individual attention to students, interpret theological problems in relation to the student's developing interests, and lessen the amount of formal lecturing by providing supplementary tutorial sessions.

One Episcopal school provides tutors during the first two years of the B.D. course, another provides them only during the third year. In the two cases the tutors have a somewhat different role. In the former instance, close co-ordination with the class work is emphasized. The tutoring session usually begins with some supplementation or development of the lectures the student has been hearing. This discussion leads to further questions, and may become the occasion for the raising of personal problems. The tutors in the third-year program are not graduate fellows but are faculty members and clergymen whom the school has found competent for this work. Here the emphasis is upon the students' special interests and upon preparation for the ministry upon which they shortly enter.

A perennial problem of every tutorial and counseling relationship is raised by the privileged character of what the student may disclose in these sessions. Tutors must make reports to faculty even if they do not give grades; yet the student must be free to disclose his personal problems without fear that they will become public even within the circle of the faculty. Much depends on the good sense of the tutor. With all the difficulties involved in this relationship which is both "official" and personal, academic and confessional, its potential value is so great the schools should make more strenuous efforts to discover ways in which competent tutorial help can be provided at some stage of the seminary course.

Other strategies for securing integration of the student's courses include comprehensive examinations, and a thesis. Such examinations are not common but a good many schools require a thesis. There are a few schools which give the B.D. candidate a choice between a thesis and some other academic requirement. In Episcopal schools a thesis is always required for the S.T.B. degree but not for the diploma.

As with all academic devices each of these has its advocates and its critics. The common complaint against the B.D. thesis is that students spend far too much time on it for what they secure from the labor, since they are rarely prepared to write a real thesis at this stage in their study. Advocates of the thesis point to many instances in which students have been able to bring their seminary course to a focus through the struggle with an important theme. This may be the one time in a student's life when he produces a systematic discussion of a major topic. Some of the significant defenses of the thesis have come from professors who give close attention to the students' development within a field or department over a long period of time. Preparatory papers written in courses are planned so that the completed thesis represents a growth of insight over a considerable period.

There are many schools which have neither thesis nor comprehensive examination in the requirement for the B.D. degree. A question must be raised in these instances as to whether graduation is being made dependent wholly on the acquiring of course credits, though some schools believe they have found valid alternatives in extensive term papers.

A number of schools have developed senior seminars which look toward an organization of the student's knowledge around the issues and situations he will confront when he begins his ministry. These seminars sometimes take the form of a discussion of the dynamic faiths in the contemporary world. Sometimes they are courses in comparative theology which discuss the main types of Christian belief. Where such courses are most successful they are probably led not by one professor but by several. Sometimes the instructional staff varies from year to year. The course may project its analysis of contemporary problems on the broad scale of world history, with interpretation of the great religions and of modern nationalism and communism, or it may stress the local context and the competing forms of religion in the communities immediately at hand. Schools which have such seminars are enthusiastic about them.

Good Teaching. What then is good theological teaching? Any answer must take into account the variety of impact which good teachers have. Some are remembered for their scholarship, some for their structure of thought, some for personal dedication and concern, and these all in many combinations and with different responses from various students. Yet certain common elements underlie the excellent teaching being done by individuals and by faculties.

The first factor which is presupposed by all the rest is that the good teacher is master of his subject and is able to give this subject and its problems such clarity and shape that the student can find his way into the material and grow in his mastery of it. The most effective teaching is often done when attention is so concentrated on the topic into which both teacher and student are inquiring that attention is no longer focused on the mechanics of teaching and learning, but solely on the question at hand. Any one aspect of this mastery of the process of communication to the student about a subject can be overvalued. Clarity of presentation may be a fetish, so that the more problematic areas in the penumbra of the subject are left untouched. Pedantic attention to detail may obscure the larger outlines of a problem. The good teacher is constantly seeking a right balance in these things, but such balance comes in part from his capacity to lose himself in the subject and not to give too much self-conscious attention to the process of communication.

This first point of course applies to all teaching. A second has to do with the teaching of theological courses. Good teaching in seminaries and divinity schools brings the student to see a particular subject in the context of the Christian faith so that he discovers his personal commitment to be bound up with what he is "studying." The objectivity which is required is not lost. Rather, the objective search of teacher and student is carried one step further so that together they face the ultimate issues of the Church's faith as approached through the particular subject in hand. The message of the prophets becomes alive for contemporary issues when the student learns to interpret the prophets in their time and discovers the relationship between the Word of God as it came to them and the issues of the common life today. Christian preaching becomes more than an "art" when it is understood as the minister's personal witness to God's judgment and his mercy, a witness which requires of him and his hearers a discipline of thought and will.

There are many ways in which good teachers secure such life and interest in their teaching. Sometimes it is done overtly. The teacher deals with his subject so that its relationship to the whole of theology and to the life of the church are made plain. He makes historical applications and finds illustrations which connect with the student's experience. To be sure, if a course is arrested too often in order to underline contemporary applications, the basic pattern will never become clear. Yet this is a point at which a little help may go a long way. A few strategically placed illustrations may stimulate the student to build his own bridges to present problems and make it impossible for him to think of any field of study as a closed room with no windows which look out upon the wider historical landscape.

Whatever the teaching style the personal commitment of the instructor will be somewhere revealed. The real proof of the teacher's dedication to the ultimate concerns of the Christian community is seen when the student gives his primary attention not to the professor but to the object of Christian commitment, God and his Word in Christ.

There are two points at which the teacher's personal vocation and dedication become especially clear. One is his fidelity to the demands imposed upon his mind and spirit by the subject at hand. The teaching which accomplishes the most is that through which the student sees the professor's mind at work on a problem, grappling with its difficulties and seeking more light. Such is the vocation of the theological teacher, to clarify, explore, and interpret the meaning of the faith. It is this which lays upon him a discipline and a demand for self-giving.

The other manifestation of Christian concern will come in his regard for, and relations with, students and colleagues. In a theological school the demands of love and justice may be so often spoken about that they become routine symbols but in the end they remain the decisive requirement upon all participants in the learning community.

Greatness in teaching is a gift for which to be thankful, not a skill which can be completely analyzed or acquired. But its consequences can be stated. The greatness can be measured by the spaciousness of the spiritual intellectual room in which the student is brought to move. He sees his problems as involving questions which challenge and threaten men everywhere. He can discover within dogma and ritual the depth of the personal meeting of God and man. He learns the infinite pains of scholarship and a sense of how a multitude of details take on order and importance in a larger setting as part of the story of God's dealing with man. A field of inert details and ideas has become a realm of ordered power. In the end it is up to the theological teacher to escape from the pedantry of narrow outlook and dogmatic blinders which threaten to overtake him. He must teach his point of view with respect for his heritage and for the demands of the logic and truth of his subject and at the same time set the students' minds free. Such teaching requires specific attention to four points which have arisen many times in our discussions with faculties.

First, the theological teacher must continually be pushing students to examine the ultimate presuppositions with which they think and with which they judge themselves and their fellows. No purely technical mastery of logic or method will suffice. In theology we are dealing with issues which involve conviction and faith. A teacher of history who brings historical periods vividly to life, and who contributes important knowledge of historical movements, has not led students to the depth of his subject until the question of the meaning of this history has been raised. How are historical causes and events to be understood, and what is the relation of a Christian view of human events to other views? Such questions ought to be inescapable in a theological course.

When those in the "practical fields" insist that they are concerned not only with methods of preaching and pastoral work, but with theological aims and standards of judgment of Christian practice, they surely are justified from the standpoint of this view of theological teaching. It is often difficult to move from analysis of some aspect of Christian ministry such as preaching to analysis of the ultimate presuppositions involved, but the difficulty is no justification for avoiding it. Every activity within the Church and every act of Christian life may yield new insight into the truth about God and man.

Here we face the difficult problem of how far the theological teacher is responsible for introducing students to points of view he does not hold. Just as the school must keep its integrity and yet not become the purveyor of a stale formula, so the individual teacher faces the same problem. Much of the stimulus in theological education comes from the ability of teachers to open up live options for the students, and to communicate the experience of sharing in a theological discussion in which major issues are at stake and concerning which absolute answers are not now, or perhaps ever in this world, completely given.

Some teachers do this best by outlining their own positions and arguing for them. In this case good teaching requires that it be made plain to the student what decisions have been made in taking this position, what consequences may follow, and also it requires that alternative points of view be presented. Other teachers give most time to the discussion of various points of view and encourage students to come to their own judgments without too much specific persuasion from the instructor. Probably most teaching combines these two strategies. In either case the student learns that he is dealing with ideas which have their growing edges and which involve real decisions.

The second trait of good teaching is that a close relationship is kept between the formal structure of thought and concrete human problems. One of the widespread concerns of students is for the "relevance" of their theological study to the world they live in. This "world" has two aspects both of which usually lie behind the search for relevance. One is the personal life of the student, his search for meaning, and for adequacy to realize his vocation of service in the church. The other aspect is the course of history with its conflict of gigantic powers which seem to be untamed by Christian principles. Students ask how the church can be effective in this kind of world.

In meeting the issue of relevance the teacher must move back and forth from the structure of the Christian faith to concrete experience. The clue is in their continual interplay. The teacher who has had much pastoral or mission field experience often has much to communicate, but he needs to detect the universal in the particular and to relate his personal experience to the structure of faith. Questions of the Kingdom of God in relation to human history, of the calling of the Christian, of Church and Society, are all significant for the discovery of "relevance." Good teaching will continually seek the meaning of God's redemptive action in the midst of the forces which shape our existence.

Third, the good teacher gives attention to the relation of his subject to the vocational commitment students have made or are considering for the Christian ministry. On this point, the students with whom we have talked are especially emphatic. The good teacher has helped them to see the Church and its ministry in such a light that they have gotten a sense of its ultimate importance and have had their own decisions clarified. For the student who is uncertain concerning his decision to enter the ministry direct talks of encouragement and inspiration may not help. Some may discover they are not called to this kind of ministry. It may be most important for the teacher to understand the student's doubts and questionings. In this realistic setting deeper conviction can come when the calling of God to meet human need is made plain. Sometimes the student will catch from the teacher the spirit of ministry which carries conviction. Above all, students need to see within and beyond the specific forms of ministry the demand of the Gospel which is the source of all ministry.

Finally, there is that aspect of theological teaching which is most difficult to formulate, and yet which is its foundation. The theological teacher has as his ultimate topic the bearing of human experience on our knowledge of God and the bearing of the Christian Gospel upon our human response to him who is the source of our being. Our teaching and learning is, like the rest of life, in the hands of God more than in ours. Yet when we try to direct our attention to this fact and seek the presence of God we seem to turn away from the analysis of ideas to the attitude of worship. We no longer speak only about God but pray to him. What then becomes of teaching?

It is difficult to say precisely how it is that our relationship to God can be the central theme of theological teaching while the process remains that of objective analysis, discovery, and interpretation. But such is the case when the teacher knows what he is about, for the most effective work is done by those who keep this ultimate dimension of their subject clear. In the theological classroom the emphasis is upon "the truth about our faith" rather than upon the immediate confrontation with faith itself. Yet in a strange way this indirect movement about the center leads at times to the center. Good theological teaching moves always within the process of seeking understanding toward the issues of faith where they become personal and ultimate. Both teacher and student are people who know sin and estrangement, and who live by the promises and the reality of grace. The Word of God is not present as preaching or as sacrament in the meeting of teacher and student, but it does nevertheless become present in a special way which is of decisive significance for the Church.

CHAPTER SEVEN

Theological Students: Varieties of Types and Experience

In a previous chapter some information was given about the number of theological students in the Protestant seminaries in the United States and Canada, about enrollment tendencies, the percentage of women students of theology, the relatively low increase of Negro enrollment, and about the denominational affiliation of the students. Certain other more or less external data have also been gleaned from the information supplied by the schools. It is clear, for instance, that by and large seminary students are, now as in past decades, graduates of church-controlled or church-affiliated colleges, though the percentage of graduates from independent and state universities is slowly increasing. Available data indicate that since 1950 this movement is slackening except in the case of the interdenominational theological schools and the Episcopal seminaries.

Questions about the academic standing and the intelligence rating of theological students are frequently raised but cannot be answered on the basis of available data. Mutually contradictory impressions and reports from college and seminary administrators, contradictory advices from experts in the testing field, and prevailing uncertainty concerning the qualifications required of men preparing for the ministry have, in view of the limitations of the study, led its directors to forego any effort to advance into this field. This decision has turned out to be well-advised since a special study highly relevant to this subject was inaugurated in 1956 under the auspices of the Educational Testing Service, financed by a grant from the Lilly Endowment. Within the limitations of the present inquiry it seemed more pertinent that an effort should be made to try to understand what sorts of men are studying in the seminaries and what effects educational procedures have upon them, by conducting a series of student interviews in a selected group of schools. Intensive interviews were held at seven seminaries, less intensive ones in many others. These conversations form the most important basis of the following reflections though much other information also contributed to them. Two points in particular have emerged from these conversations: the great variety of personality types and motivations among the students and the highly dynamic character of the educational process when it is regarded from their viewpoints.

I. *What Kinds of Persons Seek Theological Education?*

No simple answer to this question is possible. One cannot say that any particular student is typical of his generation of seminarians. There is great diversity in personality orientation, motivation, previous training, and in many other respects. Some men of high quality are shy and retiring, others are forthright and aggressive. Some poor quality men matriculate from good liberal arts colleges, and some excellent students come from very poor colleges. Each student comes with a unique pattern of conditioning experiences and decisions. His motives are complex and often uncertain. Further, one cannot assume that the motivations that lead a man to apply for admission will remain fixed throughout the course of study.

Yet certain patterns emerge. One can draw typical images of students who seem to be present on almost every seminary campus, though no one student perfectly fits the picture an analyst draws. Further, images are static, and theological students are very much in a process of change. Thus the best that patterns and images can do is to help to understand some students.

With all the risks involved, at least ten kinds of men who come to our seminaries may be described. 1) There is the student who is in seminary because his parents, pastor, and home congregation have decided for him that he will make a good minister. 2) A man may be suffering from deep wounds in himself and seek through theological education to heal his own disturbed mind and spirit. 3) A student who functions well in interpersonal relations and anticipates the prestige and success that will be forthcoming from a ministerial career will find his way to seminary. 4) A person who has prematurely tasted the fruits of success in a church career as a boy evangelist, dynamic youth leader, or student movement executive must complete what are to him often only *pro forma* requirements for ministerial status. 5) The man who decided for the ministry at an early age, frequently out of a sense of alienation in the world, and who enjoyed the protection of the pre-ministerial group in college will find his way to seminary. 6) A zealous spirit characterizes the student who has found a gospel and knows its saving power. He wishes to share his good news with the world. 7) Religion and theology present themselves as objective intellectual problems to a searching mind, and the theological school seems to be the place to pursue a study of these problems. 8) An experience of a tragically disorganized society, or of disordered minds, often leads a student to study for the ministry. He sees the Church as an institution out of which flow healing processes for the social and personal evils of our time. 9) Frequently found in the present generation is the man seeking for a faith adequate to bring order into the intellectual and moral confusions that have characterized his previous personal and academic experience. 10) Finally, there is the rare student of mature faith who lives in the knowledge that it is God who saves and justifies. He is seeking to become an adequate servant of his Lord. These types must now be more adequately described.

1) A student may come to seminary because his family, pastor, and home congregation believe he is the kind of person who would make a good minister. Perhaps he is not conscious of drifting along a course overtly or subtly prescribed for him. Other options for professional work have never been real to him. He has felt no compulsion to assert his autonomy and make a decision about any particular lifework. The coercive influences have played on him in such a disguised manner that he may think a decision his own when it is not. Such a man entering theological school may feel that he is in a strange land. The curriculum does not provide any excitement for him either in the theological, biblical, or practical courses. He meets the required standards. In addition to lack of stimulation from his studies he finds his field work to be a boring assignment. No matter what opportunities come his way, he feels no compulsion to grasp them and to work in them. His faculty becomes aware that he is not doing well in spite of the laudatory letters of his pastor and the laymen in his church. The student may be prodded by his boredom into asking questions about his fitness for the ministry. Perhaps his faculty counselor will spend some time with him, seeking to help him reflect on the purposes of his presence in the seminary.

Various things can happen to such a student. Sometimes such a student comes to a sense of self-direction within the work that others appear to have chosen for him. He may find a validation for his presence in the seminary which enables him to become an effective student and a dedicated minister. Sometimes he may be brought to a level of self-knowledge in which he has the courage to admit that he would rather be selling books or working in a laboratory. If there is a good understanding of the double calling the school may help him to move out of the study of theology into other work where he can also serve God. If neither the student nor the school becomes aware of the problem, the student may eventually be ordained without any material reorganization of his life.

Should the school effectively lead the student into a field of study or work other than theology, its involvement is not necessarily over. The president or dean sometimes becomes the object of parents' and pastor's hostility. Their high hopes that the young man would become a minister are not easily redirected.

Men who have been involved in theological education for many years believe that the number of students who commit themselves to seminary training under such subtle duress and coercion is decreasing, that in fact very few are left. Other professional opportunities are open to Christian young people in which they can render service to God and man. Parents and pastors have become more aware of the possible tragic consequences of a decision pressed too hard and too soon. Churches and schools have intensified their appraisal process of potential ministers so that they can sometimes redirect such a student before he matriculates. Students in recent generations have been given opportunities to survey the possible fields of lifework and are likely to make their own decision to greater extent than formerly. In the new situation, however, churches have found it necessary to extend their efforts to recruit capable young people for the ministry.

The line between recruitment by effective guidance and subtle coercion is often a fine one. The call to "full-time Christian service" tendered at the moment of greatest religious emotion in a youth camp may be a form of subtle duress, though made with the best of intent. Giving a young man opportunities to have camp experiences, and suggesting from an intimate knowledge of his talent and abilities that he consider the ministry, may lead him to at least a tentative commitment. Fortunately tentativeness on the part of students is found far more frequently than coerced commitment.[1] This is a hopeful sign.

2) Theological education frequently is attractive to a person who is seeking some healing for a disturbed self. He may be suffering from a sense of guilt and seek in the study of religion and the service of the church some expiation. He may be afraid to meet people and face the world, and be seeking a community in which he will be accepted and not be subjected to criticism. Theological disputation in which he engages is frequently a transposition of his own inner conflicts into the exalted and accepted language of the Christian tradition. Such a student might well bear out projection theories of religion, in which God is the projection into infinity of one's own parents, or one's own scheme of values. An excessive zealousness to reform the world may be an externalization of a personal feeling of nonacceptance in the world. Excessive concentration on objects of devotion or on the aesthetic aspects of the liturgy may betray an inadequate acceptance of the more common relationships characteristic of human society. Frequently the student whose religious orientation is dominantly directed by his own disorders does not find the help that he is seeking in the theological

[1] On the call to the ministry see *The Purpose of the Church and Its Ministry*, 63–66.

school. His problem may become intensified rather than alleviated. A radical discontinuity within himself, or between himself and his society, may come to overt appearance so that extensive therapy is needed. But another student who appears to be similarly preoccupied with the problems of the self may rise to a new plateau of self-understanding. Such awakenings and their therapeutic consequences come in a variety of ways. Sometimes the new state is the result of the process of social maturation in the school community. Sometimes it issues out of personal relationship with a faculty member or fellow student. Or the teaching and content of a particular course may be the cathartic agent. Not only courses in psychology of personality, but courses in theology, New Testament, ethics, church history, and a variety of other subjects are mentioned by students as the occasions for the working of healing processes of mind and spirit. Again field work experience and clinical training in mental hospitals have been the milieus of restoration of the self. The person whose motives center in the need for personal therapy may find it to a large extent in the course of his education and become an effective minister.

The churches and schools, however, cannot afford to take too many risks with students of this sort. As one dean put it, "We are an educational institution, and not a center of psychotherapy." The student with personal problems may take more faculty time than the total economy of the educational process can afford. To get for him the kind of psychiatric care he needs is frequently beyond the financial resources of the school. If he completes his course without some therapeutic experience he may render great disservice to the church in the ministry. For these reasons an increasing number of schools and denominations have engaged in various testing programs.

Though we have found no valid evidence to support the idea, it is believed in certain quarters that some theological schools have more personality problem cases than others, whether this be due to some power of attraction or to failures of discrimination in admission. Undoubtedly the over-all pattern for such a church as the Presbyterian Church, U.S.A., is improving with the accumulated experience of an ongoing denominational testing program. The heterogeneity of nondenominational schools appears to some observers to be a factor involved in personal discord. Students come from a variety of denominational and regional backgrounds, and some have no structure of theological tradition or church-relatedness in which they feel at home. On the surface students in ethnically, culturally, religiously, denominationally homogeneous theological communities appear to be relieved of tensions present in the nondenominational schools. But in the former sort of seminaries other external factors can bring out potential personal problems. There may be subtle or overt pressures to conform to patterns of thought and action. Dependency may be encouraged; hostility may be directed to theological opponents or "the world"; guilt feelings may be exacerbated. Hence it seems that no school is exempt from students of this type. With the increasing care given to the appraisal of applicants and the counseling of students, however, such students do not present an alarming problem.

3) Another sort of student seems primarily to be seeking a career which will bring him the rewards of secure status in society. A few students self-consciously desire the personal adulation and recognition that can be forthcoming from smooth operations in interpersonal relations. Such persons have been known to fabricate a personal history of past accomplishments, if not for the administration then for fellow students. Such a student may be sensitive to the weaknesses of particular associates and teachers, and play on their conviction that he is fundamentally "a good guy." He may even be interested in the relatively meager financial rewards that are to be gained by facility of tongue and pseudocharismatic personality.[2] Self-conscious manipulation of persons is plainly fraudulent in the ministry. The student, however, can usually point to some apparent good that he has done through his careerist pseudocharisma which tends to soften the criticism of him. Most students of this type flounder before getting out of school. If they are not checked by seminaries, frequently church examiners rule them out before they are allowed to enter the ministry. Yet there are some who remain largely self-seeking careerists and so cover their motives with "piety" and "genuineness" that they manage to deceive themselves, and get into the ministry.

The *self-conscious* careerist is a rare person in seminary. The man who is susceptible to popular success symbols of the seminary and ministry, though not explicitly seeking them, is more common. He wants to "learn the ropes" in seminary. How can he get along well with the most people? How can he take a stand on a controversial issue which is really no stand at all, but can be interpreted by both sides as commendable? The cultivation of personal loyalties is substituted for the commitment of men to the living Word of God in the name of God. In seminary he learns what the acceptable things to say and do are in the eyes of the people whose approval he most craves. He depends on "his smiling, smiling face" to carry him through crises. If one looks for a living center in such a student it is hard to detect an identifiable unity of faith and action.

Perhaps these students are harder to reach in the educational process than are those who have serious psychological problems. The latter

[2] A district superintendent reported to a group of students on the way in which a man serving a summer parish in his area "had quickly won his way into the hearts of the people." The side remark of a student of this sort was, "I don't care if he got into their hearts; did he get into their pocketbooks?"

have deeply personal questions to bring to what they are learning. The career-minded student probably does not attain such involvement in his theological thinking. The reference is external; he is an "outer-directed person" whose sense of fulfillment comes not in personal integrity, but in conforming to expectations which will bring him institutional success. For many such students, however, the probing questions must be faced simply because they live in a community of men who are constantly raising and discussing them. The superficial character of one's interpretation of the ministry may be penetrated by the critical evaluation of what he reads and hears. The inadequacy of his initial dominant motivation may become clear, and if only from the prodding of his conscience, he may find a sense of direction which is rooted in the fundamental orientation of a new life in faith.

4) Perhaps sometimes hard to distinguish from the careerist is the student that has already received the recognition and rewards of a "successful" church career, and feels there is nothing to learn in seminary. Perhaps such a student's "maturity" has come in his undergraduate course of study in religion. Under the stimulation of excellent teachers he has satisfactorily resolved all the issues of theological discussion. In some traditions he has been an effective and acclaimed boy evangelist, in other a parish minister, a dynamic youth leader, or a member of the hierarchy of the student movement. Not all students who have had these experiences manifest premature maturity. Some, however, exude a great sense of superiority, not only over their fellow students, but frequently toward teachers and courses in particular departments. As boy evangelist or dynamic youth leader, the student may have addressed gatherings of several thousand people. He has associated with people who are important in the ecclesiastical world. He knows that his youthful accomplishments will secure him a sure place in the church program at some level. As leader in the student movement or as an excellent undergraduate student he has learned to verbalize the theological jargon of the day and has established his own (or adopted another's) pigeonhole classification system for all ideas that he encounters.

The road of the successful church or theological functionary in theological seminary is likely to be a rocky one. If he excels academically, and has read widely, he may well find that some of his courses repeat work previously done. If he has had good teachers, he may find some teaching dull. Such experiences tend to reinforce his own sense of superior accomplishment. He can attain a high scholastic average by his ready articulation of material, but his teachers will feel that there is a gulf between the mental dexterity and memory content on the one hand, and the lived experience and faith of the student on the other. The hope of the school is that underneath the façade of learning something may happen to awaken the man to his personal or social immaturity.

If the student's recognition has come through national prominence in youth movements, he may have different problems. In a student body of a seminary his star is immediately dimmed. He finds men of greater ability who are not known beyond their local church or college campus. His verbalized conceptions of Christian faith and work appear to be inadequate in the light of new-found knowledge. He may have to shift from the one-night stand performance before mass audiences to the sustained leadership of a small group in his field work. Either this student will go through theological school defensively retaining a self-image that is the product of his early encounters with the church, or he will have to live through a period of painful self-analysis. Apart from such analysis his theological education remains a *pro-forma* procedure that must be undergone in order that external requirements for initiation into the professional fraternity of the ministry may be met.

Usually, however, a student of this type is awakened in theological seminary. He is generally conscientious as a student and in his commitment to a church vocation. His conscientiousness leads him to self-examination in the light of the courses and the social experiences of his seminary life. He will be helped by personal counseling as he reorients himself. When he does find an adequate unity of faith and life he is likely to become a very effective minister or teacher. The native ability that was expressed in his preseminary success finds a new focus of expression.

5) Another type of student has been sheltered from confrontation either with the intellectual criticisms of religion or from the world of sweat and cursing by an early decision to become a minister. He has conformed to an image of the morally pure and holy youth that is expected to become a minister. Perhaps he was the teenager that many parents pointed to as an example for their own rowdy children to follow, yet he probably had little acceptance by his peers. In college he found his friends among other preministerial students, and probably confined his participation in extracurricular activities to religious groups on the campus.[3] He was embarrassed by bawdy jokes and angered by profanity. When he was thrown in the company of industrial workers or farmers among whom his identity as a preministerial student was unknown, he felt ill at ease because of their manners and speech. He did not suffer from real vocational uncertainty during his

---

[3] An airline stewardess remarked to a staff member that the preministerial students on her campus were "a bunch of sanctimonious Holy Joes," and were the biggest detriment to religion in the college. Many good theological students admit that they were unwilling to be identified with the pretheological groups on their college campuses.

college career, and came into seminary with a fairly clear-structured picture of what would happen to him in the next three years. Now, in seminary he may be embarrassed by the presence of persons who do not share his moralism, and who express distaste for his piousness. He tends to work at his studies with dedicated conscientiousness, but probably brings little of a spirit of inquiry to them.

Theological schools expect to receive large numbers of this type of student, and probably are very effective with them. The school can count on their dedication to the church and the ministry. Frequently they have been guided through a pretheological curriculum which has given them a better general education than, for instance, those pre-engineering students who decide to go into the ministry in their senior year in college. The student of this type may be dissatisfied with the community life of the school because it lacks the uniformity and coziness that he expected and wanted. He may find that some of his teachers appear to be disrespectful of what has been sacred to him. The critical spirit of fellow students and teachers may disturb him. But it is very likely that he will go through a period of reorientation of motivation and conception of the ministry and the church under the impact of it all. He will probably find new theological roots, and an enlarged vision of the responsibilities and opportunities of the ministry and the church. He may go through a revolt against moralism that many of his colleagues went through during high school or college, but with the sustaining support of the community he can weather his rebelliousness and become more effective because of it. An uneasiness about the status quo of the church and ministry that had not existed before may creep into his consciousness. It will be more difficult for him to conform to any particular external patterns of what the correct behavior of the religious man ought to be. This, too, is probably for the good of the Church.

Many faculties and administrators are impressed with the present increase in the number of students of this type in comparison with the years when veterans of World War II made up the majority of the enrollment. They are aware of a certain immaturity in many members of the present generation of students that stems in large part from a lack of confrontation with diverse groups of people. The normal experiences of large portions of the American people are foreign to these students. The brutality of war, the immediate experience of demoralization of life under the impact of economic depression or wartime uprootedness, are matters of textbook knowledge and not lived experience for them. This immaturity makes it necessary for schools to provide experience in which new dimensions of human existence can become real to students. It is also one of the strongest arguments made against exemption from military service for pretheological students.

Experience in work camps, clinical training, students-in-industry programs, and the like help some men of this group to come to self-knowledge. Theological faculties tend to believe that at some point the church-sheltered student must come to a radical confrontation with the realities of human existence as they are for widespread groups of people in the world. It is an essential aspect of his education, and is basic to his becoming an effective minister. As a historian put it, "We need ministers who have a hard-headed realism." A benign smile is not enough.

6) Zealous enthusiasm characterizes another kind of theological student. Such a man has found a saving truth, and out of the abundance of its meaning for him he wishes to share it with the world. The saving truth may be an evangelical experience. In his own religious life he has found the adequacy of the Christian Gospel, and he believes that his experience is normative. For another student the saving truth is an esoteric version of Christian faith, or even a syncretism unique to himself. Out of the wrestling of his own soul, or the stimulation of college courses, he has grasped an insight that appears to be of ultimate meaning. Still another person has come to hope for the social salvation of the world through Christian pacifism or a comparable movement. A sense of courage and purpose permeates his total self as he engages in the Christian cause.

Contrary to the assumption in an article on seminarians called "Where Goes the Glow?" [4] zealousness is by no means characteristic of all entering students. While zeal is laudable the enthusiastic student often finds out in the course of his studies that he has an oversimplified purpose. Effective theological teaching tends to make him aware of the partial truths that men seize upon as total. He may find that biblical fundamentals cannot be deduced as simply as he anticipated. A new understanding of human nature may come to him. For example, his expectation that upon presentation with a rationally coherent system of values a person will act accordingly becomes untenable. Humans deceive themselves, and mind does not govern will. Or, he may find that in the realities of history there is institutional power as well as personal love, that evil needs to be resisted as well as good restored. Whatever his enthusiasm may be, in most instances he has to rethink his purpose in the light of new knowledge and new experiences.

The enthusiastic student is a good candidate for theological education. He may be disappointed by senior associates who do not have "a glow." Exposing his truth to the light of wider knowledge may be a painful experience. He may be prone to substitute for his old enthusiasm a new one defended just as uncritically. He may jump from Wieman to Barth, or from fundamentalism to unitarianism. More

4 *Christian Century,* Vol. LXX, 508, April 29, 1953.

likely he will not discard the whole of the truth that gave a center of meaning to his vocational choice, but will incorporate new insights into it. A new appreciation for the Christian tradition will modify but not destroy a novel approach to theology. Understanding of the unity of mankind and of the ways in which this unity becomes concrete may qualify an individualistic theory of salvation. Few students with enthusiasm for a single truth leave theological school without a modification of perspective or without zeal for the modified and enlarged vision.

7) Another group of students consists of those who have an objective intellectual interest in theological problems. Ostensibly such a man is concerned with truth as a perfect absolute, and is interested to check or follow out the claims of the Church to truth. If his interests are philosophical, in contemporary mode he may be interested in the logical analysis of theological statements. Or his question may be the coherence of the traditional Christian views on the nature of God with an understanding of ultimate reality given in contemporary metaphysics and based on the modern view of the physical world. The principal criteria that must be satisfied are those given by a discipline that has its roots outside the Church. He may be concerned with the structures of religious institutions, and with their dynamic interactions with other aspects of contemporary culture. He may be concerned with measuring the influence of religious beliefs on human behavior. Whatever his avenue of approach may be, the Christian religion is a phenomenon to be understood objectively, scientifically, and logically.

This type of student makes certain theological schools feel uncomfortable, and is uncomfortable in many of them. Because of the indefiniteness of his statement of belief or vocational commitment such a student may be excluded from schools in the admissions procedures. Most schools find it healthy to have a few highly critical students enrolled. They prod other students and stimulate teachers. Such students, however, become restive when they must conform to certain theological lines, whether these be given confessionally or implicitly in the "general tone" of a school. A man of this sort may feel that the church is poorly served by the reluctance of a school to confront critical issues that are raised from the outside. This may lead him to transfer to a school which is more open to rigorous intellectual discussion.

He is likely to come out of seminary, however, with a greater appreciation for the Christian tradition and for the existential quality of Christian truth than he had upon entering. Most such students are more loyal to the Church and its tradition than they are aware of. They feel more at home in a religious community than in a nonreligious one. They are more willing to review their previous theological standpoint than they would like to admit. In this respect, theological schools frequently bring a student out of an attitude of skepticism or scientism into an inner appreciation of Christian faith within which his critical faculties can work. He may find his way into further graduate training beyond the B.D. degree either in a theological discipline or some other, and become an effective teacher. He may become a good preacher and pastor.

8) A common type of theological student is the humanitarian. He has come to believe for at least several reasons that the Church is a great healing force. For some students of this type the fractured and unjust social order is the object of the Church's activity. They may have had experience in deteriorating urban centers or in political reform movements during college. For others, the Christian religion with its law of love can bring the warring nations together. They may be enthusiastic pacifists or world federalists. For other humanitarians the Church provides a ministry for healing the individual ills of people. The counseling ministry, meeting the psychological needs of the people, seems to them to be the center of the Church's vocation.

There are many indications that the humanitarian interest among students has been shifting from social reform to individual care. A growing knowledge of the complexity of economic, social, and political affairs dulls the edge of social moralism. In a time of national prosperity the issue of economic justice does not seem to be important. The revision of the theology of social action adds further uncertainties. For various reasons the problems of individuals seem to be more pressing.

In the case of either of these humanitarian outlooks, the student is likely to encounter theological insights that modify his preconceived approaches. He becomes aware of the total ministry of the church, and sets his concerns for counseling and social action in this wider context. In seminary there will be times of frustration for him in social apathy or in the assumptions that preaching is so efficacious that counseling is unimportant. Through his education, however, his special humanitarian concerns will probably mature, become more wisely directed, more deeply founded, more established within a larger faith.

9) A ninth variety of theological students consists of those who are seeking for themselves and the world a faith that is adequate to bring order into the intellectual and moral confusions they see. Such a student frequently is uncertain about a vocation within the Church.[5] He has a certain loyalty to the Church, and a feeling more latent than manifest that the Christian faith offers a means of salvation for the world. Frequently his concerns are more theological than ecclesiastical. Either out of his college religious life or some vocational experiences after college he has come to raise profound questions about the meaning

[5] In this respect the Rockefeller Brothers Fund fellows are by no means untypical of the contemporary generation of students.

of human existence. He matriculates as a religious seeker, and not as one who is certain that he has found an answer to the confusion of the times. He is more likely to enroll at a nondenominational seminary because of his skepticism about a church vocation, but there are many of this type in denominational schools. He may express doubt about the efficacy of the ministry. The institutional responsibilities of guiding committees, doing administrative work, routine calling, fund raising, and the like, generally appear to him to be dead weight that hinders the essential work of the minister.

He may have a predilection to disparage the practical courses in the curriculum before he takes them, for he is convinced that what he needs to get is a theology. "If one gets a thorough grounding in theology and the content of the Christian faith, the practical things will work out by themselves." His intellectual concerns are not dealt with in a purely objective manner; rather he is personally involved in almost every idea that crosses the threshold of his mind. In church history he may find himself "rooting for the Arians" while studying the Christological controversies, and not just absorbing data. What is most important in biblical courses may not be the mastery of the content of the Bible nor the study of the formation of the canon, but rather an understanding of the authority of the Bible for Christian faith and life. He is likely to feel restless under the pace that course work requires him to go. He does not have the opportunity to think through the implications of each new idea for his own theological position. His mind may wander from a lecture to pursue an insight suggested by some particular phrase. He will sometimes forget about his assigned or suggested reading and pursue the study of Hartshorne or Kierkegaard independently of any course work. During his study he will probably look critically at his own ecclesiastical tradition, and may entertain the thought of joining another denomination that appears to bring him "into the mainstream of the tradition" more than his own does. Or he may resolve to work within his present denomination to bring it to a better understanding of its message and mission in the world.

Some members of this group find it necessary to locate companions engaged in the same quest, or among those who have reached some resolution of their religious problems. A student may find his campus snack bar to be a "citadel of learning," where he can engage in theological conversation. On many occasions "his verbalizations extend themselves far beyond his knowledge," but out of the dialogue comes the kind of insight which brings coherence to his own selfhood. Because theological problems, whether they come alive in biblical, theological, or homiletics courses, become so all-absorbing, he is likely to entertain the idea of graduate study. His intent may not be so much on the teaching ministry as on "getting an extra year to think through all the impressions" gained in the regular course of study. A career in teaching may be attractive because he sees that theological teachers constantly live with the problems that currently excite him, whereas parish ministers seem to be preoccupied with things of lesser importance.

The number of students of this type in seminaries is large. They are not going to accept any particular formula of function or belief before they have wrestled with it thoroughly, and have come to regard it as an expression of the faith which is both the Church's and their own. They are not looking for the security of ecclesiastical status or time-honored dogma, but rather for a faithful certainty of the goodness of the living God. They are not trying to construct a theology *de novo* out of a variety of empirical sciences, but are coming to grips with the meaning of biblical faith as it is relevant to all of contemporary human experience. While they may be critical of the churches, they tend to come to a real sense of the living Church which spans history and cultural boundaries. They are not looking for an authoritative pastoral role that gives them power over laity. Nor are they satisfied to be the friendliest man in the village whose pleasing personality wins the admiration of all. They seek ways of ministering which maintain communication with the laity of the church, and yet preserve the integrity of the Christian Gospel. This type of student is characterized by an earnestness of spirit and a humility that make for rapid growth in Christian maturity during theological education.

10) A final category of students consists of those few of mature faith who have come to a genuine acceptance of their environment and themselves in a lived experience of the justifying graciousness of God. A student of this sort seeks with as much earnestness as one of the previous type, but he possesses an equanimity of spirit that enables him to carry on a dialogue with his books, his teachers, and his fellow students without the intensive personal involvement of the seeker. He is not without doubts about particular statements of Christian truth, but he knows that he is justified even in his doubt. He may question many aspects of denominational programs and prevailing conceptions of the role of the minister, but he recognizes that programming and ministerial chores are necessary. He lives in the hope that through the routines of parish life he can witness to God who acts both through the Church and through other institutions and experiences. He may be critical of some of the work in the practical courses, but understands that an effective ministry requires knowledge of church school curricula and administration, good sermon construction, effective administrative procedures. He may be excited by theological and other content courses, but knows that apart from the incorporation of a theological point of view into the daily functions of the ministry, knowledge is irrelevant.

In a sense such a student possesses the kind of maturity that most students are approaching after their three years of study. He is likely to be more interested in learning than in high grades. His commitment to the parish ministry and to his own denomination will not come under radical questioning. Yet he does not accept any given stereotype of the function of the parish ministry, nor is he satisfied with the superstructure and programming of his church. He does not hold his college religious experience or his high school youth work or the excitement of theological education to be normative for himself or the Church. He recognizes that he has only begun in seminary a process of continued education that will continue throughout his years of ministry.

The theological students of America are at least as diverse as these ten images indicate. Qualitative distinctions cut through all the types. Students' self-understandings change during their course of study. The intense growth of three years in a seminary community has profound effects.

II. *The Dynamics of Theological Education*

Not only is the great variety of student types frequently forgotten by faculties and ministers, but the dynamics of education as it centers in students is also often lost sight of. A minister may recall the intensity of his personal struggles in seminary with an air of amusement and detachment. Frequently he has come to some ease in Zion either by resting in a structure of unity that emerged in the course of his own experience, or by turning his attention to activities that do not force critical and disturbing questions upon him. Some faculties seem to believe that curricular integration will bring unity to the life and activity of the student. Following some educational or theological orthodoxy loyally, they may expect that all the students, regardless of individual differences, will come out as integrated beings. Students themselves may look for escape from intense personal involvement in theological education. They may take refuge in objective scholarship, or in dogmatic acceptance of one aspect of Christian truth as the whole truth, or in the recognition and rewards that come in their field work. Because the great mass of Protestant Christians rarely have an opportunity to become closely acquainted with theological students in the process of their training, the anxieties and rewards of theological study remain outside of their experience.

Most students quickly learn, however, that theology is not studied like ancient history or chemistry. The student cannot be content to master a set of objective principles and data which he can then objectively apply to the various pastoral situations in which he finds himself. The ultimate data of theological study are fundamental personal and social beliefs about the nature of reality, divine, human, and physical, on which the life of the student rests. What he must in part objectify, evaluate, and make decisions about are not historical cases of legal precedent, or anatomical and chemical phenomena, but the fundamental assumptions of his personal existence and those of the historic community in which he professes loyalty. The student frequently reorders not only data and thoughts, but also that center of meaning that gives coherence to his life and his understanding of all reality. Theological education involves the total man. If we desire to understand men so involved in their studies we must analyze their lived experience during the process of learning and maturation that we call theological education.

The individuality of students in preparation, personality, and purpose makes the dynamics of education distinct for each person. Yet not only faculties but the students themselves may lose sight of this fact. A student frequently accepts what has happened to him as the norm for all his fellows. If his enthusiasm centers in his field work he may deprecate the studiousness of the budding scholar. If theological concerns consume his mind and spirit he may be impatient with a neighbor who wants to learn how to run a church school and a youth group more effectively. To be sure, there are many common denominators among students, and in some schools there is more homogeneity than in others. There is usually greater diversity among students in nondenominational seminaries than in denominational schools. Yet even where most of the students come from a common ethnic, religious, and cultural background they do not respond in the same manner to the same books or teaching. The meaning of what they read, hear, and do is always in relation to what they are and what concerns are important to them at that time. When one couples the individuality of students with the diversity of seminary teaching and experience, it becomes clear that not every student is going to "come alive" in the same manner, place, or time.

The process of education as it centers in students can be stated in another way. In the midst of various heteronomous pressures, the student seeks to become increasingly theonomous. He seeks to make his self-directed motives and his other-directed stimuli come under the service of the Lord God. He will always be moved by impulses that arise from within and the consciousness of what is expected from without, but in the light of his professed obedience to and love for God he is impelled to bring both the external and internal direction into coherence with the meanings of Christian faith. All truth is to a large extent deeply subjective truth for him. The process is further complicated because the student believes that what is true for him must to a large measure also be true for the Church, for the biblical witness, and for the universal human community. Any ordering of the self in

Christian faith is an ordering within a given community and tradition, and these can never be subjective in a solipsistic sense. Out of the impact of his personal impulses, his conception of the expectations given by Church and tradition, his direction by family and culture, and his increasing sense of bringing all this under the ordering of God, there begins to develop a structure of meanings. The personal anxieties and confusions of the self, and the seemingly contradictory elements to which he is exposed at some point, are relieved by a sense of coherence. Some personal center of meaning comes into being.

We have previously noted the variety of motivation among persons seeking theological education. But any individual student may have some of this variety and hence conflict within himself. Moreover, the variety of experiences to which he is exposed is at least as great as the complexity of his motives. The normal state of theological students is one of becoming more than one of being. The process of becoming involves tension and anxiety even when the self is sustained by the goodness of God and by the company of understanding and forgiving fellows. Out of the process of becoming there emerges a new center for the self. This occurs in different places and times. Three aspects of the process must be elaborated. First, what are some of the experiences that appear to students to be in conflict with each other and with the state of being they bring to the schools? Second, how do students handle the consequent tension and use it creatively? Third, how does unity begin to emerge out of the diversity and confusion of the total experience?

A. *The Variety of Experience.* Many schools have orientation programs for the first-year students in which an effort is made to interpret in advance some of the problems and rewards that are forthcoming. The novelty of the school and the unreality of discussion about events not yet experienced all work against the effectiveness of such orientation. To tell a student that he will find that the teaching in a New Testament course may not agree with what is said in constructive theology courses is one thing; for him to experience the disparity is another. To predict problems of time budget between field work and study is one thing; for a student to be equally interested in his youth group program and in church history is another. The variety of experience has personal consequences for almost every student.

One of the student's dialogues is between the old and the new. In his religious training and college study he may have come to accept a theory of the authority of the Bible. It may be one of verbal plenary inspiration or it may be one that emerged out of a historical-critical approach to Scriptures. In the former case an introduction to the critical-historical approach to Bible study thrusts upon him the need to reformulate a new ground of certainty for his faith. In the latter case he may find his previous critical study of the Bible had been wedded to an inadequate theology so that he too must revise his understanding of Scriptures. Tension about the authority and relevance of the Bible for modern life is one of the most common among students.

Not uncommonly the student from a liberal college has rejected tradition as irrelevant. He has been overwhelmed by the novelty of the modern age, and believes that a new day requires a new theology and new approaches to the ministry. If he has not rejected tradition, he may have absolutized his own particular tradition. Since all he has known is pietism or Anglo-Catholicism he tends to identify part of the tradition with the whole. In either instance courses in church history and history of doctrine expose him to the richness, variation, and continuity of the Christian movement. He comes to see himself in relation to Augustine and the Reformation as well as Spener, to the free forms of worship common to evangelical Protestantism as well as to the Catholic liturgical tradition. Sympathetically interpreted, old phrases and symbols take on fresh meaning. Groups previously identified with the Antichrist or with rigid orthodoxy are seen in relation to their time and place. Theological education gives the student a view of the broader Church of which he is a part. He comes to such a view, however, only by wrestling with the variety of the tradition as it bears upon him.

In even the most denominationally oriented theological schools students come to some understanding of the One Church which bears up their particular denomination in its unique life. The struggle of many students is to see the relation of loyalty to their denominational point of view to a dawning sense of the oneness of the Christian community. Southern Baptist students read books by Anglican and Lutheran theologians, and have to understand their relation as Southern Baptists to the Body of Christ which includes persons whose writing has contributed to their own lives. Fundamentalists have to admit that one's salvation is not dependent upon belief in plenary inspiration, but on the goodness of God. In the light of their theological studies Unitarian students are forced to apply the critical spirit out of which their denomination arose to its presently prevailing theology. In the critical awareness of the insufficiency of the sense of Church with which he began his study of theology, a student is likely to entertain the possibility of joining a church which appears to him to embody the "main stream" of church life more than his own does. Sometimes he takes such a step, but never without some agony of spirit.

The tension and the dialogue of a theological student is not only between what he was and what is new to him. It is also between aspects of the new. Is his time better spent preparing his Sunday School lesson, or preparing for examinations in theology and Bible? If he serves a church ought he to make parish life the center of his focus, or is it his primary vocation to be a student? What are the relative merits of spending time discussing theology with his peers, and reading theological classics that have shaped the Church's thought? Should he try to use all the opportunities for growth in interest in the arts before he gets lost in the semi-isolation of a rural or small-town parish, or ought he to stick to the studies? Should he participate in the local political campaigns and in ameliorative social work, or are these things that can be delayed until he leaves school? The decision on the use of time is always a decision between aspects of the good. It requires a weighing of the various factors which may contribute to the student's maturation. It also sharpens the dilemma between the desire to be of immediate service to others, and to concentrate on the seemingly self-centered assimilation of information and experience which will be used at a later time.

A further dialogue and tension goes on between aspects of the new. Courses are taught from different points of view. In schools with large faculties a student may have two courses in Old Testament, for example, which interpret both the authority of the Bible and its content in different ways. Rarely is one teacher so much more persuasive than the other that the student can immediately make a decision about the validity of the perspectives. Even where all courses are taught from a defined confessional point of view students seek and find crucial distinctions between the perspectives of faculty members.[6] In addition to the variety of theological opinion that comes in lectures, students are exposed to a more or less extensive spectrum of contemporary and historical theology in their reading. The problem that a student faces is not objectively to try to make Barth coherent with Tillich, or Luther coherent with Augustine. Rather each author (for at least the better students) raises issues about his own developing theological position. For some students the larger part of theological education is spent wandering in what appear to be uncharted wastelands of theological opinion. Yet they are under the compulsion to have some ordered faith, life, and thought that will give integrity to their ministry.

For other students the dialogue is carried on around the problem of communication. How does one "translate" what he is taught in theology into the curriculum of the church school? What is the relevance of the Synoptic problem to "meeting the needs of people"? What is the validity of the Church's historic liturgies in the light of their development through history? Some students are frequently impatient with the

6 Students in a seminary of one of the more conservative Calvinistic theological schools in America rated their faculty on a scale of "conservatism-liberalism," all within an explicitly "plenary inspiration" theory of the authority of the Bible. There was remarkable consensus on the ordering of men at the two extremes.

"impracticality" of their "content courses"; others are impatient with the "superficiality" of their "practical courses." In either case the judgment arises out of an effort to see the relation of one thing to another, and the whole to the task of the minister. To be sure, many a student matriculates with prejudices about the order of importance of what he hopes to do. Not uncommonly he assumes that "the theoretrical is the most practical," and that if he can only find a satisfactory theology matters of church administration and Sunday School curriculum will take care of themselves. Other students have prejudged the "insignificance of theology" and believe that if one "knows how to work with people" an effective ministry is assured. The bulk of theological students, however, confront existentially the necessity to forge their theological, biblical, and historical studies into a living unity with the practical fields. If the conversation between fields does not go on in the minds of the teachers, it is likely to take place in the mind of the student.

The catalogue of student experience of dialogue and tension is not exhausted by a list of theological problems. Theological tensions are personalized and personal tensions are "theologized." Also, the theological student tends to be self-critical and introspective to a greater extent than some other graduate students. He stands before God not only as a student before an object of knowledge, but also as an estranged and sinful son. He brings to his studies not only curiosity, but guilt. His relation to that about which he learns is not disinterestedness, but love, adoration, and obedience. What is assessed and objectified in his studies is the faith by which he lives. To ask questions about that faith is to ask questions about himself. To raise doubts about the adequacy of a theory of the authority of the Bible, for example, is frequently to raise doubts about the sufficiency of the beliefs by which the student directs his thought and behavior. Theological education can be a refiner's fire, and no dross is consumed without changing the character of the metal.

B. *Bearing the Strain.* Ministers easily forget the personal struggles of their seminary years. This is illustrated time and again by the questions they address to recently graduated candidates for ordination. In liberal denominations they may ask, with some attempt at humor, "Do you believe in the Virgin Birth?" They are surprised to find that the candidate views this as an open question. In conservative denominations the same question may be asked with great seriousness. There the ministerium may frown on the unsettled mind of the candidate. The student, however, lives with this question, and many more searching than this. His problem is that of the man who questions that in which he believes, and believes that which he questions. Through this he must maintain his identity and integrity.

The ultimate answer to the question "How does the student handle his tension?" is a theological one. He is carried by the gracious mercy and power of God. But God's action is through the acts of his servants, and the manifestations of his gracious mercy and power must be concrete for the student who is becoming and not being a Christian. How does the student find his way into a center of meaning which gives him both personal integrity and a sense of being God-directed?

Membership in the seminary community assumes great significance for students who are undergoing personal reorientation. The over-all impact of the community is that it sustains one in his doubts and gives hope of what he might become. The community is concrete in a man's relations with other students, to the faculty, and in the worship life and service activities of the school.

While some students believe that the common life in their school is "too cozy" or "too much like the rah-rah spirit of college, only covered with piosity," other students do not find the kind of personal intimate relations they anticipated. They are caught between the school as institution enforcing certain obligations, and as a Christian community in which there is mutual acceptance of persons. The dilemma students do not always understand is that the seminary is both school and a manifestation of the Church. For some students the seminary is not enough like a small town, and for others it is too much like such a town. Some students feel cheated if they do not know the personal history and present events in the lives of their fellow students and faculty; other students long for more anonymity than is possible in even a large seminary.

Within the differentiations of expectation, however, there is a general acknowledgment of the importance of social relations in theological education. The theological "bull session," in the dormitory, the snack bar, or in "cell groups" of couples, is one of the most important aspects of the educational process. Frequently the communication is among peers going through the same courses. In the light of their readings and lectures, they attempt to work through problems of thought and action that come to their attention. Just as frequently students who are being initiated into theological discussion find greater stimulation from more advanced students in their midst. At times the advanced student who has come to some identifiable theological position appears to the seeker to be dogmatically orthodox. Usually, however, he gives constructive guidance through his statements and questions. Social relations function not only as pedagogical devices; the presence of students who have passed through uncertainty into a greater coherence of life and thought is itself a symbol of the worthwhileness of what sometimes appears to be a hopeless enterprise.

Faculty members also are both participants in the dialogues and symbols of hope. A common complaint of students in larger seminaries is that "the faculty members are inaccessible," or that "we don't get to know the faculty as persons." Students recognize some of the demands made upon faculty time and generally accept the inaccessibility that exists as their fate. Many students do not use available opportunities to engage their teachers in conversation. Time and again, however, the private or small group session with a teacher and the conversation after a lecture will bring clarity to the confusion in which students live. Though at a distance, yet faculty members are "present" in almost every discussion of theology or practical church life that goes on. They are the stimulant and the sounding board for student creativity. Students find not only some direction leading to personal wholeness, but can come to accept the almost insuperable character of certain theological problems. Acceptance of the faculty's fallibility makes fallibility more acceptable to students. To see teachers, both great and poor, wrestle as believers who dare to question, and as inquirers who dare to believe, makes the same status more palatable to the students.

Community, as it sustains the student in his tensions and doubts, is more than a process of communication between its members. It is directed outward to the glory of God and to the service of man. Thus in common worship and common action the spiritual and intellectual tensions find a wider context of meaning. The student tends to lose his preoccupation with himself as he self-consciously relates himself to the Sovereign Lord in worship. Not every student is pleased with the patterns of worship that prevail in his school. There is less dissatisfaction in denominational schools that have a liturgical tradition than in denominational and nondenominational schools that must develop an ordered life of prayer and praise. For many students, however, the chapel period is a time of religious nurture of a different order from the rest of his school life. Here, in a more than intellectual way (except when faculty members use their preaching to expand their courses, a frequent complaint), the reason for theological study comes into focus. The experience is not an individualistic one, for corporate worship reminds the student that he is one of a company of God's people. Before the throne of grace distinctions between persons which sometimes take a place of inordinate importance in the minds of students are leveled. Faculty and students, good students and mediocre students, all join in the praise of the ultimate object, not only of their study, but of their life, the Deity.

As the community acts in a Godward direction in its worship, so it acts communally in a manward direction in various projects of service. "The community of deed," like the community of worship, brings students out of their preoccupation with self into service of others. Part of the frustration of seminary life is that the altruistic motives which are parts of Christian life seem to have no effective expression. There are tasks, however, in which students act together. They join voluntary associations to canvass for a political party at election times, gather clothing for students abroad, give blood to the Red Cross, and form choral groups that visit churches in the vicinity of the school. Local problems come to their attention and are met with corporate action. The common life in Christian service is a normal part of church life that keeps students aware of a vocation beyond that of study and their own redemption.

They also relieve the tension of theological study with a variety of diversions. In actuality most of them live in several worlds. A Rockefeller Brothers fellow, for example, found that the voluntary acceptance of a field work assignment in a semirural parish took him away from a falsely accelerated pace of theological problem solving. His experience is common. To meet and talk with farmers, for whom theological problems are as uninteresting as problems in animal husbandry are to most theological students, keeps a wider reality of human life in focus for the student. In addition to field work various forms of recreation keep students on an even keel. Some seminary book stores sell as many copies of a new edition of Pogo as they do the works of any single major theologians. Baseball, the opera, political debates on television, symphony concerts, movies, all have wide appeal to the theological student audience. Students in one school grieved when the handball court was transformed into a wing for the library.

For the married student his home life, often with fatherly care for one or two children, is a major diversion. Married students rarely complain about their family responsibilities unless unusual events cause great financial hardship. The stability and normality of family living is for most students an asset to their theological education. Emotional tensions may occur in early marriage, and on rare occasion a marital problem becomes serious, but in the main marriage and family life appear to make a contribution to the student's total development that outweighs the consequent distractions.

Diversions keep a student's own development in the perspective of social and cultural reality out of which he came, of which he is a part, and into which he will return with a special vocation. Experiences not directly related to study bring fresh insight into the nature of human reality and have a significant impact on his theological orientation. Opportunities to participate in more than one sphere of life, while necessarily curbed during the period of study, do give realism to seminary life that might otherwise be lost.

In addition to the common life and the diversions that occur, the student in part bears the strain of a state of becoming through his opportunities formally to articulate both his problems and the answers he has found. Students speak of the importance of writing term papers and preparing sermons in this connection. Where a term paper is not only an exercise in scholarly bibliographical research, but also gives the student an opportunity to develop and express his own emerging point of view, it is a creative experience. There are students, however, who misuse such opportunities. One who is preoccupied with himself to an unusual degree may come to believe that theological education is only coming to self-knowledge. He may turn every assignment into the grinding of a personal ax. Most students who write a constructive paper, however, come to some self-knowledge in the light of a growing awareness of the faith and life of the Church. In objectifying his subjective problems and seeing some order emerge in his interests and point of view, emancipation from the self in the agony of becoming a Christian occurs. Such an experience comes frequently in sermon preparation. Laymen who listen to a student preaching in their churches have commented on the growing clarity and unity of sermons as he develops in his theological education. Student preachers often find the discipline of regular preparation of sermons to be "a course in systematic theology," in the sense that it forces them to order their thought.

C. *Coming Alive.* We have noted that students have a variety of experiences and bear the strain of uncertainty in various ways. The implication that students "come alive" at different places and times must be brought into sharper focus. Students generally have some point of orientation which unifies thought and life in the Christian faith and Church before they leave the seminary. Some have developed a sense of integrity that is explicit and can be articulated. Others only dimly sense the direction in which they are moving as graduation time comes upon them. A common motive for graduate study or a fourth year of work is the desire further to develop and nurture a faith and life that is only coming to birth. There is no one midwife that attends each birth. Every school has more than one Socrates.

Some students come to Christian self-knowledge and maturity largely in one course. For others this occurs in tensions between lectures and reading. A few students can point to one place where the pieces fell into a pattern for them, but for most students the process is more complex. Certain experiences of illumination recur. Yet no one of these can be established as efficacious for all.

Students more often point to good teaching than any other experience as crucial in their personal development. Yet one is hard pressed to define the qualities of good teaching from a student's point of view, for the same student will find different styles of teaching equally stimulating, and different students have different preferences. However, certain names recur as "effective teachers" in conversations with students.

What qualities frequently appear in teaching that affects the center of students' existence? Some men find that a comprehensive presentation of material in a delightful, if not entertaining, manner is the best general orientation in a field. Lectures in which the line of march is clear and historical or contemporary figures are developed as if from within, seem to be important to students, particularly in the initial stages of their education. Many students, however, find that if reading assignments and lectures cover the same material in relatively the same order, comprehensive lecturing is a waste of time.

Many students prefer lectures to present a point of view or thesis in the light of the content that is drawn into the course in class and reading. They are looking for a structure that they can tentatively adopt, or think against, which draws a variety of impressions into unified order. If the theological motif of divine action in history, for example, comes through time and again in a survey course in Old Testament, students have a framework in which they can comprehend a great diversity of reading material. If an epistemological "bias" is reflected in the teaching of contemporary theology, so that the course is not only a survey of present-day theology but an interpretation of it in the light of a theory of theological method, the course takes on more meaning for many. If the thesis is a controversial one, perhaps not in line with the prevailing theological point of view, students frequently find stimulation.

Other students look for the relevance of the course in its relation to other subjects and to the ministry. For them the good teacher is one who makes allusions to the way in which New Testament study contributes to systematic theology, or theology becomes part of preaching. But students tend to react negatively to self-conscious attempts to be relevant. They do not want a teacher to stop in the midst of a lecture on Luther or a discussion of international relations to inform them of a "snappy sermon starter." But they are sensitive to overtones of relevance to things other than the topic under present consideration. The exciting teacher for many students is one whose lectures and discussions show that he is widely read and appreciates many sources of information and insight. He can touch upon their prior experience or study in such a way that they can relate what he is saying to themselves. But they still respect and want competence in the field of special responsibility. The teacher who "builds bridges" between disciplines cannot be glib and casual; he must show that he grasps the fundamental point of view of the disciplines he is relating to each other, and is well read in them.

The teacher who has enthusiasm about his subject matter helps many students see what issues they must face and gives them support in solving problems. A passionate display of interest in a subject, however, is no virtue in and of itself. The teacher who has scholarly competence coupled with personal vitality communicates more than one whose lectures lack enthusiasm. But teaching need not be dramatic nor be illustrated with physical and emotional antics in order to be lively. The dimension that is helpful is the teacher's own personal involvement in the questions under discussion. The problems he is developing must be *his* problems. He must have entered personally into the exposition of his materials.

Students demonstrate the weaknesses as well as the strengths of this kind of teaching. They may respond more to the impact of a personality than to ideas communicated. They may become enthused, but be hard pressed to define what ideas and data they are enthused about. They may become almost exclusively dependent upon oral presentation as the means of learning. Their loyalty may be directed more to a person than to any objective position about Christian faith. They may take "an exciting point" out of its intellectual context and develop it beyond its intrinsic importance. The danger of enthusiastic teaching lies in its tendency to evoke a limited and emotional response from students.

Often a somewhat disorganized teacher is more helpful than the one who has a very clear outline to which he is bound. A lecturer or seminar leader who draws in materials only tangentially related to the subject at hand may broaden horizons and provoke thought. A course may become something of a long annotated bibliography through which the student becomes acquainted with a great diversity of literature and may be motivated to do research long after his formal education is over.

Such is some of the variety of teaching that is effective with students in fostering the process of coming to theological and personal integrity in Christian faith. Few students become disciples of teachers in the sense that they enslave themselves to the opinion of a master. For most, one or several teachers can be lifted out as particularly crucial in their personal development. Teaching, whether in lectures or seminars, is probably the most common situation in which students come to focus.

A second major enterprise of theological students, at least as far as time consumption goes, is reading. However, along with the complaint that students do not know how to write good English goes the complaint about their inability to read well. Teachers hope and expect that students will be able to absorb the material of a book either by grasping the structure of the argument or by carrying on a dialogue with the writer as they read. But on the basis of students' reports about themselves, few seem to have "come alive" in the course of reading. To be sure, the memory of students is no better than that of most faculty members and ministers. Also students are often so engaged in thinking about problems of faith and life in the Church that the ideas they gain from reading are absorbed into their own intellectual equipment. This is better in the long run than it is for a person to recall chapter and verse of documents. Most of the students interviewed, however, by their own confession and by demonstration in the discussions read mainly to meet requirements in courses. Occasionally one met a student who had excellent recall of what he had read but found that he had done little constructive thinking about it.

Students cannot be expected to recall the structure of ideas of all the literature they read during seminary training. Yet one might normally anticipate that each student would have a few key books. They would represent points of view with which he could tentatively identify himself, which he could articulate. To be sure, some students are more articulate in writing than in conversation. In the interviews, however, many students who had some anchorage point in thought and life did not mention any authors as important contributors to their thinking until explicitly pressed to do so. In answer to specific questions about what writers contributed to their personal maturation, some were hard pressed to give names, others could give names and be unable to give book titles, and still others gave names and titles, but could not inform the interviewer what ideas in the books were provocative. This leads one to hazard the generalization that reading plays a role ancillary to oral teaching in the development of most theological students. In many instances the significance of reading is almost negligible.

There are good students, however, whose center of theological and personal existence has been clearly forged in dialogue with both oral teaching and reading. Paul Tillich's method of correlation in theology may be expounded and obviously reflected in the way a student thinks and speaks. H. H. Rowley's books on the Old Testament and the relevance of the Bible have not only become part of the personal equipment of some students but are objectively discussed with a considerable degree of faithfulness to Rowley's own statements. English and Pearson's book on emotional problems have intensified self-knowledge and yet a student can discuss the work critically and objectively. Occasionally a man can even point to a footnote in an essay, or to a brief article that was highly illuminating and stimulating to him.

If reading is not as important as it ought to be in the growth of theological students, this presents a complex problem. The previous training of the student, from grammar school through college, is involved. Students, however, frequently point to the overburdened schedule they are forced to meet. One minister recalled his three years in seminary as an affair of being "talked, and talked, and talked, and talked at." So much time is spent in classes in some schools that students do not have opportunity to assimilate the reading that is required and to browse through the available storehouse of unrequired reading. So many long term papers are required that a man does not have time to read broadly on his topic and to think his way through the ideas. Some reading is done prematurely before students have the equipment with which either to assimilate or criticize what they have read. To be sure, equipment for reading comes in part out of reading, but many students would appreciate more time to develop their own points of view in dialogue with what they are reading. In this connection the pressure for high grades is frequently emphasized by students as detrimental to real education. Many men who learn best from books must emancipate themselves from the compulsion to make high grades by meeting external course requirements.[7]

Students arrive at a center of life and meaning in different courses and in different areas of reading. Self-knowledge and maturation come in relation to wider aspects of experience. In some schools an effort is made so to pattern the curriculum that each student has the experience which the administration feels is most important for self-awakening. Thus in one seminary a course in apologetics, centering on the Apostles' Creed, is designed to raise theological issues in the first semester of residence. Normally the student follows his first year with a summer in clinical training. In another school a course in human personality is required in the first year partly on the supposition that it will bring students to self-awareness.

Yet self-awareness and integration of the self occur around different centers for different students. A course in church history in which the student has the history of his own sect or church objectified for him may be as important in the process of maturation as a course in which he sees himself against various psychological theories of the self. For many students reading the Bible may be as integrating as reading a systematic theology. A course in preaching that develops both style and content in relation to style may have as significant an impact as field work in a mental hospital. Furthermore, a student may come to focus around the theology of Luther and build his theory of Church and

[7] One might suggest a hypothesis at this point. The opinion that many pastors are not doing the kind and the amount of reading that they need for the nurture of their resources in Christian faith is widely held. The increasing popularity of "canned" sermons and other material from organizations such as the Ministers' Research Foundation must be noted. The lecture series presented for ministers by seminaries, denominations, and councils of churches gain wide response. Perhaps one of the factors in this configuration is the inability of ministers to read comprehensively and critically. Because they have not learned how to study in the isolation of man with books and because they have become dependent upon the stimulation of oral presentations, they are somewhat at a loss when separated from the seminary community.

ministry on this foundation, while also gaining self-knowledge and modifying his approach to the ministry in a course on the psychology of personality.

In addition to course work, many aspects of communal life are important in the process of becoming a Christian. Worship, discussion groups, action programs, and the like not only sustain a student in his tension, but frequently become the occasion for the gaining of those insights that bring a man to greater coherence of life and thought. Thus students refer to conversations with particular friends as sources of illumination. They speak of the importance of particular chapel services—for example, a Good Friday service—in which a new level of integrity came into being. The questions of teenagers encountered in field work jobs may tie theological study and the work of the ministry together in a vital way. Because of the variety of situations in which learning takes place, students can never agree among themselves what pattern a "good theological education" should have. The sequence of courses and experience that suffices for one ought to be reversed for another. Ought theology precede or follow sociology of religion and psychology of personality? For some it is more helpful one way, for others another way. Ought field work be omitted the first year? For some students church responsibility is a distraction and confusion; for others it is a constructive diversion from study.

The problems of theological education from students' points of view probably center on the facilitation of the process of personal growth and maturity in Christian faith and church commitment. They recognize the need for enough rational structure to the process so that they may receive the basic intellectual and practical equipment to become effective ministers. Yet they need enough flexibility so that they may develop around those centers of meaning in Church and faith which give personal coherence and make possible an orderly Christian interpretation of nature and human existence. Mixed and conflicting motives, expectations projected on them from family, church, and school, and a great variety of new experiences must be forged into the being of a God-directed man. This is the process that brings both anxieties and rewards to theological students.

CHAPTER EIGHT

The School as Community

I. *The Common Life and Its Institutions*

A medical leader once pointed out that an indispensable part of the education of a doctor is supplied by his participation for many years in a community devoted to the work of healing. All the elements of the curriculum were very important, to be sure, but, beyond all this, a person who aspired to become a physician needed to be for a long time the member of a group infused with a certain spirit and will. The similar role that community life plays in the education of a theological student cannot easily be overestimated though concern for curricular rearrangements may often lead faculties to overlook it.

Community life contributes to the development of theological students at almost every point. For three years or more his mind is molded and his spirit nourished by his interaction with his fellow students and teachers. The seminary is both his church and his school. In it he is drawn to love and serve both God and man. His relationships have value not only for himself; he serves his teachers, his fellow students, and churches as he is being served. Manifold institutional regulations are developed to facilitate this communal life. Yet some of its most personal meanings can never be rationalized and articulated. It constitutes an occasion and context in which God's actions are made known to men called to serve him in the churches.

As in the churches, so in the schools there is never a perfect correlation between the officially defined and rationally developed structures of common life on the one hand, the processes and needs of its constituency on the other. Administrations and faculties, sometimes in consultation with students, try to create those forms for the common life and the educational process that will most facilitate the desired end of mature Christians ready for the ministry. The curriculum undergoes periodic revisions due to restlessness with the established pattern. Although students sometimes call curriculum revision "the favorite indoor sport of the faculty," the need for change arises out of the inadequacy of the given course of study. In some schools the common life of worship is a perennial problem. In seminaries of denominations without established liturgical patterns, or in nondenominational schools, there is likely to be a great deal of diversity in preferences for orders of worship. The pattern established to the satisfaction of the majority of students may be very unsatisfactory to the minorities; the liturgy of one generation may be offensive to students in the next. Some schools seek to create a common bond among students by arranging frequent social functions in which all the students are drawn together. Such functions sometimes appear to be artificial and to develop a sense of unity at a superficial level. In many other areas restlessness with the defined structures of common life instigates change by students, faculties, or churches.

Changes in institutional structures do not always take place when they ought to. Patterns become ossified; old forms refuse to die. For various reasons they are perpetuated and tend to disrupt rather than foster the processes of education and community life. A complin service continues to be read, though only two or three students gather for it. A student committee on academic life is named each year, although it does not meet and act. Students often attend teas more out of a sense of obligation than with pleasure. Frequently there arise alongside of the formally established patterns of life certain expectations to conformity that perpetuate a program or organization meeting no real need and having no real purpose. Students attend meetings because "if you don't, you are breaking community." They may not desire "community" in the sense manifest at the particular meeting, but a stigma is attached to those who do not attend.

Since there is always tension between the institutional forms and the common life of the student body, schools have come to accept and even encourage the formation of unofficial groups centering around particular interests. The interest of a group of students in the religious implications of modern art may be encouraged by informal gatherings rather than by either a course in the curriculum or an "arts committee" in the student organization. "Cell groups" for worship and discussion that supplement both the formal services and the seminars and lectures are formed. Student groups come into being around ephemeral needs and situations. Occasionally the zealous interest of some members of the community leads to the imposition of their concern on the whole school by institutionalizing it. This may be done on some occasions with much profit, on others without any value accruing to the community.

The situation of the theological schools is analogous to that of the state and nation, the institutional church and the Christian community. The common life and individual growth they foster cannot take place without guidance by rationally developed patterns of action and expectation. Intellectual growth needs the course of study as a directive. The common life of the spirit needs patterns of corporate worship. Yet growth in intellectual and spiritual life can never be identified with the forms. The community needs the institution, yet the community and the institution are not one.

II. *The Selection of Students*

Something has previously been said about the selection of the older members of the theological community—the faculty members. In choosing them schools are bound to consider their qualifications as scholars and teachers but must also be concerned with their potential contribution to the common life as friends and advisers, as pastors and priests, as members of one body able to live in harmony with all the other members while performing their peculiar services. Increasing attention is now being paid to the selection of the younger members of the community—the students.

The necessity of better selection procedures has become clear to many administrators and faculties. Regularized procedures giving insight into the qualities and characteristics that make for an effective ministry have not been adequately developed. Yet in their search for students who will become effective ministers, schools and churches cannot rely on intuitive insight and recommendations from kindly pastors alone. The use of psychological tests for measuring intelligence, aptitudes, and getting personality inventories is still in an experimental stage. Other more or less objective criteria used are the college transcript of the student and the record of college activities. Before interpreting further the efforts that schools and churches are making to become more accurate in their evaluations of students, it is important to understand what some of the desired qualities are.

The qualities of mind and spirit making for good theological students and effective ministers cannot be precisely stated. The difficulty is at least twofold. In the first place, effective communication of Christian faith involves an integration of the self around deeply personal, yet God-directed, meanings. If the task of the ministry required the memorization of fundamental principles and their application to specific situations, one might more readily objectify the traits of mind needed. Or if it required only the establishment of rapport of person with person in such fashion as to win confidence and loyalty, one might more easily decide who would be effective. Since, however, the effectiveness of the ministry involves relations to the Divine Lord, and commitment of the self to Him, obvious qualities such as intelligence and personal affability are not of absolute importance. While the life of man in faith has psychological and social consequences, and while certain psychological and social characteristics make for effective communication of the Christian Gospel, any effort to list in serial fashion the qualities needed for the ministry is bound to become trite.[1]

[1] Many such lists, in part set up by committees of churches in search of pastors,

In the second place, a definition of qualities needed for the ministry is difficult because a diversity of gifts is needed in the total life of the Church. If, for example, a standard definition of emotional stability were made the principal criterion for evaluation, a modern Jeremiah or Kierkegaard would probably not be permitted to study theology. There is clearly a place for a few "off-beat" personalities in the work of the Church. If high intellectual competence becomes the principal criterion, some men who could become effective pastors are excluded. If the capacity for easy social relations is lifted to pre-eminence, the Church will lose some potentially good scholars. Even within a given vocation, such as the parish ministry, diverse qualities can make for equally effective work.

Because it is not possible to define precisely what kinds of persons make good theological students and ministers, schools and churches tend to draw the outside limits beyond which a person is found not acceptable, rather than to set forth a perfect model their candidates must approximate. They are seeking men with adequate intellectual ability to carry on a program of graduate professional study. For information on this point they rely heavily on college transcripts and exclude those applicants who have not completed a college course. Generally they are as interested in signs of improvement in performance in college as they are with an over-all average. The minimum average that constitutes outer limits of acceptability varies with schools. At least a C average in college is the general requirement, although where other factors seem to compensate, schools occasionally accept students with slightly lower standing. Where a school with limited enrollment has a large number of applicants it can set a higher average grade requirement. Some schools have very few students with less than a B average. Others that for various reasons accept more applicants may have the bulk of their students in a lower bracket. In some denominational schools the intellectual achievement requirements are very flexible because they are encouraged, if not compelled, to accept all students who have the approval of a church official or body.

The college transcript often includes the student's score on one of the standard intelligence measurement tests. Increasingly, however, church agencies and schools are requiring that students take special tests. These are administered at various times from the date when the

---

have been made available to the staff of the study. A typical one finds that the members of a church rate the qualities desired in their minister in the following order of importance: "Sincerity, friendliness, scholarliness, sense of humor, initiative, progressiveness, cheerfulness, resourcefulness, simplicity, imagination, decisiveness, evangelistic, adventurous." The same group of church members rated the "skills" desired in the following order: "Pulpit speaker, administrator, youth director, pastoral counselor, teacher, public relations, community builder, informal speaker, ritualist, social reformer."

student comes under care of his local presbytery or bishop to the first weeks of school after admission. In some instances the Graduate Record Examination scores are available as a further record of the academic achievement of the student.

Records of intelligence and achievement, however, are always set in the context of other data. Probably every school can cite several instances in which a student showed a great deal of promise on the basis of transcript and test scores, but did not develop significantly in seminary. An equal number of instances can be cited in which a school was skeptical about admitting a student on the basis of these objective data, but because of new motivation or other factors he did well in his course of study at the seminary. Yet every school finds intelligence test scores and college transcripts to be generally the most reliable evidence it has for evaluating the intellectual ability of an applicant.

In addition to intelligence, schools are looking for evidences of emotional stability. Again, the line is so drawn as to exclude those who are obviously very neurotic or psychotic, and those who show signs of aberrant social behavior. In recent years a good deal of attention has been given to the selection of students who are free of critical personality problems. As was previously indicated, theological education tends to attract some men who are seeking answers to their emotional problems. Also since there is a good deal of personal strain involved in the study of theology basic stability is required of those who wish to pursue it.

The seminaries, however, have no clear definition of the emotional stability they are looking for. In such churches as the Protestant Episcopal Church, the Presbyterian Church, U.S.A., and the United Lutheran Church in America there are programs for interviewing and testing prior to application for admission to the school. An effort is made to discover the marginal persons through personality inventory tests or psychiatric interviews. The experience of the administrators of these programs lends itself to various interpretations. There is some consensus, however, around the opinion that the normative scores for the general population on personality inventories cannot be used as the norm for theological students.

The general problem raised by reliance on tests is the adequacy of an institutionalized standard for judging candidates for membership in a theological community. Outer limits can be drawn, but apart from acute cases of emotional disturbance other evidence must be brought to bear in the evaluation process. One veteran teacher stated that the longer he tests, the less he relies solely on testing for pertinent data. No admissions officers or test administrators have been found who believe that psychological testing is the wholly sufficient guide in the selection process. Most of them are extremely cautious about their expectations from such programs. They emphasize the value of information gained in testing for personal and academic counseling of students, but as screening devices, tests need always to be set in the context of other information. The hesitation to rely exclusively or decisively on testing is not only a recognition of the inadequacy of present instruments, but also of the diversity of gifts and qualities that make for an effective ministry.

A third ingredient quality in good students is religious conviction. There are a few Bible schools that require students to sign a particular creedal statement upon entering. Most schools, however, expect that there will be intellectual development of students' religious convictions during the course of study. The amount of certainty required by schools varies. For some, such as the University of Chicago, a serious interest in religion has been sufficient. Such schools are willing to take the risk that the student may leave seminary in a short time. They hope, however, that he will develop religious and vocational concerns. For some schools a conversion experience is the adequate sign of religious seriousness that merits enrollment in the seminary.

Unless a school or denomination has a very specific orthodoxy to which it expects all of its graduates and ministers to conform, it leaves a good deal of pliability in the definition of religious certainty. If too precise a statement of adequate religious and theological certainty were imposed upon students at the time of enrollment, the education process itself would be denied. Education for the ministry is a process of religious and theological development; development involves a change. On the other hand, few schools can afford to take the risk of becoming Christian universities in which subjects are taught for all who have curiosity about Christian faith. Without a general consensus of Christian loyalty on the part of the student body educators would be hampered at every step. Divinity study cannot begin at the beginning. The school must assume that students have both a willingness to learn and some fundamental convictions about the course of life on which they are embarked. Recognizing the variety of conviction and understanding among candidates for admission, schools generally have defined the requirement loosely. They tend to rely on a statement by the student, and on letters of recommendation from teachers and pastors.

A fourth quality in which schools are interested is vocational commitment. Most American seminaries concentrate on education for the parish ministry. Yet in the light of the diversities of ministry in the service of the Church, the diversity of students, and the unformed character of student decisions, schools generally do not demand that a student be committed to the local parish ministry. Again, little objective evidence as to vocational commitment is available. Some students who are trying to solve their personal religious problems are only tentatively enrolled in the fraternity of the pastorate when they matriculate. Others are certain that they want to be local pastors, teachers, missionaries, or institutional chaplains. A few can designate the area of vocational interest even more precisely. Flexibility in requirement at the time of enrollment must, however, be the general rule, for a common experience of schools is that a man who enrolls with an interest in the inner city church, for instance, may graduate with an interest in the Dead Sea Scrolls and become a theological teacher, or that the student who was certain he wanted to teach religion in a college ends his seminary career as one who is in love with the parish ministry. Schools that are most open in admitting men with a minimal religious and vocational commitment seem to have a greater number of "drop-outs" than schools that have clearer expectations of students in these areas. Yet no school wants to prescribe the definition of vocational commitment so closely that a potentially good minister is ruled out by either youthful or mature uncertainty.

Several other qualities of lesser importance can be described. For example, schools require some certification of the good health of the student. Yet schools are flexible enough in their definition of adequate health to allow persons with some handicaps to enter. Administrators feel that they have a responsibility for the placement and adequate adjustment of a student, and may guide a man with great physical defects into some less arduous work. Yet the standard of "good health" is a broad one. The financial status of the potential student has become increasingly important with the high percentage of married students. No seminary is under legal obligation to provide for the care of a student and his family, yet every school will want to stay clear of potential moral obligations to assist one student to the extent of being unjust to others. In the present time of prosperity the financial problem is not as acute as it has been in the past. Yet not a few schools have a high percentage of students whose course of study is radically handicapped by their expenditure of time and energy in earning a livelihood for themselves and their families.

Various devices used in the selection of students have been mentioned. Schools are seeking to get a better picture of the student in advance of his matriculation. This image is useful both in screening candidates for admission and in guiding students through their course of study. Most significant among the procedures used are various psychological tests, college transcripts, letters of recommendation, personal histories written by students, and interviews. Some of these have been discussed above, but it is important to see some of the relative merits of various efforts.

Psychological testing has been going on for more than a decade in many seminaries. It is designed to give insight into the student's basic intelligence, his personality pattern, and his vocational aptitudes. The testing programs are administered in various manners. In some churches, as we have noted, the programs are administered by denominational officials prior to matriculation. In other instances, for example Andover-Newton Theological School, the schools have tests administered at the college prior to admission to seminary. Others administer tests after the student has matriculated; in such cases the function of the results is to give insight useful in counseling. Schools and denominations have experimented with a variety of tests. After many years of experience with a special test developed there, Andover-Newton has come to rely heavily on the insights gained from it. Other schools have tried various tests and given them up as not very helpful.

In general it is clear that the whole testing program needs to be more thoroughly studied. While the present study of theological education has been in process, significant developments have taken place toward this end. Dr. Elmer Million of the Department of the Ministry of the National Council of Churches initiated the most complete survey of the use of tests that is now available. During the same period individual seminaries and teachers discussed the need for an evaluation of testing programs. The Educational Testing Service, a nonprofit organization, under the leadership of Dr. Henry Dyer has made tentative explorations and proposals for research. In April, 1955, various groups and persons interested in the evaluation of testing gathered in Princeton and endorsed proposals of the Educational Testing Service. In 1956 the Lilly Endowment provided funds for such research. A thorough study project is now under way. What seems to be required is: 1) a thorough study of the present use of tests and the evaluations that have been made of their use; 2) a study of what characteristics of effective ministers and students can be tested with some reliability and validity; and 3) if the previous phases warrant it, the development of an instrument that might be widely used in the seminaries and churches. The cautiousness and willingness to accept criticism that characterize the approach of the Educational Testing Service create confidence. Its representatives have repeatedly stated that the first phases of the research may indicate the futility of trying to develop an instrument that would give insight into the fitness of a man for the ministry. In this regard, the professional psychologists and testers are more skeptical and cautious than are some theological seminaries.

Most schools find that the college transcript gives very useful objective information. The difficulties it presents, however, ought to be noted. The principal one is the diversity of standards used in grading. After years of experience with the same colleges, registrars and admissions officers develop their own rules-of-thumb in assessing the college records. One denominational seminary, for example, that gets most of its students from four church-related colleges now knows that "an A in philosophy from College X means that the man has had good training in the field and is competent to handle philosophical ideas, while an A in philosophy from College Z indicates neither of these." A second limitation of excessive reliance on transcripts is that they emphasize the intellectual capacities and achievements of students. These are only a few of the factors in the syndrome of qualities that schools are looking for in students. Fortunately, many transcripts include a record of students' participation in extracurricular activities.

The value of letters of recommendation varies greatly. Schools tend to use letters from ministers with great caution. College teachers, they say, are likely to be more objective in their evaluations of students. The experience of the seminaries with letters from ministers supports the contention of college administrators and scholarship selection committees that ministers tend to deal in generalities and overestimate the virtues and potential capacities of students. "He is a fine young man, and comes from a good Christian home" and "He is sincere and loves people, and will make a good minister" are unfortunately typical of key passages from their letters.[2] Fortunately there are many exceptions. Discriminating alumni are often particularly helpful in giving a fair assessment of the capacities and potentialities of an applicant. College chaplains and members of departments of religion frequently give the most reliable evaluations. The responsibility of American ministers not only to recommend a man but to give a critical evaluation of his fitness for theological study and the ministry needs to be emphasized. Well-meaning kindliness is less than fair to both the student and the school. A careful letter from someone who has known and worked with a student during formative experiences can disclose significant characteristics of behavior. Ministers should be sensitive to qualities needed for effective professional study.

One former seminary president spoke highly of the revealing quality of personal histories required of all applicants to his school. His successor in the seminary agreed. Through years of experience, both men developed something of a "sixth sense" in the interpretation of these histories. They became sensitive to fabrications of hopefully impressive histories. Such efforts themselves disclose something about the student. Where honesty and candor were evident the administration was able to predict with some accuracy the adjustments a student would make to the community he was about to enter. Most schools require some autobiographical statement. In some instances students use the require-

---

[2] One school reported that a pastor was enraged when it took the faculty almost two years to discover that a student from his church had psychotic tendencies. Yet this pastor knew of previous periods of mental illness in the man's life and had not disclosed this in his letter of recommendation.

ment as an opportunity for self-disclosure, others present only the most external facts. In the former cases, seminaries get a useful picture of the deeply personal qualities of the applicant.

Most schools find it impossible to require that every applicant be interviewed by a member of the seminary staff. In instances where there is geographic proximity, or where a member of the seminary staff is visiting a college, interviews are sometimes given. Denominational seminaries that recruit largely from their own colleges find that annual visits to the campuses which include interviews and group discussions are helpful. The difficulties in interviewing are at least twofold. Some students are reticent and never disclose their greatest assets and potentialities in an interview situation. Others are adept at making good first impressions that do not always stand the test of later educational experience. The second difficulty is that the interviewer must be a person who can establish rapport without losing his critical faculties. Not every dean or college visitor has this ability. Most schools believe, however, that an interview is necessary only in doubtful cases.

Institutionalization and refinement of admission procedures are obviously essential in theological education. Not all persons can become effective participants in the seminary community. There remains beyond the qualities and achievements that can be objectively measured, something of the mystery of personality. In the light of this all evaluations are most relative and stand under judgment.

III. *The Physical Condition of Theological Education*

Community life also includes a physical setting. North American seminaries are as variously equipped with buildings and grounds as any other educational institutions. Some schools are in the hearts of cities, others in luxuriant country settings. Some have ample space for student living and activities, others suffer from serious overcrowding. In some places apartment developments are part of the campus so that married students are not physically isolated from the center of the common life; in others married students are scattered widely through cities and neighboring country towns. Some libraries are forbidding in their darkness and dustiness; others are light, spacious, airy, and conducive to study. Not a few schools have recently had the pleasure of moving from sites depressing because of their location and the condition of their buildings to magnificent new plants.

Perhaps the most difficult building problem in the last ten years has been that of housing married students. A fundamental policy issue lies at the heart of the question. To what extent is the seminary responsible for the wives and the children of its students? The principal argument for the provision of housing on or near the campus is that it facilitates the incorporation of married couples into the community life. The experience of schools that have made such provisions, however, is not uniform. Some married students prefer to center their "community" life in their homes, or with a few congenial couples. Couples in one house may have a significant common life, but hardly know couples in another house. In addition to this, human incompatibilities may cause dissension within houses. The question arises whether the provision of housing for married couples leads to a moral obligation to meet further student family needs. A few administrators believe that the school ought clearly to state that it is under no obligation to the student for the housing and care of his family. Other questions have also been raised. In university-related schools a case must be made to medical, law, and other schools for the need for divinity student housing. Otherwise the university will be overrun by requests for apartments. Again it is pointed out that student couples have opportunities for common recreation and discussion in small groups in spite of the lack of central housing and that no matter what physical facilities are provided, married students will not participate in the common life of the seminary to the extent that most single students do. A further question regards the stability of the present trend of married students' enrollment. If for economic or cultural reasons there should be a shift to later marriages, schools do not want capital tied up in real estate that is not producing either income or other goods for the school.

Housing for the single students is almost universally provided. There are a few exceptions such as Temple University's theological school, the Seventh-Day Adventist Seminary, et cetera. When women are enrolled their accommodations are usually not as well planned as those for the men. Many men's dormitories, however, are overcrowded and in need of redecoration and repair. Some, like many married students' quarters, are converted homes. Others are very old and bear all the marks of institutional housing of several generations ago. A very few schools, such as Chicago Theological Seminary and Colgate Rochester Divinity School, either overestimated their enrollment trends or did not consider the possibility of the married student trend, and now have more single student rooms than they need. In some places there is good provision for recreation; in others the need for recreation apparently never entered the minds of administrators. Coffee shops and snack bars are in current vogue, and are an asset to community life.

The importance of providing facilities on campus for day students is not always recognized. At Oberlin, where a high percentage of the students commute to school, a very attractive social room was recently developed. The commuting students have expressed unanimous gratitude for this, for it enables them to have a common life of discussion and recreation during lunch hour and between classes. The room also aids in bringing resident students and commuting students together.

The new student center at Princeton Theological Seminary serves similar purposes.

Very many seminaries seem to be dissatisfied with their present facilities for common worship. In Luther Seminary, for example, a large student body gathers in a low-ceiling basement room for their services. At the University of Dubuque they gather in a small room at the end of a corridor. At Princeton the historic chapel is far too small for the present student body. While efforts are made to give inadequate facilities the outward marks of a house of God through the provision of organs, lecterns, pulpits, and altars, the environment is not conducive to an experience of the majesty and goodness of God. Yet the members of the community gather faithfully, and live a genuinely significant common life of worship. In other instances, such as at Chicago Theological Seminary and the Divinity School of the University of Chicago, impressive churchly buildings are available for worship. Impressive chapels, however, do not of themselves attract worshipers. Schools that have facilities accommodating far more persons than attend regularly, and are outwardly conducive to reverence and piety, are in the minority. It is important for denominations and boards of directors to realize the need for adequate chapel facilities.

Since the adequacy of library buildings and accommodations has been dealt with elsewhere in this report it is sufficient to call attention here to the significance of the library as a center and symbol of the common life. To the members of the seminary community no less than to the casual visitor the attention given by a school to its library is an index of the intellectual tone and expectations of the community.[3]

Class and seminar rooms have not always been expanded as rapidly as the enrollment. Large lecture halls are often provided for required and popular courses, yet in some schools students scramble for seats, and raid adjoining rooms for the needed chairs. Adequate airing and lighting are often neglected. Instructors often need more blackboard space than is now available. The dominance of the lecture method of education is reflected in the common lack of good seminar rooms. The allotment of space is not just a matter of convenience, but of fundamental educational policy. Schools must provide the conditions under which creative intellectual development can best take place.

In recently built seminaries such as Boston University School of Theology and Pittsburgh-Xenia, the administrative offices are both efficient and attractive. On the other hand, at one school the president shares an office that is subject to much intrusion with a part-time member of the faculty (the president emeritus). More frequently faculty offices are makeshift. Many are former dormitory rooms. In

[3] See above, Ch. Six, Sec. IV.

some instances there are two men to an office. In others the offices are scattered over a campus wherever there is room for them.

Faculty housing is more commonly provided by denominational seminaries than by nondenominational. The intention of schools in providing faculty housing on campus is to facilitate the unity of the community. There are bound to be more frequent contacts between students and teachers under a variety of conditions when they live in a small area. For instance, Union Seminary, New York, and Union Seminary, Richmond, have provided substantial, if not luxurious, housing for members of their faculties; the former with apartments in and adjacent to the quadrangle, the latter with individual homes. In contrast to this, faculty members at Boston and Yale live as far as fifteen miles away from the campus. At Boston a self-conscious effort is made to overcome the barrier of distance and to get students into faculty homes. Some faculty who live away from the campus believe, however, that the independent life and privacy gained by the separation is more important than the contribution they would make by physical proximity to the students at all times.

The diversity of physical facilities in the seminaries is matched by the diversity of their location. General, Union, and Biblical Seminaries, for example, are located in the heart of New York City. In Chicago, McCormick, Bethany Biblical, and Northern Baptist are all in rapidly changing inner-city neighborhoods and apparently intend to stay there. There are suburban seminaries such as Garrett and Seabury-Western in Evanston, San Francisco in San Anselmo, and Andover-Newton in Newton Centre. Other schools have been established in deliberate isolation from the noisy world, though in some instances the cities are moving out to them. Episcopal Theological Seminary at Alexandria, Virginia, and Mission House in Plymouth, Wisconsin, are examples of such schools. Their location adds to the sense of emancipation from worldly concerns that makes for a strong internal community life. Many schools are located in university centers, as, for instance, the seminaries of Berkeley, California; New Haven, Connecticut; Austin, Texas.

Their location imposes dilemmas on many theological schools. If a seminary is to expand in the metropolis or in an inner-city area property values are high, and it has no control over the surrounding area. In some instances the only expansion possible is to purchase old homes and try to make them function efficiently for educational and religious purposes. Yet, location in the city can give a sense of social, cultural, and religious realism to education. The changing areas in Chicago, for example, offer sociological laboratories at their back doors to students at McCormick, Chicago, Bethany Biblical, and Northern Baptist Theological Seminaries. The presence of East Harlem a short distance from

Union Seminary, New York, has helped to provoke an important experiment in urban church life, the East Harlem Protestant Parish. To these advantages one can add the accessibility of field work jobs, cultural opportunities, and the possibility of acquaintance with a wide variety of Christian faith and practice. On the other hand, proximity to urban life is distracting. Some remoteness on the part of students and faculty from urban centers may lessen the demands made on them by local churches and may allow for greater concentration on study. The members of somewhat secluded theological communities are bound to become more fraternal and interdependent. Also there is more space for expansion in rural or suburban settings.

Relocation is a real possibility for very few schools. Boston, Pittsburgh-Xenia, and New Orleans Baptist have relocated within a metropolitan area since the war. Golden Gate is in the process of moving. Other schools wish to move, but lack the capital resources to do so. Still others are debating the desirability of relocation. With rapid transportation available, urban schools have access to rural fields, and seminaries in small communities and suburbs have less difficulty than heretofore in enjoying the opportunities of the city. There are, however, faculty members who confess loneliness and the danger of creeping intellectual sterility brought on by isolation from other seminaries and from vital cultural and academic life.

One cannot construct a master plan for theological school buildings and their location any more than one can make any given curriculum universally normative. There are seminaries at the doorsteps of great universities that enter into no important conversations with these neighbors and might as well be a thousand miles away. There are relatively isolated seminaries whose faculty members maintain intellectual alertness and wide cultural interests. There is a sense of community in some poorly housed schools surpassing that of others with fine buildings. Geography and physical property by themselves do not determine the nature of community life and the educational process. Yet schools ought to have resources to find that kind of physical environment that is most conducive to good theological education.

IV. *Common Work in the Community*

A principal integrating force in any community is common work. Frontier and farm families in America had a center of unity that no longer exists for most contemporary urban families. Their cooperative endeavors brought about a kind of interdependence among their members not known in urban life. The meeting of psychological and social needs was grounded in work. To some extent theological communities are "communities of the deed," that is, their members are united not only in a common purpose but in corporate action.

Some common work is carried out in accordance with developed procedures of the institutions. Some of it goes on in spite of institutional procedures. Some arises because such procedures have become obsolete and irrelevant to current problems. Some comes into being through the ingenuity of individual innovators, persons impelled to develop activities where they sense needs unmet by established routines.

The principal area of common work is theological education itself, in which work is shared by students, teachers, administrators, boards of trustees, and churches. Theological education cannot be carried on in isolation; scholars depend on other scholars and upon insights gained from students. Students depend on other students as well as on the guidance of their teachers. The communal character of theological education exists in both its phases as intellectual inquiry and as training for professional responsibility.

In furthering the intellectual inquiry into theological subjects the dependence of the student on the work of the faculty is more obvious than the reverse. Students come as novices in the vocabulary and literature of theology and biblical studies, whereas the teachers have a competent if not extraordinary grasp of them. Also, there are schools and individual teachers who do not admit the contribution of students in the ongoing task of theological study. The vocation of the man of knowledge for them is to transmit information and a pattern of thought to young people expected to conform to type. Such rigidity, however, is not widespread. Students contribute to the work of theological study by bringing to bear in their discussions and papers fresh points of view developed out of the unique syndromes of their previous life and academic experience. They may suggest readings to the professor that have tangential bearing on the subject matter at hand, yet are illuminating. They provide the context of intellectual stimulation that is necessary for continuing scholarship. Graduate students, of course, having achieved greater intellectual maturity in theological matters, can contribute even more to the common inquiry than B.D. students. Yet it is not uncommon for B.D. students to do significant work that, though never published, affects the minds of the teachers. Of course, under the stimulation of the vitality of a new idea (for him), a student may exaggerate the contribution that he is making. Yet the struggle for solutions to age-old theological problems goes on in such genuine exchange of thought between professors and students in seminary communities.

Students also help to develop their own practical training through the processes of communication in the seminary. The clearest example of this is the growing use of colloquia, workshops, and "practicums." Not all the significant techniques and illuminating ideas about church programs come in unilinear fashion from the teacher to the student.

Much is learned as students help one another come to clarification of their problems and solutions, albeit this is done under the guidance of a teacher with wider experience. Even though the institutional forms of communication may appear dull to many students they often find stimulation and receive correction in unofficial ways as in the dormitory and coffee shop conversations.

Just as the community of inquiry frequently extends beyond a given seminary to related colleges, and, through books, to communities of philosophers, social scientists, et cetera, so the community of training includes the churches. Schools and churches are drawn together in the development of curricula for church schools; they work together in field work projects. Several schools, including Augustana, Yale, and Boston, carry on programs in local penal institutions where students teach courses in a variety of subjects and act as unofficial chaplains. A Connecticut pastor once proposed that he take as many as eight men in his large parish to work with them in problems of church administration, church school supervision, counseling problems, and funerals. But just as more could be done to enlarge the community of inquiry, so the community of training could be extended.

Special vocational groups within the theological schools frequently engage in common work without academic credit. For example, under the leadership of missionaries on furlough enrolled as students, the candidates for mission field appointments often develop intensive study programs on problems of theology and missions, and international and intercultural relations. A group of persons particularly interested in inner-city churches have developed similar study fellowships. Persons concerned with political and social action at various schools have formed centers of common study and effort.

Often such groups supplement course offerings. They carry out implications of work done in classes with reference to a particular concern. It is not the part of wisdom to add every such particular area to the curriculum, though in some schools student interest in the significance of modern art and literature for Christian faith and the church have led to the introduction of relevant courses. Not every interest can and ought to be so institutionalized. One or two generations of students may be enthused about the arts, or the inner city, and then the interest may wane. Administrations have wisely allowed extracurricular interests to coexist with the institutional patterns of education. Perhaps some relief from present heavy academic loads would allow for more of such significant unofficial ventures. Certainly all schools ought to recognize the educational significance of noncurricular programs developed out of student initiative and freedom.

In addition to common educational work there are other forms of corporate action. The refectory services are often student ventures managed according to the principles of the co-operative movement. Book stores are usually owned and operated by students and faculty. In some schools such business ventures are controlled by the student association. Ventures in publication combine academic and business interests. Wartburg, the University of Chicago, Union, New York, and other seminaries issue attractive student publications. Such activities flourish and die but have their value for the student generations that participate in them. They do require a good deal of student time, usually operate on a financial shoestring, and involve business obligations.

Flexibility in institutional arrangements is necessary if patterns of common work are to be developed that meet current, and often ephemeral, needs. There must be enough freedom from directed obligations if student and student-faculty groups are to make explorations important to them. Seminaries sometimes could also provide the necessary institutional assistance for such ventures in common work. Where voluntary programs have permanent value they can be built into the official program of the school. On the other hand, seminaries need to be sensitive to signs of declining interest and importance in certain projects, and not keep them artificially alive.

V. *The Community of Worship*

Worship has several important functions in the educational process. It is for students and faculty in general the most important alternation from study; in the context of praise and adoration the objects of theological study are set again in the context of churchly devotion. Diversity of points of view on questions of theology and church strategy is set in its proper light. The anxieties and guilt of students in the throes of becoming Christians are relieved in their renewed certainty of the faithfulness of God. For some students the life of worship and devotion brings the maturation process to its culmination; in worship they come to themselves.

Although many schools do not have an adequate place of worship, a program of chapel services is part of the institutional structure of every school. Though very few schools require chapel attendance in most of them students are expected faithfully to worship together. Continued absence from services frequently becomes the cause for consultation with a dean or faculty adviser. In schools where students come from diverse religious traditions the stated chapel services are sometimes poorly attended.

The orders of worship in theological schools are as diverse as they are in American Protestantism. In Episcopal and Lutheran schools the services follow the liturgies established by the churches. Yet within the family of Episcopal seminaries there are noticeable differences. In some the services are sung, in others they are read; in some the altar is reverenced by the officiating clergy, in others it is not. As one moves from church schools within the well-established liturgical traditions to other schools there is less unity even within denominations. Although new interest is developing in the liturgical heritage of the Reformed churches, American seminaries in this tradition have not been greatly affected by it. The diversity of patterns is greatest in the free church schools and in some nondenominational schools. In some the order changes with each student or teacher officiating for the day. Freedom of expression in worship is policy in some schools. This sometimes leads to bizarre novel forms and blind aping of misunderstood traditions. At other times freedom makes for the expression of genuine piety. Some nondenominational and free church schools have more discussions and tensions about the worship program than do schools in the liturgical tradition.

Some growing coherence of form in seminary worship is developing. Perhaps its maximum definition can be stated as an appreciation for orderliness and dignity. Schools where pulpit gowns would have been frowned upon thirty years ago now use them freely and regularly. Stately hymns of the church tend to replace the gospel songs of revivalism. Even where the basic physical facilities are obviously makeshift, the decor aids to give the worshiper an attitude of reverence.

The communal character of seminary worship is manifest in many ways. Worship is the great leveler of distinctions within the institution; faculty, students, and administrative personnel share a common practice and attitude. In most schools the responsibility for the services is divided between students and teachers. Representatives of the denominations often take the services in their schools. In many seminaries there are voluntary student choirs. To be sure, chapel services can also become the sounding board for parties in the school; "high church" and other groups conduct worship according to their interests. But nonpartisan concerns, too, are brought before the community through emphases in certain services, as on missions and social action.

In addition to the stated services (held only weekly in at least one school, in most daily), there are spiritual retreats. At some seminaries, such as Colgate-Rochester, the retreat is held on the campus, but all classes are dismissed for the day. Other schools hold their retreats away from the campus in order to be relieved from the distractions of academic pursuits. Western Seminary and Pittsburgh-Xenia, for example, have an annual day of prayer together at a church in the Pittsburgh area. A common practice is to have some outstanding Christian leader visit the seminary to lead the retreat.

The life of worship, however, is not encompassed in official programs. Prayer groups like special study groups are to be found on almost every campus. At the University of Chicago, for example, a group of students and faculty meet for a Thursday morning communion service, celebrated according to an ancient usage of the church. Frequently residence houses have their own programs of worship. Again, groups that gather for prayer and Bible study represent particular theological and religious parties in the community, while others cross such lines. Some meet to make particular intercessions, for instance, for a mission field. Other groups follow the principle that to work is to pray and share common worship in connection with their prosecution of relief projects or their discussions. These voluntary worship programs paralleling the stated services do not include all students. There are persons on almost every campus who rebel against what appears to them to be excessive piety. It is not uncommon for them to seek refuge in recreation or discussion that marks their own special community.

Common worship is supplemented by the life of private devotion. Among students interviewed during the study many expressed dissatisfaction with their devotional life. Most students feel that they ought to have a disciplined and sustained life of Bible reading and prayer, but very few meet their own expectations. This leads some to a sense of guilt and unworthiness. Others state that study is their form of devotion. There are, of course, many students who practice devotional exercises with great diligence and fruitfulness. Periods of self-examination, disciplined devotional reading, and prayers are part of their daily routine. While this is not a communal activity, its existence is an important ingredient in the community life.

As in the case of other areas of seminary life, worship never brings institutional forms and student practices together in a perfect way. That the two are not one is good. The unofficial programs are for some students more significant than the stated chapel services. Schools without an established tradition, however, often exist in a perpetual state of tension, if not conflict, over ways of worship. Without being able to develop a pattern that is normative, they are pressed by student parties and changing generations to shift to and fro. The existence of some structure of common worship to which most groups in a community are willing to bend their personal whims gives stability and meaning to the common life. Nothing seems to compensate for chaos in a seminary's practices of worship.

VI. *Faculty-Student Relations*

"We do not get to know the faculty as persons" is a common complaint among theological students. This means a variety of things. Some students desire such intimacy with faculty that they can call them by first names and know the day-to-day events of their family lives. Others feel that the faculty are so much in the role of teachers and scholars that they never come to understand them as men living in Christian faith and life. Still others respect the autonomy and privacy of the faculty and wish only for more contact with teachers as men with greater knowledge and wisdom about common problems.

Seminaries try to develop procedures to foster the meeting between teachers and students. Teachers have stated office hours. A few keep an "open door" policy to be accessible to students at all times, but this makes for hectic and interrupted days. Most instructors feel that the maintenance of a regular schedule of office hours gives students ample opportunity to discuss pertinent problems. Yet almost every teacher is willing to make appointments outside of the regular hours to help a student who has particular needs or shows particular promise.

The counseling of students is both pastoral and academic. In most schools an instructor is responsible for a number of counselees who come to him for assistance and direction in developing their academic programs. In addition to this, consultations are required for term papers, reading reports, and other assignments. One part of "academic counseling" that students frequently feel is inadequate is what one student called "theological counseling." If a student has a particular theological problem that is consuming his interest and attention, and is perhaps in some tension over its resolution, he may wish to discuss it with a mature theologian. Such discourse is outside the bounds of instruction that can be evaluationally graded, but within the bounds of education. To be sure, discussions with other students and seminars are of some assistance in this regard, but often they are inadequate.

Teachers also function as pastors to students. Just as all parish ministers are not equally adept at pastoral counseling, so a variety of this talent exists among teachers. Thus in most schools a large amount of pastoral counseling is done by particular instructors with whom students confer about personal and religious concerns. The teacher, like the local pastor, must be aware when a problem must be referred to specialists more competent than he. Some students are loquacious, and wear their hearts on their sleeves. A willing ear extended by a well-meaning teacher may lead to diminishing returns. Other students need guidance through theological problems that have personal dimensions. Still others are disturbed by guilt stemming from their imperfections and misunderstood natural desires.

Teachers who are effective in establishing rapport with some students are literally feared by others. Deans frequently get an overload of counseling responsibility, making it necessary to find a secluded place to get their administrative and academic work done. A few schools, such as Concordia in St. Louis, provide resident pastors or counselors who relieve teaching faculty from some of this work. Deans of students also assume this role.

Pastoral care of students leads to fairly strong bonds between some students and their teachers. In the present arrangements for counseling, however, the competent student may be neglected. The exceptionally good student may draw attention in seminars and be encouraged to spend time with his teachers. But the quiet competent B student doing his work adequately but inconspicuously may be overlooked in favor of others with some particular problems.

Most students respect the regular office hours of the faculty. They are cognizant of the variety of demands made on a teacher's time and do not want to invade his privacy more than necessary. Yet many desire the opportunity to talk to an instructor when some concern is particularly pressing. Where teachers are well known undoubtedly the prestige factor enters the motivation to know them. Other students desire more opportunity for "off-the-cuff" remarks that can be intellectually stimulating and reveal the way a teacher's mind works. Many students, however, are reticent and do not initiate conversations when the opportunities do arise.

In addition to the counseling situations, there are many occasions when faculty and students meet socially. Teas are common. School family suppers are held. Picnics are planned in the fall and spring. A Christmas party is often part of the agenda for the year. Occasionally there is recreation such as volleyball in which both students and faculties participate. Some teachers make an effort to have their students in their homes during the course of a year, though this is often more costly than salaries can bear.

On some occasions social intercourse is pleasant and helpful, but it is admitted from both sides that this is not always so. Deliberate efforts to "create community" frequently become evidence for the hypothesis that community cannot be manipulated into existence. Some teachers and students do not enjoy folk songs and parlor games. A few teachers cannot refrain from delivering lectures even on social occasions. Not all students and faculty members are equally pliable in social situations. Where there are traditions of festivals and class skits, they often begin to assume significance beyond their due. A student in one seminary, for example, reported that he spent every evening for about three weeks working on a class skit.

Both through and in spite of institutional efforts to strengthen the bonds between students and faculty there emerges a strong identification with the school and each other. Warm friendships arise. Interest in each other's work frequently leads to continuing correspondence and mutual assistance. The loyalties of seminary alumni are frequently pinpointed to certain teachers. A common spirit exists through the changing generations of students in which all members of the community participate. The existence of such a spirit is important in the educational process.

With the increase in the number of married students, efforts are made to include students' wives in the life of the school. Many seminaries have developed wives' groups that meet socially for a program of instruction. They study problems of the mistress of the manse, as well as theology, comparative religion, and ethics. In some schools wives freely audit courses. Even though most of them are either regularly employed or taking care of families they have many opportunities to participate in seminary life.

VII. *Pressures to Conformity*

"At X Seminary if you are not theologically orthodox and politically liberal, you just do not belong." Such was the statement, exaggerated to be sure, of a student who had been in divinity school for a month. That it was said with some vehemence by more than one student would indicate some partial truth. Unwritten expectations are real to students. Sometimes they are not aware of pressures even while they are bending to conform. The images differ in the various seminaries. Like suburbia or the street gang, members of the theological community are enveloped by a host of taboos and expectations.

It is a mistake to think that only theologically conservative seminaries embody subtle images of beliefs to which students feel bound. At a Methodist seminary, for example, one student suggested there was such a sense of community because everyone was expected to think somewhat alike. At a Lutheran school students complained that the inquiring spirit was always pushed into surrendering to an orthodox position. In the same school the faculty felt pressure in the same direction from students and alumni. There are schools in which believers in the verbal inspiration of the Bible feel ill at ease, and others in which nonbelievers in the same doctrine feel out of place. Where a prevailing philosophy of religion dominates, whether personalism, process metaphysics, or some other, students sometimes feel that they must become converts. To be sure, many denominational schools stand on historic confessions within which all theological teaching develops. This does not necessitate, however, compliance to the extent of the lack of freedom and inquiry.

In addition to theological images, there are others. We have noted that some students at one school think that blind acceptance of contemporary political liberalism is a part of belonging to the community. While the generalization is somewhat unfair, it is likely that schools with a tradition of social action make students who are not interested, or who are politically conservative, feel ill at ease. There is more than one kind of heresy. Pressure to conform to certain theories about liturgy and liturgical practices is felt in some places. A student in an Episcopal seminary complained that although his school claimed to be "liberal," it was as militantly low church as one of its sister schools was high church. In many seminaries students who like to sing gospel hymns are afraid to admit it publicly. In some others those who are interested in modern art and literature assume an air of condescension toward their less "cultured" brethren. Elsewhere students who have such interests feel accused of being esoteric and effeminate. Other patterns of behavior of less importance in relation to the total vocation of the student become dogmatized.

Some students regard every manifestation of expectation an infringe-ment on their freedom. Though they are few, these radical individual-ists in seminaries are most sensitive to pressures. Their witness to the existence of heteronomy frequently must be discounted. On the other hand, many students are so other-directed that they conform to every wind of doctrine without being aware of their lack of self-direction.

Perhaps the most crucial pressures are the "intellectualist" and the "anti-intellectualist." Sometimes they war against each other on the same campus. At other places one of them is clearly in the ascendant. Intellectualist pressure takes two forms. One is the competition for high grades. Since theological schools are graduate professional schools, competence of intellectual performance is expected. Yet there are students who make a fetish of this. Comparative rating of students in the community is frequently made along an axis of academic achieve-ment, usually measured by grade reports. Students believe their status depends upon the external mark rather than upon intellectual growth and maturity. "My education began only when I was emancipated from striving for grades," one man reported. Another at the same school said that the grading was too easy, and that tough grading would make him work harder and learn better.

The other form of intellectualist pressure, probably confined to a very few isolated university schools, is for "objectivity." Students tend to feel that their religious commitment is something immature and to be ashamed of. Religion has to prove its validity in the competition of ideas. Thus the point of expected loyalty moves outside the circle of faith to doubt. Critical inquiry can and does take place within faith in most schools; when it becomes wedded to an objectivist attitude it harasses the life of devotion and faith for many students. The question becomes not how Christian faith illumines our existence, but how does a Christian doctrine of God stand up against the modern metaphysics with its roots in the physical sciences. For others the truth is a Freudian theory of personality, or social and historical determinism. If Christian doctrine is not coherent with such points of view, it must be either re-created to conform, or it must be dropped in favor of a *de novo* theology. Tendencies also appear to become preoccupied with questions that are given top priority, such as epistemology, while it is forgotten that something of the given exists in every point of view.

The alternative to this pressure is not anti-intellectualism; rigorous study and criticism can go on within examined but accepted presuppositions. The striving for complete objectivism is probably waning rapidly in schools where it has been in vogue. Where it has been dominant, however, the personal turmoil of many theological students has been intensified.

Anti-intellectualist pressure is more prevalent at the present time. Its existence is manifest in diverse ways. At some places the student who entertains the idea of graduate study is subject to subtle forms of derision. His fellow students believe that the only valid and important ministry is the parish ministry, and that one need not be scholarly in order to be effective there. Elsewhere most of the energy and time goes into a variety of practical courses and field work. If one knows the techniques of administration and counseling, or preaching and community organization, the important things are thought accomplished. In some instances, as one student strongly put it, theologues are taught to "play church," to go through certain rituals and act out certain roles. Sometimes theology is taught only homiletically, biblical courses only inspirationally, and church history only entertainingly. Faculty members who attempt to turn the tide against anti-intellectualism must fight every inch of the way. The sense of community may be greater in schools dominated by anti-intellectualism. In some instances this is due to the time and effort put into the cultivation of personal relations. In others the vocation of the school to develop parish ministers according to a particular mold appears to be involved. Anti-intellectualism crosses the various theological boundaries with no difficulty. In a theologically conservative school it may take the form of emphasis on the techniques of soul-saving, in a liberal school on the techniques of counseling.

Such and other pressures to conformity are rarely institutionalized; they are seldom given official sanction in written documents. Yet they are as real as charters and regulations. They become heteronomous bases for common life, and for many sensitive students and teachers greatly complicate the fulfillment of their vocations.

VIII. *Breaches in the Community*

To describe disruptions in the life of the seminary community is not to propose that the ideal is a monolithic structure. Diversity within community is healthy. Sometimes, however, differences lead to breaches in the common life and merit special attention.

Allusions have previously been made to the "problem of the married students." Through providing housing, classes for their wives, and other aids, schools have often attempted to retain the communal life they knew when the proportion of married students was small as when they require that couples in seminary apartments eat several meals a week in the refectory. The seriousness of the consequences of the division of the married and unmarried is an open question. Single students appear to be more concerned about the lack of opportunity to know married students than the reverse. Among some married students one finds a sense of obligation to develop closer relations with single students, but not all feel a great need to belong to "the seminary family." For commuting students, most of whom have major church responsibilities in addition to their study, the relationship to the student body is necessarily tangential. There is no doubt some loss to everyone concerned.

Theological educators agree that the level of academic achievement has not suffered with the increase in the proportion of married students. They do regret, however, that by sheer facts of separated housing and the focus of interest in the marriage, informal discussion that is educationally important has declined. Since theological education involves the total self, to be physically separated from the community diminishes the total effectiveness of the school. Yet married students associate a good deal with each other, and the consequences of this are as significant as their associations with single students. One ought not to underestimate the prevalence and importance of the contacts that do exist between married and single students; single men are invited to their colleagues' apartments; they share lounges and snack bars; post-lecture conversation is common. New patterns of community life may emerge as schools experiment with various approaches to keeping married students in the community. Although the present breach is not a serious one, it is the most obvious and puzzling one.

Many schools have had the experience of seeing student parties develop over particular interests, become antagonistic toward each other, and then in a generation disappear. There are "neo-orthodox" theological parties and "liberal" parties. Rarely do they engage in creative disputation with each other; generally they ignore each other publicly and make caustic remarks about each other among themselves. In seminaries where strong teachers hold different theological points of view, student parties tend to focus around them. Where a dispute arises about the pattern of worship life, extremists soon develop parties and often hold unofficial services to meet their needs and prove their points. On most campuses there are parties that cannot name an opposite number, but by their enthusiasm over a cause bring about alienation from other students. This occurs with radical social action groups from time to time. Although there have been instances in which a particular faculty-student party has either left or been encouraged to leave a school, the breaks are almost never so severe. Within bounds of humility and reason, the existence of student parties can be stimulating, though painful. Some seminaries would be far more exciting if such groups, concerned with significant issues, were active in them.

CHAPTER NINE

The Line of Advance

The foregoing chapters have offered facts and reflections about theological education in the Protestant seminaries of the United States and Canada as these have become available to three students during a year and a half of fairly intensive inquiry. In general the facts indicate a considerable advance in the course of a generation toward increase in the number and improvement in the preparation of young men and women entering the ministry of the Protestant churches. But they give little basis for complacency; while the advancement of theological education has begun its road builders see many obstacles as they look ahead. It remains for us now to project as best we can the line of further progress, to offer a brief restatement of the critical issues that must be met by schools and churches, and to give what recommendations we can about measures that may be taken to overcome obstacles and to expedite the advance.

In part this task has been essayed in a previously published volume of reflections on the aims of theological education, issued under the title *The Purpose of the Church and Its Ministry*. In that small book an effort was made to interpret the unity present in the puzzling variety of American Protestant churches and seminaries and to call attention to their need to realize that unity and to clarify their goals. It was suggested that the society in which all the diverse institutions work is always the universal Church and that the purpose of the Church is the increase among men of the love of God and neighbors; the ultimate goal, however, is often forgotten in the pursuit of proximate ends which, being treated as final, become sources of division and confusion. It was further maintained that the uncertainty about the nature and task of the ministry, evident in a previous generation, continues to plague the members of the profession and the schools in which they prepare themselves for it; but also that a new conception of the minister as pastoral director is emerging in the Protestantism of the United States and Canada. Finally, the idea of a theological school was defined as the idea of an intellectual center of the Church's life and it was pointed out that such an understanding of the seminary meant that the study of theology must be considered a kind of ministry and not only a preparation for other service; that, further, in such a center of the intellectual life of the Church a continuous and lively dialogue needs to be maintained between theology and other church activities, between the thinking Church and the thinking "world."

We shall not in the ensuing reflections and recommendations try to deduce from such general statements about the purposes of Church, ministry, and seminary what specific educational steps should now be taken by the schools. We shall address ourselves to less far-reaching though not to more practical or more immediate matters of concern. We shall assume that the problem of action in education as elsewhere is always *how* to pursue proximate goals and solve current dilemmas in such fashion as to contribute to ultimate ends. Those proximate ends and immediate issues arise for us within the complex of all the internal and external forces that play upon us in our situation. While they are not rationally deducible from ultimate principles of action, the ways in which we meet them can and must be shaped by reference to final principles. So from the conviction that man's last end is to glorify God one cannot deduce that he should eat and drink, marry and beget children, sow and reap, construct and demolish, organize governments and suppress crime, but only that as he does such things demanded of him by his nature and situation he so do them as to glorify God. The democratic ideal of freedom and equality does not in itself impel American mayors and judges to deal with problems of housing and slum clearance, of traffic and of juvenile delinquency, but this ideal can deeply qualify the ways in which they meet contingencies which arise in all modern civilization and which officials in nondemocratic nations must also surmount in similar yet divergent ways. If the purpose of the Church is the increase among men of the love of God and all neighbors; if the emergent new conception of the ministry is that of the pastoral director; if the theological school must be an intellectual center of the Church's life, then, to be sure, certain deductions may be made concerning the content of the theological curriculum and the qualities desired in teachers and students. But on the whole the consideration of such principles will affect the *manner* of theological education. While the schools are clarifying their goals they need also to carry on a tradition and to meet issues arising out of their situation in the institutional religious, cultural, and economic life of the present. If the two sets of problems cannot be separated neither can they be identified. Hence in the following discussion of the main emphases now needed in theological education we shall assume that for reader as for writer the previous reflections about goals is a background against which the apparently more proximate concerns of the seminaries can be set and that we can address ourselves to the latter without constant explicit reference to that background.

I.   What Is the Key Problem?

The proximate problems and concerns of theological education are numerous and various. Many of them represent difficulties that educators at all times and in all kinds of teaching encounter. Among these are the difficulties of reconciling the needs of individual students, having varying capacities, interests, and rates of personal growth, with institutional habits, needs, and concerns. Another is the difficulty of so mediating a heritage of knowledge and so using a tradition that the powers of the living present be not choked or thwarted but released and directed so that a living generation become not the slave but the heir, conservator, and perfecter of its ancestors. Also recurrent and constant in education are the difficulties of finding the unity of wisdom in the multiplicity of knowledge, and of fostering the integrity of the self while its manifold needs are being met. Some of the problems of theological education are peculiarly modern but not peculiarly theological. When seminary faculties debate the question of the relative weight to be given to general preparation for life on the one hand, to vocational preparation on the other; or when they contend with the problem presented by increasing specialization in subject matter or professional activity, they are dealing with values all teachers in all fields must balance in some fashion. Such problems in theological education are not the less pressing because they arise in all kinds of teaching or in all periods. But they can be met only by gifted, concerned, thoughtful, and experienced *scholars* and *teachers,* solving them daily and annually in their personal meetings with subject matter and students, in their communal adjustments of institutional processes. While certain generalized formulae may be offered, as has been done in the preceding chapters, the criticism and refinement, the application and adjustment of such generalizations is something that only alert and wise faculties can undertake.

Other issues in contemporary Protestant theological education are given with the existence of Christian faith and of the Church in the world. What is novel about them today may be only the special form in which they appear as a result of the historic development of the Church and the movement of the human world into the era of modern culture. Among these are the problems of a faith that seeks to understand itself with the aid of contemporary ideas; of the communication of the gospel in the modern tongue; of the interpretation of a Scripture from which new light constantly breaks forth while ancient illuminations are obscured by passing clouds or long eclipses; of the interrelations of faith and history, of revelation and reason, of theology and "secular" science and philosophy, of Church and State, of Church and economic society, of this world and the other. Here belong also the special forms in which such questions arise in specific areas of action, as when religious education deals with Church-State and faith-history problems, or pastoral counseling encounters the question of the relations of psychiatry to religion; or when seminary administrations are concerned with the connections between their work and that of universities on the one hand, of parish churches on the other. When we think of these questions it again seems obvious that while much advice may be given or transmitted, the issues must actually be met day by day and year by year in the schools themselves, by administrators and teachers who are indefatigable students of the Word of God, of human nature and the human situation before God, by theologians who are keenly aware of the problems and able to meet them with wisdom and grace.

Considerations of this sort lead us to the conclusion that the key problem in theological education in the Protestantism of the United States and Canada is that of providing and maintaining the most able corps of teaching theologians and theological teachers possible.

We are led to a similar conclusion when we begin our reflections at another point. The description of a good school as consisting of a Mark Hopkins at one end of a log and a James Garfield at the other has been repeated *ad nauseam;* it has been subject to caustic criticism and to historical demythologizing. At the least a school requires a log large enough to accommodate several teachers and several students; singular intellectual parentage is likely to be sterile; the only child in an educational household is exposed to unusual hazards; communication cannot take place unless Mark Hopkins and James Garfield have some kind of a laboratory in which both attend to common realities; the log must have at least a niche for books. Nevertheless the old saw calls attention to the three necessary elements in an educational process. The question is: on which element—teaching corps, students, or equipment—do we need to concentrate attention today if theological education is to maintain and accelerate its advance in accordance with the demands made upon it?

The Physical Equipment of the Schools. In general the equipment of the seminaries is good. Deficiencies in their libraries continue to make themselves felt but the movement toward the improvement of this situation is well under way; provision for housing the enlarging enrollment and the increased proportion of married students continues to require the attention of many boards and administrators. Not a few schools show their lack of concern for more advanced teaching methods by their failures to provide seminar rooms, faculty studies, library cubicles, et cetera. But in general equipment does not seem to be a major problem; or, otherwise, where it presents such a problem the observer must often conclude that the lack of desirable equipment points to lack of concern on the part of the faculty or administration or both. Moreover it appears true that in theological as in other forms of education the supporting group—whether of churches or of individuals—can be stirred more readily to underwrite the improvement of physical property than the improvement of a faculty. Exceptions must be made. There is at least one seminary in the United States with an excellent faculty and a fine *esprit* for which the overriding problem at the moment is equipment. But this is the exception. The need for good equipment, especially libraries, chapels, and classrooms, cannot be ignored, but on the whole it is receiving adequate attention today; in some instances too much.

The Recruitment and Selection of Students. A large body of opinion in the schools and churches favors concentration on the students. The increase of their number and the improvement of their quality are the subjects of many discussions and the goals of many experiments. Several denominations in the United States and apparently all the churches of Canada are plagued by the shortage of candidates for the ministry, or at least by the shortage of candidates who are willing and able to complete a theological course of study. More frequently the complaint is that too many men are entering the ministry without adequate preparation and that too many of those who are attending theological schools are either too poorly prepared or too lacking in native gifts. Hence there is concern in many quarters for the development of recruitment measures, for the enforcement of a requirement that all ministers be seminary-trained after completing a good liberal arts college course, and for the development and more rigorous application of selection procedures.

There is ground for complaint and attention must be given to all three measures; yet the increase in the number and the improvement in the quality of theological students does not constitute the key problem of theological education today. As was pointed out in the first chapter, the number of students enrolled in theological seminaries has tripled during the last generation; the rate of increase of theological enrollment has exceeded that of the growth of Protestant church membership, while at the same time somewhat more effective use of available man power has been made by the churches.[1] There is no guarantee that the rate of increase will continue though there is a good prospect that the seminaries will continue to participate in the accelerated movement of American youth toward higher education, that the churches will increasingly demand a theological-educated clergy, and that continued religious concern in the culture together with the

[1] With the exception of a few denominations the average size of local churches has increased significantly in the United States during the period 1934–54.

heightened prestige of the ministry will attract an increasing number of men and women to the calling. If this is the case, as seems likely, then added motivation will be given to the movement toward more rigorous selection of candidates, while the need for a larger number of well-equipped teachers will be even more evident. The numerical increases in theological students, especially since the close of World War II, are in part due no doubt to the improved recruitment programs of denominations and schools and these need to be continued and refined. Some efforts of this sort are almost puerile in character and call for a thorough reappraisal; the best procedures in the field need to be studied and communicated so that denominations can learn from each other to a greater extent than is now the case. Recruitment, however, is not the primary problem in theological education.

Greater claims may be made on behalf of improved selection procedures. A considerable advance has been made in the past generation insofar as under the influence of the general movement in the American population toward higher education and under the pressures of the accrediting agency, the number of seminaries admitting only college graduates has greatly increased. Though it cannot be taken for granted that the ministry will be recruited only from those who have demonstrated their ability to achieve a bachelor's degree from a reputable college, nevertheless the movement is in this direction. And so far as the theological seminaries are concerned it can be taken for granted that this principle of selection has been established.[2] A small proportion of schools calling themselves theological seminaries with an even smaller proportion of the theological enrollment do not enforce this standard of selection. In a few others the established standard is imperilled by denominational pressures or by the rivalry of institutions that undertake to prepare men for the ministry by means of Bible study at the collegiate or subcollegiate level. Hence watchfulness needs to be exercised in various quarters lest standards be relaxed. But on the whole it seems most unlikely that a movement sustained by a great popular trend—the trend toward higher education—is in danger of reversal.

If this can be assumed, then the question is whether theological education can look for its next advance by becoming more selective in

[2] The present report is concerned with "the *work which the theological schools do in preparation of persons who are to serve in the parish ministry*," not with preparation for the parish ministry in all the American and Canadian denominations. Hence we do not raise the question whether all aspirants to the ministry should attend theological schools, whether other roads into the ministry should be provided besides the graduate seminaries. The importance of theological education provided by the seminaries as preparation for the parish ministry has been established. It needs to be understood and improved, whatever be the improvements required in preparation programs of other sorts.

admitting students to the seminaries. Shall it add to the requirement that they be college graduates new measures which will ensure to a larger extent than is now possible that such students have the spiritual, moral, and intellectual qualities necessary or desirable in the ministry? A connected question is whether recruitment procedures can be devised which will attract to the theological schools more men who possess the very highest intellectual and personal gifts. It seems clear that the selection procedures of schools and of denominations need in most cases to be more closely correlated; that through more careful admissions and counseling procedures, men and women who do not belong in the ministry should more frequently be directed toward other vocations than is now usually the case. Moreover, the ministry, like every Christian vocation, needs more first-rate characters and minds than it can now muster. A variety of measures commend themselves as desirable in order that these ends be achieved. One of them is the further development by denominations of "in care" programs that provide for the careful selection, supervision and counseling of aspirants to the ministry by presbyteries, associations, dioceses, and other constituent bodies of the national churches. Though these programs could not be carefully studied in the course of the present inquiry sufficient information on the point has been gathered to make it clear that a few denominations are now taking their responsibilities in this matter more seriously than had been the case; that, however, even within such denominations local groups vary greatly in the carefulness and effectiveness with which they discharge these duties; that certain denominations, especially those organized on congregational principles, encounter special difficulties in adjusting their institutional structure so as to meet this need. It is to be hoped that the relatively new Department of the Ministry of the National Council of Churches will provide an agency through which denominations will be able to counsel with one another on this point and to learn from one another's successes and failures. What needs to be stressed is that while schools need to improve their selection procedures this responsibility should not be left to them alone. In medicine and law, states and professional associations support and complement the standards of the schools; in the case of the ministry the churches must—as indeed in many instances they do—work alongside the schools to enforce good selection procedures.

A second line of approach to the solution of selection problems is offered by the development of intelligence, achievement, and personality tests such as are being used by many schools and some denominational agencies today. Since this matter is being especially studied at the present time by an independent group of inquirers—the Educational

Testing Service—no further specific recommendations seem to be in place.[3]

The recruitment for seminaries and ministry of more persons of the highest potentiality is an objective of the Rockefeller Brothers Theological Fellowship Program and is an important interest in the best recruitment procedures of some denominations and seminaries. A number of things, however, must be remembered in this connection: first, that there are in the seminaries, as in the ministry, a not inconsiderable number of men and women whose collegiate records show that they belong to such a group; second, that all the professions and professional schools tend to stress the same point so that competition for the most highly qualified college graduates is very great; third, that, as a recent study points out, so far as intelligence goes only 55 per cent of the most talented group of young people in the United States graduate from college and that therefore seminary recruitment programs among college students are by themselves inadequate.[4] As the report of that study states:

There are never enough of the most highly qualified workers in any field. Getting more of this bright group into college, giving them a broader view of the things they might accomplish, and then letting each specialize in the field of his own choice would benefit all fields of specialization and be of profit to the nation as a whole. On this score the country has a poor record: giving a college education to only half of the potentially most promising seven per cent of the nation's youth constitutes a gross under-utilization of some of its highest talent.

The great stake the churches and the seminaries have in the improvement of college education in general and in its availability to all qualified young people appears at this point as well as elsewhere. Finally it is to be remembered that the best talents are attracted to any profession by the challenge it presents and the significance of the work that it is doing. This is true in the schools: "In general, and at both undergraduate and graduate levels, fields which have the reputation of being 'hard' get somewhat brighter groups of students than do fields which have the reputation of being easy." [5] The moral theological schools and departments of religion may draw from this observation needs not to be made explicit.

Continued improvement of recruitment and selection procedures by churches and schools is very important and must not be neglected. Yet as matters stand the primary problem of the seminaries in general is

---

[3] See above, Ch. Eight, Sec. II.

[4] *America's Resources of Specialized Talent*, The Report of the Commission on Human Resources and Advanced Training, prepared by Dael Wolfle, director. New York, 1954. Cf. summary statement, 181–84.

[5] *Ibid.*, 202.

not how to increase the number of their students or select a higher quality, but rather how to make the best out of the goodly number and the good quality of the applicants they accept. The main problem is neither that of finding more five-talent geniuses nor of excluding more one-talent men with a penchant for burying that talent, but of helping the large number of two- or three-talent men, present and willing, to double their gifts. Evidence on the comparative quality of students preparing for the various professions is hard to come by and more difficult to evaluate. On the basis of the data available and of the judgments of many educators it would appear that while, indeed, some seminaries enroll students representing a rather low average of ability and achievement, on the whole the theological students are young men and women of good average intelligence and achievement. If they do not constitute an intellectual elite, there are nevertheless many first-rate minds among them, while insofar as other qualities are concerned they are—again with exceptions—not unfit to stand in the succession of the sort of men who have given the Church its leadership from the beginning. The question about theological students is not how their intelligence and achievement tests compare with those of physicists and psychologists, agricultural students and domestic science teachers, but whether they have good potentiality—spiritually, morally, intellectually, personally—of developing into faithful, thoughtful, competent servants of God in the Church. It is the conviction of the study staff, based on various experiences and inquiries, that this question must be answered with a fairly emphatic "Yes." Hence we conclude that necessary as it is to maintain constant pressure on the improvement of recruitment and selection procedures, yet the main problem remains that of the better education of the presently available men and women.

II.   *The Improvement of Education*

The measures that can be taken to improve the educational process are many and various, yet they can be easily grouped under the main heads of the improvement of teaching methods and the strengthening of the faculties of theology.

A. *Improvement of Teaching Methods.* To the members of the study staff—all of them teachers in theological schools—the fundamental problem has presented itself in terms of the question: How can we do a better job? They have been led to self-criticism as individuals and as members of the group of theological teachers by their observations of what is going on in the schools—frequently a reflection of what they themselves have been doing singly and in corporate faculty groups. That self-criticism has been strengthened by the observations and criticisms offered by seminary administrators, teachers, and students and by churchmen not directly engaged in the work of the theological schools. The net result of these observations and critiques may be stated simply: *The greatest defect in theological education today is that it is too much an affair of piecemeal transmision of knowledge and skills, and that, in consequence, it offers too little challenge to the student to develop his own resources and to become an independent, lifelong inquirer, growing constantly while he is engaged in the work of the ministry.* The fact that similar self-criticisms are made by faculties of law and medical schools and of many colleges does not lessen the sharpness of the judgment. Indeed it is the impression of the staff members that colleges and nontheological professional schools are more frequently doing something to remedy their defective practices than are the seminaries.

It is not necessary to review the points made in a previous chapter concerning the educational methods of the theological schools. The question is: What measures can be taken in order that the traditional-istic, uncriticized repetition of established patterns may be stopped; that teaching may become more vital, learning more adventurous and zealous. Certain habits, often unconsciously followed, need to be broken, especially the habit of thinking of education as transmission of knowledge rather than companionship in learning. The cliché that seeks to solve this problem by means of the formula that education should be student-centered rather than subject-centered is of no help, nor is it useful to raise once more a complaint against the lecture system of classroom instruction. If a student does not concentrate his attention on a subject he is no student but a narcissistic self-pollinator; a student-centered pedagogue is not a teacher but a nurse. The question is whether teacher and student are companions in inquiry into a challenging subject or whether the teacher conceives of himself as a retail distributor of intellectual and spiritual commodities. The lecture system of classroom instruction is no more tied to the latter idea than discussion methods and group dynamics are in themselves representative of the former. Yet it is not enough that bad habits of thought and false philosophies be abandoned; truer philosophies of education must be given fit modes of expression and this indeed implies revisions of instructional systems, reduction of class hours, increase of personal instruction and guidance, provision for seminars, honors courses, et cetera.

Certain general and negative observations may be made. The rule in the seminaries is to require attendance of too many classes in too many subjects on the part of the student; instruction in too many subjects by each teacher. Students too often are led to confine their reading to textbooks or to a limited reserve shelf. They write too few sermons and papers and these are too cursorily criticized—mostly they are simply graded. They attend too many survey courses and dig deeply into too few subjects. The schools provide too few seminars and too little tutorial assistance. Yet if each of these criticisms were met, one by one, without a change in the fundamental philosophy of education it is questionable whether anything would be accomplished. Improved methods of imparting knowledge remain methods of imparting knowledge rather than teaching methods. The student who profits by such improvements also suffers loss if he is led to believe that he has "completed his education."

How then can the methods of teaching be improved in such fashion as to serve more adequately the *desideratum* of all education—the encouragement of students to remain lifelong seekers of larger knowledge and ever more understanding professional workers? Taking for granted that movements toward a change in the intellectual and spiritual climate of the seminaries are present and that dissatisfaction with a prevailing philosophy of education is growing, how can these movements find expression in positive action?

Concerted action on the part of all the schools can never go far enough. Nothing can take the place of individual experiments by the more adventuresome and least complacent institutions. The advancement of education in all other areas has been dependent on such pioneering movements by individual schools. The innovations introduced into medical education by Johns Hopkins University seem to have been as significant in the reorganization of the medical schools as was the Flexner report. Langdell's introduction of the case method in Harvard Law School—a method now under attack—changed the traditionalist pattern of legal education. Recent developments in college education have been pioneered by Swarthmore, Princeton, Antioch, Harvard, Yale, and other schools that have grappled independently and thoroughly with problems common to all the colleges. Nothing can take the place of such experiments, though errors are unavoidable in all new trials. What direction the pioneering efforts of individual theological seminaries should take cannot be prescribed, yet it appears desirable that some should attempt to move toward tutorial methods of instruction, that in them or in others the effort be made to offer a plan of directed studies to a selected group of students who have been freed from many of the standard obligations of the curriculum while assuming other obligations, that some seminaries should recognize the integral nature of theological study and allow their students to concentrate heavily in one field with the understanding that the implications of that field will lead them into inquiries apparently remote from the point of departure.

A second step, closely related to the first, would be the provision of educational conferences in which theological educators could learn from their colleagues in those colleges and those schools training men for other professions that have thoroughly examined their procedures and made new departures in their methods of teaching. Such conferences could be held at many levels. Individual theological faculties or their curriculum committees would profit from direct study of experimental programs carried on by college, law, and medical faculties in their immediate vicinity, often in the universities with which divinity schools are connected. Consultations could profitably be held by the representatives of a group of theological schools with thoughtful administrators and teachers from colleges and professional schools. Consultations at regional and national levels among theological seminaries would be helpful. The development of the work of the American Association of Theological Schools made possible by recent gifts from John D. Rockefeller, Jr., through the Sealantic Fund, Inc., may well include the promotion of such consultations. The dissemination of information and stimulation of interest in this field could also be furthered through publication, perhaps through the bulletins of the Association. The minimum step that can be taken is the thorough self-examination by theological faculties as wholes of the meaning and effectiveness of their common work. In too many seminaries the teachers do not constitute an educational community but function as individuals who confine their collective attention in faculty meetings to the trivia of educational procedures while the educational process in general goes on in a traditional way. Doubtless these individuals are constantly continuing their self-education as scholars but are not educating themselves as a community of teachers.

The improvement of teaching methods is not an end that can be gained by following certain prescriptions. It is a matter that concerns every teacher as well as every faculty. Constant study, self-criticism, and experimentation are required of the teacher who would help students become, in their own field, constant students who are self-critical and experimental in their attitudes.

B. *Strengthening the Faculties.* Improvement in the methods of teaching and the strengthening of the teaching corps are almost two sides of the same coin. The enlistment and thorough preparation of theological teachers and the maintenance of high morale among them need to become matters of great concern to all supporters of the seminaries. It has been observed above that the schools are hard put to it to find well-prepared teachers for the various fields of theological study. If the growing number of departments of religion in colleges were taken into consideration the difficulties of finding enough well-prepared and otherwise capable men and women would appear even greater. If theological enrollment continues to increase, the lack of teachers is bound to become even more distressing than it is now. The shortage is apparently not due to a lack of possible candidates but much more to the long period of training required, to the inadequacy of resources with which to finance that training, and the very modest salaries with which young people must be content for many years after completing their preparation. It is made more difficult of solution, of course, by the requirement of many schools, that members of their faculties be also members of the supporting denomination, since it cannot be expected that supply and demand will be correlated in every denominational group. A second problem arises when the question is raised how young teachers, following a Th.D. or Ph.D. program, may be prepared not only for creative scholarship in their field of specialization but also for their work as teachers. The third question administrators and governing bodies need to face is how to maintain the effectiveness and *élan* of their faculties. The following measures are suggested as aids toward the recruitment, preparation, and strengthening of the faculties without reference in each instance to the way one of these particular problems is met by it.

1) It is evident that greater attention needs to be given by the churches, the schools, the American Association of Theological Schools and other groups to doctoral programs in theology. The emphasis in denominational promotion of theological education naturally falls on the B.D. program and on the work of those schools that confine themselves to it. The concern of the American Association of Theological Schools has also been focused on this program. Partly in consequence of this, partly for other reasons, the doctoral programs have not been subject to the same helpful criticism that the B.D. course has experienced, nor have they been as adequately financed. Standards in the field of doctoral study vary much more from school to school than do the highly various standards of the B.D. seminaries. Graduate work is often dealt with as an appendage to the three-year seminary course, much as the M.A. program of many colleges is appended, almost for honorific purposes, to the liberal arts course. Whether uniform standards can be developed in this field may be questionable, especially in view of the fact that the graduate schools of the major universities have not been able to agree on standards for the Ph.D. and that standards vary from department to department in individual schools. Nevertheless consultation and exchange of information among the schools offering doctoral programs in theology or religion would offer some help toward raising standards where they need to be raised. It may be possible to rescue the Th.D. degree from continuous depreciation similar to that suffered by the Ph.D. degree in the late nineteenth century. The Council on Graduate Studies in Religion, an informal body, has been at work in this field for several years but many of the schools offering doctoral programs in theology or religion do not participate in its deliberations. The new committee on advanced study set up by the

American Association of Theological Schools will presumably give to the doctoral program larger attention than it has received in the past. It is to be hoped that concern for thorough scholarship in theology will prevail over the desire of many men for an honorific degree.

The need at the present time does not seem to be for a larger number of schools that will offer education at the doctoral level. A number of denominations are, indeed, considering the development of such programs in denominational seminaries, partly because they have found that their teachers are likely to take their advanced work in the interdenominational schools.[6] On the whole, however, there seems to be little objection in the denominations to the interdenominational training of their scholars so long as the denominational character of their B.D. education is safeguarded. The need is not for more schools but for better work in those now occupying the field.

2) Doctoral study in theology or religion suffers, at least so far as students engaged in it are concerned, from lack of adequate financial support. Partly because the denominations have stressed the work of the seminaries in training men for local church ministries, partly because theology has been held in low esteem in the churches themselves, partly because the tradition of many schools led to the recruitment of teachers directly from the ministry without concern for special preparation, partly because the teaching profession in general has suffered a great decline in status in modern society, the financing of graduate work has not occupied the attention of church constituencies and has

[6] The members of the faculties in denominational as well as interdenominational schools have done their doctoral work at a relatively small number of graduate schools. The statistics published by the American Council on Education (see *American Universities and Colleges,* 6th ed., 1952) show that in the period 1939–40 through 1949–50 1,133 doctoral degrees were awarded in religion. Of this number 269 were granted by the Catholic University in Washington. Other schools granting a considerable number of doctoral degrees in religion were the following: Southern Baptist Theological Seminary (200), Chicago University (99), Yale University (86), Southwestern Baptist Theological Seminary (84), Drew University (61), Boston University (60), Columbia University (35), Harvard University (31), University of Southern California (26), Princeton Theological Seminary (25), Hartford Theological Seminary (23), Temple University (19), Union Theological Seminary (18), University of Pittsburgh (18), Duke University (16), New York University (13), State University of Iowa (7), Northwestern University (4), University of Pennsylvania (4), and University of Virginia (4). In recent years Southern Baptist and Southwestern Baptist have restricted their doctoral programs to a certain extent; however, both of these schools continue to train a considerable number of faculty members of theological schools, particularly, of course, those of the Southern Baptist Convention. A not inconsiderable number of theology professors have done their doctoral work in other departments than departments of religion. Many Old Testament professors, for instance, have taken their degrees in departments of Oriental Studies and many professors of social ethics have done their final graduate work in departments of sociology, political science, et cetera.

been left largely to the endowed universities and a few endowed seminaries. These have been able in recent years to attract no large additional gifts for the support of theological studies while returns from endowments made for such purposes in earlier decades have become inadequate. On the whole these institutions have succeeded better in maintaining the salaries of their teaching staffs than in supplying sufficient scholarship aid for students pursuing the advanced program. Even more frequently than in the case of B.D. students the doctoral candidates of today need to finance their studies by serving in churches. In consequence their period of advanced study is greatly lengthened; it is subject to many distractions; they begin their work as teachers at a much later age than is the case with European theologians and with teachers in America in most other fields; many of them drop out along the way because of the difficulties encountered by their families. It is imperative that more and larger scholarships for advanced study in theological subjects be provided if the American churches are to produce a corps of scholars and teachers sufficient for their need. A small number of seminaries do provide scholarships for a few of their graduates who wish to pursue advanced studies; one denomination at least—the Methodist Church—has had funds made available to it which allows it to grant rather sizable fellowships to qualified graduates of its seminaries. The National Council on Religion in Higher Education offers some Kent fellowships to graduate students in theology, but these are not intended for future seminary teachers and the Council must look largely to its own members for the financing of its program. On the whole, however, the small number of schools that carry on doctoral programs must carry the burden of providing this student aid and their resources are in general quite inadequate. Hence most students must finance themselves.

Whence shall the funds come that are needed for this part of a program of strengthening theological faculties in the United States and Canada? Since in their field, as well as in others, tax moneys are unavailable to theological education, only two sources seem available— the churches and the foundations. While the latter—apart from the recent gifts of the Sealantic Fund, Inc.—have probably made fewer and smaller contributions to this area of professional study than they have to teaching in general, to medicine and law, they have on the whole done better than the national church bodies. The latter must take the place that federal, state, and municipal governments occupy in the field of general and other professional education if theological work, especially in its advanced stages, is to be adequately financed. More must be said on this subject in the final section of the present chapter.

3) A third step or series of steps that may be taken toward the

strengthening of the faculties lies more largely in the competence of the schools themselves though they will require the aid of outside agencies. As was pointed out in Chapter Four, "the greatest single difficulty in many schools is their tendency to become intellectually and spiritually 'ingrown.'" This tendency makes itself manifest even in the way in which the teaching methods of a school may be uncritically continued generation after generation. Two specific measures seminaries need to adopt far more frequently than they do at present in order to overcome intellectual and educational isolation is to give their faculty members sabbatical leaves for study at other schools and to provide for exchange professorships. As we have noted, sabbatical leaves are few and far between for most theological teachers and are frequently inadequately financed when granted. Exchange professorships have a double value—for the teacher who is exposed to new practices and ideas and for the school which receives a new perspective on its work from the visitor. Interdenominational exchanges are desirable but where they are not feasible exchanges within a denomination or between schools belonging to closely related denominations—such as the various Lutheran, Baptist, and Presbyterian groups—might contribute in the course of years to a strengthening of the schools through the invigoration of faculties. Such exchange, like the sabbatical leaves, will require some additional financial resources but the investment would be relatively modest in view of the returns that may be hoped for.

4) The strengthening of the faculties requires other steps. The number of teachers needs to be increased in those seminaries in which, as was pointed out in Chapter One, increase of student enrollment has not been matched by faculty increases. The increasing burden of administrative and counseling duties carried by a considerable number of professors—often the best teachers—needs to be lifted from them by the provision of a larger administrative staff, of secretarial help, and perhaps, where the situation warrants it, by the appointment of seminary pastors or counselors.

5) In theological education, as in the whole teaching professions, the monetary inflation of recent decades has not been accompanied by corresponding salary increases. (See above, Ch. Two, Sec. V.) In many seminaries the activities of teachers outside the school are multiplied not only because of the claims of the churches on their time but on account of their personal financial needs. In consequence their attention is often distracted from their primary work and their energies dissipated. The burden lies heaviest, in general, on the younger faculty members with their low salaries and growing families.

To be sure, various studies of faculty salary scales, including our own, show that increases in instructors' and assistant professors' salaries have kept better pace with inflation than have those of professors. But this mode of reckoning fails to take into account that the former ranks were notoriously underpaid in the past so that even an accelerated rate of increase has not eased their situation appreciably. Very few theological schools, even those that have relatively high salary scales, are paying their young faculty members salaries that are commensurable with what the same men would receive in their alternative profession— the parish ministry. The salary needs of faculties as a whole are met in greatly varying degrees in the different schools and the different denominations. It seems clear from the data summarized in Chapter Two and from the observations of the staff that in at least one-fourth of the schools the scale is so low that faculties must supplement their earnings by additional employment. In most of the remaining seminaries the faculties share with the teaching profession in general the loss of earning power that has accompanied inflation, the redistribution of income, and other phenomena of recent economic and social change.

6) There are other provisions that can be made to strengthen the teaching corps of theological scholars. Improved teaching methods will liberate teachers from spending so many hours in the classroom and from endeavoring to be expert in so many different subjects, as is now the case in most schools. An increase of the teaching corps will reduce the student-faculty ratio which is at present too large in the growing seminaries. Improved libraries will serve faculties no less than students. Administrators alert to the needs of providing both good teaching and good counseling will relieve from some teaching responsibilities those of the faculty who bear the heaviest burden of counseling duties. The addition to the school staffs of more administrative officers will set free for teaching and scholarship a considerable number of professors who at present spend much time in the administration of admissions and registrarial procedures, in the supervision of field work, and in similar enterprises.

7) A special question is whether provision should be made by graduate schools for the training of their young scholars in teaching methods. It has often been observed that these schools focus their attention on the education of their students as specialist scholars without keeping in mind that such specialists will be teachers. It has therefore been recommended that the doctoral program in theology as well as in other fields should include courses in pedagogical theory and method. It seems very questionable whether the recommended procedure would achieve the end desired since the necessary concentration of the young scholar on his specialized study would probably lead him to regard such studies as distractions. Graduate students who have been approached with this proposal show a marked lack of enthusiasm. It would be a far better procedure, in the judgment of the present inquirers, were seminaries to encourage and aid their young teachers to attend summer schools of education after they have encountered some

of the problems of education directly in their early classroom and tutorial experiences.

III. *The Reorganization of the Curriculum*

The emphasis lies on the improvement of teaching methods and the strengthening of the faculties but other measures, closely related, also commend themselves as desirable or necessary if the advancement of theological education is to be furthered. Among them is the lengthening of the period of theological study. Three years are evidently too short a time for the theological and professional education of ministers. When the theological curriculum is regarded from the prevailing point of view as a course of study in which the student is not only given orientation and adeptness in biblical studies, theology, and church history but also prepared for the performance of all the functions of the ministry by theoretical studies and practical exercises, then it seems clear that more time must be given to it than the three years afford. The analysis of required courses in typical seminaries, offered in Chapter One, indicates that the effort of the schools to meet all the internal and external demands made upon them has led to a multiplication of subjects, increased rigidity in the requirements, the increase of introductory and diminution of advanced studies, and, in general, to the atomization of a course of study into "courses."

It is frequently suggested that the problem may be met by the addition of a fourth year of preparatory studies. The addition of such a year, it is felt, will provide time for more adequate study of the basic disciplines, for the addition of the necessary new subjects in the practical and theoretical fields, in theological and social sciences; and it will allow for the inclusion of the field work program, the importance of which is generally acknowledged.

The solution seems reasonable if the premise is granted—namely, that the seminary course of study should prepare men and women to carry on all the functions of the ministry. It follows the pattern established in the past in seminaries and in other professional schools. These have consistently moved for a long time toward increasing the period of preparation. But reasonable as the proposal seems to be it must be challenged on two grounds. The premise is to be questioned and it is to be objected that even were the premise accepted insuperable economic and social obstacles stand in the way of this solution of the dilemma.

To take up the latter objection first: before the seminaries in general venture on this road of increasing their regular course of study from three to four years they will need to make a choice between an "*Either-Or*." *Either* they will need to reduce by a quarter the number of students they will graduate each year *or* they must increase their facilities so that they can take care of one-third more students than are now in residence. If the demand of the churches for well-educated ministers is not now being met the schools will not be able to meet it if they reduce their graduating classes by a fourth. A four-year curriculum evidently requires them to do this or to expand their staffs and faculties. A school which can provide for 300 students with approximately 100 men in each class would, in the case of a four-year curriculum, be able to have only 75 men in each class. With the increased desire of the members of the American denominations for theologically educated ministers, with the increase of Protestant church membership, and with the growth of population, the pressure is now all in the direction of enlarging the seminaries so as to provide for more rather than fewer graduates. If reduction in the number of graduates cannot be considered by the schools in general, expansion of their staff and equipment is the only alternative. Only a few seminaries can increase their enrollments without such expansion. The addition of a fourth year to the theological curriculum, as established at present, would mean therefore that the schools in general would need to expand their facilities by one-third, quite apart from the expansion required to meet historical trends or for the sake of improvement. It would mean that if the plan were generally adopted the 150 schools that have reported to this study would need to add to their 1,500 full-time faculty members another 500, *without improving the present student-faculty ratio which is in great need of improvement in many instances,* particularly in the rapidly growing schools. Corresponding increases in administrative staff would be necessary. At the present time all of the schools are hard put to it to provide housing for their students in view of the lower age of marriage in the American population in general and among students in particular. Theological as well as other professional schools have had to spend large amounts of money during the last ten years to provide apartments for their married students. The addition of a fourth year to the theological curriculum will make this demand proportionately greater than it is now. Libraries, chapels, classrooms, refectories, and other parts of the schools' physical plants will need to be correspondingly augmented and enlarged. Finally, there is the ever-pressing question of financing the students. It is now difficult to find adequate scholarship aid and work opportunities for them. Far too many students are spending far too much time outside of their studies not only in field work but in any kind of remunerative employment they can find. The addition of a fourth year will complicate this problem further. How the schools and the churches will be able to add to their responsibilities those imposed by a fourth year of theological study remains in the minds of the directors of this study an unanswerable question. The expenditures of the schools during the last twenty years have not kept pace with both the increase of enrollment and the increase in the cost of living. The financial status of theological education is not encouraging.

Under these circumstances the addition of a fourth year to the present curriculum would seem to constitute a threat to theological education. Individual, independent schools doubtless can proceed in this direction if special financial resources are available to them or if they can afford to reduce the number of their graduates, but for the seminaries of the United States and Canada in general to accept this as the way out of their dilemmas seems most undesirable.

However, the chief objection to the addition of a fourth year—at least at the present time—to the curriculum is that it leaves the fundamental problem of theological education unanswered and, under present circumstances, will only help schools to evade it. That problem, as has been said, is how to help students to become self-educating men who will continue to prepare themselves throughout their lives to meet the changing problems of their ministry, to carry on their theological inquiries and criticisms continuously and progressively in the midst of changing religious and cultural climates of opinion. The addition of a fourth year of study that does not have this end in view cannot result in better preparation of students for the ministry; if this is not the end in view throughout the previous three years a fourth year cannot be directed toward it; if the three years can be directed toward this goal then not a fourth year in seminary but some other kind of provision for continuing education seems called for.

A second device for lengthening the course of theological study in such a way that the institutional problems may be met and the educational aim of lengthening study into a life-time pursuit may be served has more promise. This is the "internship year" which has been adopted by several denominational systems and by some individual schools. In effect all versions of the plan provide for the addition to the three years of studies of a fourth year of practical training in the parish ministry. The advantages, problems, and limitations of this program have been discussed above.[7]

Despite the limitations and difficulties it presents, the plan offers some real opportunities for improving theological education. To be sure, as administered at present it impresses the observer as being on the whole a makeshift arrangement but it has considerable potential, particularly in certain highly homogeneous denominations and schools. That potential cannot be realized unless much greater attention is given to the administration of the program than is now the case; such attention cannot be given unless an adequate staff is employed with primary responsibility for the selection of appointments, for the enlistment of pastors in the educational task, and for the direct guidance of students not in residence.

[7] See Ch. Six, Sec. II.

A third proposal for lengthening the course of study is herewith recommended to the schools, the denominations, their special boards, and to the American Association of Theological Schools by the staff of the present Study. It is not conceived as a measure that rules out the two former plans for lengthening the period of study though under certain circumstances it may become an alternative to them. The proposal is for the establishment of a summer school program for graduates of the seminaries. This program would be analogous to the kind of work which has been successfully carried on in the teaching profession for many years by teachers' colleges and by universities. Its purpose would be to provide continuing training and intellectual stimulation to young men and women during the early years of their professional experience, to allow for the correlation of actual experience and theoretical understanding, and to offer opportunities for specialized preparation for specialized ministries.

The in-service training programs of the denominations and seminaries are at the present time regarded as exceedingly important but they are unorganized, frequently poorly administered and unregulated by adequate standards. They consist of short courses offered by a few seminaries (leading, unfortunately, at times to the Th.D.), of many summer conferences and institutes on such specialized subjects as the rural ministry, foreign missions, inner-city work, pastoral counseling, et cetera, of a very few summer sessions held by seminaries, of one or two fairly well-developed programs such as that of the College of Preachers in Washington, D.C., and of various extension courses offered to ministers of their neighborhoods by seminaries. The desirability of in-service educational programs is widely recognized. The demand on the seminaries by their graduates and pastors in the neighborhood for provisions in this area is considerable. It is pointed out that young men who are encouraged to maintain their intellectual alertness, curiosity, and capacity for self-criticism during the first ten years of their professional work are likely to continue to do so throughout their remaining lives.

The summer school program in view would provide for correlation of actual experience with theoretical understanding. At present teachers of religious education, of pastoral counseling, and of church administration often complain that their students return to them after a year or two in the ministry to ask for aid on problems which had been thoroughly discussed in the classroom. Even field work does not usually suffice to overcome the sense of unreality in academic explorations for which the student has not been prepared by direct encounter with the problems considered. The complaint of students that their seminary work was abstract is more frequently due to their own lack of a sense of concreteness than to the abstractness of the teachers. Summer schools, coming after a year or two or three in the ministry, could supply a correlation of practice and theory not ordinarily possible in B.D. study.

Preparation for specialized ministries cannot be effectively carried on until young ministers have found their particular calling within the calling. Not many men in theological schools can predict whether they will serve in rural or urban areas, in the suburb or in the inner-city; whether they need most to concentrate on preaching or on counseling; what particular needs they are going to encounter among the young people or the adults of the communities they serve. In certain relatively few instances, the B.D. course must provide for such specialization. By and large it cannot do so without impairment of fundamental studies and without considerable misspent effort on the part of young people who cannot accurately predict what they are going to be challenged to do in a specific way. A summer school program could provide opportunity for such specialization not prior but subsequent to a young person's engagement in specialized tasks.

Furthermore, this proposal would enable the schools to meet some of their problems without encountering so insuperable a demand for additional personnel and equipment as the four-year program brings with it. A summer program, providing for eight- or twelve-week sessions, would be able to make use of existing equipment during that portion of the year when it now usually lies idle. It would also make the problem of increase of staff more amenable of solution since it would be possible to employ not only a limited number of seminary professors teaching in the regular sessions but also college teachers, pastors, missionaries, hospital chaplains, religious education directors of denominations, and other highly qualified persons who could give some time to the summer schools. A much larger reservoir of man-power is available for this program than for the four-year B.D. plan.

It is not within the competence of the Study of Theological Education to suggest in detail how such a post-B.D. program might be worked out but the following suggestions are offered to the agencies ultimately concerned: The summer schools should provide work in two areas: first, in the further preparation of men for the parish ministry; secondly, in preparation of men for specialized ministries. Work, therefore, in the summer schools could be concentrated on such subjects as pastoral counseling, religious education, church administration, rural, suburban, and urban church work, church social action, church council work, college chaplaincy work, and perhaps foreign missions. Additional work in preaching should also be carried on in them. While all the work should be carried on in the context of theological study and while provision should always be made for continuation of the study of Scriptures and of theology, yet the practical program should be kept distinct from the present Ph.D. and most Th.D. programs. While the latter programs are also in need of clarification and some standardization they clearly ought not to be developed in the direction envisaged by the proposed plan. Whether or not such an in-service educational program should lead to the granting of degrees will depend on the thoroughness with which it is developed and administered. Granted that the summer school sessions are of sufficient length and that standards are sufficiently high the S.T.M. and even S.T.D. degrees might eventually be granted.

It may further be suggested that schools of the sort proposed be established on a regional and interdenominational basis so that pastors may be able to attend them without incurring the expense of long-distance travel and of employing supplies for their pulpits. It has been noted that denominations are more ready to co-operate with each other in the conduct of graduate programs than they are in the carrying on of the fundamental B.D. work. Though some summer programs might be organized denominationally, if interdenominational co-operation is feasible other advantages besides those arising from regional location might accrue. For instance, funds might become available that are inaccessible to purely denominational schools. Ultimately, of course, summer schools for the ministers of the churches should be supported by the churches but in the initial stages of the movement new funds must be looked for.

It seems clear, however, that though a regional organization is desirable the suggested program should be administered by extant theological schools working in co-operation. Experience in theological education is highly concentrated in their administrators and faculties. The wide participation of denominational boards needs to be sought but the responsibility for theological education still lies on the seminaries.

The provision of post-B.D. schools with or without the adoption of the internship year cannot solve the many problems faculties face in their efforts to make the B.D. curriculum more effective. But it would relieve some of the pressure and so allow more room for experimentation and concentration. It would not eliminate the need for field work, since participation in the life and work of the churches is highly important not only as preparation for the active ministry but for successful theological study. It would, however, allow for the reduction of present field work requirements in many schools. The stronger emphasis in the summer schools on the theoretical understanding of practical work would not allow the seminaries to concentrate the three-year curriculum solely on the biblical, theological, and historical understanding of Christian faith, but it would give them the opportunity to postpone advanced work in the practical fields to the later period and to concentrate on the all-important task of helping their students to gain a sense of the whole in which all partial inquiries and tasks have their place. The relation between the B.D. and the post-B.D. programs would be that of parts of a continuous movement in which the emphasis would fall in the earlier period on the understanding of the faith without excluding practical participation in the work of the Church while during the later period the emphasis would lie on the practical without exclusion of continued work in the study of Bible, theology, and history.

IV. *Financing the Advance*

The fundamental point to be made in considering the problem of financing the past and future advancement of theological education is that this remains the responsibility of the churches with such aid as they can receive from foundations and individual donors. Insofar as churches carry on other types of education they receive increasing help from governmental sources; but the seminaries will remain their care so long as the privileges and burdens of religious freedom are theirs and so long as Church and State remain separated.

As was pointed out in Chapter Two, federal, state, and municipal funds are becoming increasingly available to all other schools. When all institutions of higher education in the United States are considered these received 56.1 per cent of their income from public sources in 1951–52; in 1931 32, 38.6 per cent of income had been received from such sources. The theological schools have not and will not receive support from the one source which is most able to keep up with the demands of increasing enrollments, improved methods, and monetary inflation. The situation in which these schools are placed by the separation of Church and State may be succinctly indicated by the following table:

Percentage of Income Received from Various Sources

	All Institutions of Higher Education U.S.A.*	76 Medical Schools †	27 Theological Schools ‡
Tuition	22.1	15.2	18
Endowment	5.6	11.9	32
Gifts and grants private sources	7.4	17.5	15.6
Tax moneys	56.1	50.1	
Denominational grants			20
Other sources	8.8	5.3	14.4

* *Biennial Survey of Education in the United States,* 1950–52, Chap. 4, Sec. II, p. 24. The figures are for 1951–52.

† Deitrick and Berson, *Medical Schools in the United States at Mid-Century,* p. 85. The figures are for 1950–51.

‡ Cf. above, Ch. Two, Sec. III. The figures are for 1954–55.

Theological schools have traditionally been the best-endowed private institutions, but as has been pointed out, income from endowment is not keeping up with increased costs. The percent of income from this source is declining. The only two sources of income that contribute increasing percentages are the students and denominational boards. Some additional increments may be gained from the former source since there are still many seminaries which do not require tuition from any students. The general tendency is toward imposing and increasing tuition charges while at the same time liberal scholarships are made available to students who are scholastically qualified and economically in need. This tendency, as it extends to the seminaries in general, may increase their receipts from students' fees. But this increase cannot by any means cover the increasing costs of present education not to speak of the costs of those improvements suggested in previous paragraphs. Indeed the gap between the costs of education and the students' contribution to those costs is likely to widen.

The only sources that can take the place of governmental agencies are the denominational organizations that are now contributing 20 per cent of the cost of theological education, while tax moneys account for 50 per cent of the income of medical schools. The denominational organizations have through their national budgets organized the giving of the churches to foreign missions, church extension, and other ecclesiastical concerns. If a guess may be ventured in the absence of opportunity for detailed examinations of the situation, it would be that such programs for raising and distributing money have been more effectively administered, have kept better pace with the growth of denominational enterprises and membership and with monetary inflation in almost all other areas of church concern than they have in the case of theological education.

That there are certain dangers connected with the kind of denominational support that is here pointed to as the only real recourse of the seminaries is self-evident. The loss of local independence represents no new problem in education, however; and it is also to be pointed out that the wise administration of national church funds could contribute to the reduction of the uneconomic number of seminaries some denominations try to maintain.

Though the primary solution of the financial problem of an advancing theological education must be sought in the denominational agencies it remains evident that an important segment of theological education will need to find its support elsewhere. The nondenominational schools might indeed receive some support from denominational boards since they prepare their students for service in denominations, since moreover they train so large a number of the teachers in denominational seminaries. Such support is most likely to come from boards and other organizations that will grant scholarships to men and women preparing for denominational ministries in nondenominational schools. Hence it will remain inadequate to the needs of the latter since their costs per student will always greatly outrun the amount of any charges they can lay on their students. These divinity schools, therefore, will remain dependent on the gifts of private individuals and of foundations. The latter, to be sure, with the notable exception of John D. Rockefeller, Jr.'s, Sealantic fund, have not made any considerable investments in the advancement of theological education. The question whether the difficulties which have stood in their way can be surmounted must be left like many other unanswered questions in this book to the wisdom and ingenuity of those primarily responsible for the continuation of the advance—the deans, the board members, the faculties, the directors of the American Association of Theological Schools, and all other interested and responsible groups.

The support of the seminaries by the churches is, of course, not primarily an economic matter. Without constant and pervasive concern in the churches for the increase of a faith seeking understanding; and of a ministry wise and knowledgeable in devoted service, theological education cannot flourish, even though the schools in which it is carried on receive liberal gifts of money. Our next step in the advancement of theological education must be the better instruction of the churches in the meanings and problems of that enterprise.

The Theological Education of Negro Ministers

Frequent references have been made in the main body of this report to the problems of Negro students of theology and of the Negro seminaries. But the questions raised for Protestantism in the United States by the depressed status of the ministry in the Negro churches needs to be underlined more sharply than has been possible in the course of the general description of theological education. The appalling shortage of well-trained Negro ministers, the financial plight of the dominantly Negro seminaries, the unattractiveness of the ministry to many of the best Negro college graduates, the relatively slow rate of increase of Negro B.D. enrollment, and many other factors call attention to a major problem that American Protestantism as a whole must deal with. It seems clear that while the Negro community is rapidly becoming an increasingly important group in the national life, Protestantism as such is not coming to grips with its responsibilities for the church life and the ministry of this dominantly Protestant segment of the society. Pending the inauguration and findings of a more complete study of the situation the following observations are offered on this complex problem.

I. The Sociological Context of the Problem

"When discussing the Negro church as it is and as it might come to be, it must never be forgotten that *the Negro church fundamentally is an expression of the Negro community itself.*" [1] Myrdal's statement appears to be true in the main. The Negro church, however, is not only an expression of the culture. It relates the common life of its people to the Lord of all life. With this qualification one must admit that "when the Negro community changes, the church also will change." [2] The validity of this latter observation is borne out by the present situation ten years after the publication of Myrdal's book, for any effort to understand the Negro church and ministry is complicated by the geographical and social mobility of Negroes in the past fifteen years. Prior to defining the problems of Negro theological education it is well to

[1] G. Myrdal, *An American Dilemma,* Vol. II, New York, 877.
[2] *Ibid.*

recall some of the social and cultural factors involved in the Negro church and community.

While one can say that the problems of the Negro church are the usual church problems in an exaggerated form, it becomes apparent that the exaggeration is great enough to create a problem that is almost different in kind. One cannot define precisely the limits of a Negro culture within American culture, for in all respects the configurations of values and meanings that seem to characterize Negro life in the United States bear the marks of the wider culture in which this life is set. So-called primitivism in Negro religious life reflects the prevailing pattern of American frontier Protestantism in the period of Negro conversions. The indifference to religion of many professional people in the Negro community and the secularization of Negro higher education mirror parallel movements in the total American culture, though these movements became effective among Negroes at a somewhat later time. Someone has suggested that in part the present change in Negro life in America reflects a cultural lag of twenty to thirty years. Urbanization, secularization, and acculturation processes among Negroes are similar both in source and in consequence to those that immigrant groups and other native groups have gone through since the beginning of the present century. Yet the present intensity and extensiveness of these forces in the Negro community are such as to create an identifiable problem.

The mobility of the Negro is geographical. Population studies indicate the following increases in Negro population in the designated states between 1940 and 1950:

State	1940	1950	% increase
California	124,306	462,172	271.8
Michigan	208,345	442,296	112.3
Illinois	387,446	645,980	66.7
New York	571,221	918,191	60.7

The percentage of increase in Indiana was 42.8; in Pennsylvania, 35.8; Maryland, 27.8; New Jersey, 19.3. In large part this represents rural to urban and South to North migrations. The consequences of these movements are many and various; new patterns of work are involved for many people as they move from agriculture to industry; community forces of social control in the small town are relaxed in the anonymity of urban existence; in some instances the increase in cash income comes at the cost of greater job insecurity; new movements appeal for the loyalty of the Negro—labor unions, political parties, and the like. In most cases the transition is from rural slum to urban slum, from the bottom of the social scale in the caste society of the South to the bottom of the scale in an only slightly less caste-structured society in the North.

The mobility is also "vertical"; that is to say, the social dynamics within Negro culture and society are intensified in several ways. Increasingly professional opportunities are opening in the service of the large Negro population and the total American society. The partial breakdown of segregation in Northern urban life offers new opportunities and creates new personal problems for Negroes. New rewards are forthcoming in recognition, but the threat of loss of self-respect is always present because the cultural interpretation of the color line still makes for the "daily crucifixion of the soul." With the rising level of general education among Negroes aspirations for different satisfactions are intensified. The rejection of the cultural past out of which the mobile generations are emerging is not easy and can never be complete. The most frequent outcome of the process is an emulation of the whites' configurations of values and meanings. The marginal man, whether the son of an immigrant from Poland or a Negro moving into a new cultural world, has to come to some satisfactory acceptance of his position. The failure to do so issues in tragic personal consequences. Symptoms of such tragedies are frightfully obvious in every Northern urban Negro community.

The mobility process is reflected in the increasing diversity of patterns of life within the Negro community. The stratification of Negro society can be observed in the institutional loyalties of Negroes, including religious institutions. The pattern of movement from lower-class sects to upper-class churches is being repeated within the American Negro society.[3] The functions of the church in meeting a variety of human needs differ as widely among Negroes as they do among whites. The stratification pattern is reflected in the Negro press as well. The concrete realization of meanings and values usually shared with the dominant white community becomes the external sign of status within the Negro community. Place of residence, association with in-groups of peers, and other aspects of the American style of life are important in determining the relative status of a Negro family.

Any discussion of theological education of the Negro ministry that is not cognizant of such sociological and cultural factors is bound to be oversimplified. They are reflected in many of the current practices and problems in theological education among Negroes.

II.   *Negroes in American Church Life*

The most obvious thing that can be said about the participation of Negroes in American church life is that their common life in the Body of Christ remains segregated. As a group, Negroes are not much more

[3] Cf. St. Clair Drake and Horace Cayton, *Black Metropolis,* New York, 1945.

church related than are whites. Myrdal's analysis of the 1936 religious census indicates that "44.0 per cent of the Negro population are members of Negro churches, as compared to 42.4 per cent of the white population in white churches." [4] Whether the number of Negroes in white churches is large enough to change this proportion significantly is doubtful. The largest number of Negroes in a dominantly white church is in the Methodist Church. Frank Loescher's figures on Negro members of white denominations belonging to the Federal Council of Churches, published in 1948, were as follows: [5]

Denomination	Total Membership	Negro Churches	Membership
Northern Baptist	1,555,914	232	45,000
Congregational Christian	1,075,401	230	19,374
Disciples	1,672,354	500	60,000
Methodist	8,046,129	3,115	330,000
Presbyterian, U.S.	565,853	54	3,132
Presbyterian, U.S.A.	2,040,399	410	40,581
Protestant Episcopal	2,227,524	347	60,326
United Lutheran	1,690,204	5	1,774
United Presbyterian	193,637	13	1,166

Comparable membership figures for Negro denominations were as follows:

National Baptist Convention, Inc.	4,021,618
National Baptist Convention	2,352,339
A.M.E.	868,735
A.M.E. Zion	489,244
C.M.E.	382,000

Loescher also secured data on the integration of the Negroes into predominantly white congregations. The following figures give some indication of the number in six denominations:

Denomination	Churches reporting Negro participants	Negro attenders	Negro members
Congregational Christian	81	399	337
Northern Baptist	80	236	149
United Presbyterian	10	19	15
E. and R.	1	1	0
Church of the Brethren	2	7	8
Protestant Episcopal	116	470	816

[4] Myrdal, *op. cit.*, 864.
[5] Loescher, *The Protestant Church and the Negro*, New York, 1948, 52.

Undoubtedly these figures are no longer accurate.[6] They do indicate, however, that Negro members of dominantly white denominations are overwhelmingly in segregated local churches. White churches of which Negroes are members have on the average less than five Negroes in the congregation. Since 1948 many inner-city churches have become interracial. It must be noted, however, that frequently these churches are interracial only during a period of transition in the ethnic and racial population within a given geographical location. Insofar as these churches appeal to Negroes they tend to attract those of middle class and professional status. Francis McPeek, of the Chicago Mayor's Commission on Human Relations, estimates that from twenty to thirty churches in that city are to some degree racially integrated.[7] How long churches can remain racially integrated while housing is by and large segregated is an open question. This is particularly a question in large urban centers where the Negro migration extends outward from a Black Belt established through the years by restrictive covenants.

The Central Jurisdiction of the Methodist Church is the outcome of an effort to achieve integration at some levels while maintaining segregation at others. In a national church in which the basis of jurisdictional division is geographical, the Central Jurisdiction is superimposed on the basis of race. In 1950 there were 346,945 "full active members" in the Central Jurisdiction. According to Dwight Culver, those who defended the establishment of the separate unit believed that

this form of organization gives (1) assurance of equal representation to Negroes in the governing bodies of the church; (2) an opportunity to develop leadership by "managing their own affairs"; and (3) an opportunity to demonstrate what Negroes can do.[8]

In the years of debate that preceded Methodist reunion the question of what to do with Negro Methodist churches appears to have been one of the most difficult issues to settle. Much of the discussion was carried on under a mask of other issues, such as polity. While the way was left open for local Negro Methodist churches to become members of the conferences that belonged to the geographical jurisdictions, the

[6] A recent study of 405 racially inclusive churches in three denominations was made under the auspices of the National Council of Churches. Of 237,476 members of these churches, 6,422 or 2.7 per cent were from minority races. Church membership by minority racial persons ranges from approximately 1 per cent in one denomination to approximately 7 per cent in another. There was less participation by the minority race members in church groups than in worship services. *Outlook*, Dec., 1954.

[7] *The Christian Century*, Feb. 16, 1955, 206.

[8] Dwight Culver, *Negro Segregation in the Methodist Church*, New Haven, 1953, 83.

process of transfer from a conference in the Central Jurisdiction to another conference is very difficult. Culver's study indicated that most of the leadership in the Central Jurisdiction would prefer a non-segregated church. The white ministers and leaders who answered Culver's questions appear to be more concerned with opportunities for Negro self-realization within a segregated pattern than did the Negroes. On the whole, it is clear that the Methodist Church has by no means achieved a satisfactory solution of its segregation-integration problem. Yet this church more than any other denomination has sought to keep Negroes and whites together in one national organization.

By and large, Liston Pope's analysis of the situation still holds true. He pointed out that there is a growing contrition among Protestants about the fact that Negro church life remains highly segregated, but that effective institutionalization of the professions churches make in denominational and interdenominational statements is yet to come.[9] One must admit that not only is the Negro church fundamentally an expression of the Negro community, but that to an alarming degree the white Protestant churches are expressions of the American pattern of life in race relations. The fact of segregation together with all of its cultural, social, economic, and religious consequences makes theological education of Negro ministers a distinct problem. Because churches cannot be brought under the edicts of public law with reference to their policies on membership, the pattern of segregation may well break down in public schools, labor unions and the hiring policies of industry before it is overcome in religious institutions. This means that the tardiness of the churches to reckon with segregation and its consequences in their own institutional policies may become more noticeable in the future.

III. *The Negro Ministry*

The ministry was for many years the principal professional opportunity available to large numbers of Negroes. Churches continue to be important in the life of Negroes both in the North and the South but the status of professional work in the church has shifted. The capable young Negro college graduate frequently rejects the conception of religion and the ministry that prevailed in his earlier experience and finds beliefs that appear more relevant to his situation. A family may be willing to sacrifice savings and other good things to assist a son who is going into medicine or law, but will give only verbal blessing to one going into the ministry. Many a Negro humanitarian regards the legal profession as more concretely helpful to the Negro in his present social situation than the ministry.

[9] L. Pope, "Caste in the Church, the Protestant Experience," *Survey Graphic*, Jan., 1947.

Undoubtedly the general educational level of the Negro ministry is rising with the level of general education in America. According to C. Luther Fry's analysis of the 1926 religious census in three Negro denominations 77.8 per cent of the ministers had neither college nor seminary education, and only 7.4 per cent had both seminary and college education.[10] The New England, Middle Atlantic, and Pacific regions had the highest percentage of educated Negro ministers. Urban areas had a higher percentage than rural. In Mays and Nicholson's study of urban ministers, published in 1933, 80 per cent of their group were not "college trained," 86.6 per cent did not have B.D. degrees, 81.6 per cent had neither the B.D. nor the B.Th. degrees, and 72.3 per cent had neither college nor seminary degrees.[11] Mays and Nicholson concluded that on the whole the younger ministers were better equipped academically than their older colleagues. They reported two other important findings. While the number of college men in Negro seminaries was increasing, "the total number of students in Negro seminaries has decreased in the last eight years." The second is that "the number of college students contemplating the ministry is small in comparison with the number that is entering some other profession." [12] Among the rural ministers studied by Mays and Nicholson, 96 per cent were not graduates of either college or seminary.[13] Rural ministers tended to be older, to serve more parishes simultaneously, and to move more frequently than urban pastors.

There are no recent over-all studies of the Negro ministry that give us data on educational background. Murray Leiffer's 1948 study of the Methodist ministry gives some indication of the improving educational status of the ministerial members of the Central Jurisdiction.[14]

Central Jurisdiction

Age Group	Graduates of College and Seminary	College graduates	Some college	No college
58–72	5.4%	8.1%	43.2%	43.2%
43–57	20.6%	9.5%	44.5%	25.4%
42 and under	30.2%	20.7%	32.1%	17.0%

[10] Fry, The U.S. Looks at Its Churches, New York, 1930, 154.

[11] Mays and Nicholson, The Negro's Church, New York, 1933, 55–56. Reid's study quotes E. P. Allridge as follows: of 23,490 Negro Baptist ministers in the South, .92 per cent have college degrees, 1.85 per cent have "had theological courses," 6.12 per cent have "only high school training," and 91.1 per cent are "without any special training." Ira Reid, The Negro Baptist Ministry, 1952, 92.

[12] Mays and Nicholson, op. cit., 56.

[13] Ibid., 239.

[14] Leiffer, The Methodist Ministry in 1948, Evanston: Garrett Biblical Institute, 1948.

More of the younger ministers are better equipped academically than are older men. When one sets these figures against those of the total effective Methodist ministry in 1948, however, the differential between the Negro and white ministry becomes clear.

Total Methodist Ministry

Age Group	Graduates of College and Seminary	College graduates	Some college	No college
58–72	36.7%	27.2%	21.9%	14.2%
43–57	51.1%	26.0%	15.7%	7.2%
42 and under	70.5%	24.2%	4.2%	1.2%

While the better educational background of the younger ministers is a sign of progress, it must be set in the context of further data about the Central Jurisdiction ministry. An age distribution chart indicates that half of its ministers are past 51 years of age. The median age of the ministry in the dominantly white jurisdictions is about 47 years. In his 1952 study Leiffer indicates that the number of effective ministers in the Central Jurisdiction dropped in four years from 1349 to 1244, or 7.8 per cent. "Of the 1139 men in that jurisdiction for whom age data were secured (91.6 per cent of all effectives) only 146 were under thirty-eight years of age." [15] The better education of the younger Negro clergy is an encouraging sign. Leiffer's study of the age grouping of Central Jurisdiction ministers, however, depresses any over-all optimism that one might have about the improvement of the Negro ministry. There is no reason to believe that the recruitment problem, so acute in the Central Jurisdiction of the Methodist Church, is much less acute in other Negro churches. The ministry is clearly not attracting young college educated Negroes.

IV. Negroes in Theological Schools

Several recent surveys indicate that enrollment of Negroes in graduate theological schools is increasing. Frank Dorey's recent summary comparison of such studies indicates that from 1942 until 1954 there was an increase from 178 to over 329. (The latter figure is believed to be low because the coverage of white seminaries in the 1954 study used by Dorey was incomplete.) It seems likely that the seminary enrollment of Negroes has almost doubled. In the same period the number of B.D. degrees granted to Negroes has increased from 61 to over 96. Using the inadequate figure for 1954, the increase in the number of Negroes getting the B.D. degree is over 50 per cent. From 1946 to 1954 (again

[15] Leiffer, *The Methodist Ministry in 1952*, Nashville, Tenn., 1952, 20.

using the incomplete figures of the 1954 study), the enrollment of Negro students in dominantly white seminaries increased from 77 to more than 105. In Negro schools it increased from 166 in ten schools to 224 in seventeen schools. (Dorey questions the legitimacy of the figure seventeen since in 1950 he found only twelve Negro theological schools that required college graduation for admission.) Dorey makes two important summary statements. "The significant fact is that there has been a slow increase in the number of Negro students going to white schools, yet proportionately, the white schools continue to get one-third of all the students. It is significant also that while the number of Negro college graduates enrolling in Negro schools has increased substantially, the proportion enrolling in the two accredited schools has declined sharply." [16] These two schools are Gammon Theological Seminary and Howard University School of Religion.

The decline in enrollment in A.A.T.S. Negro schools has been noted in Chapter One. The three Negro schools included in our sample for intensive study dropped from 110 students in 1949–50 to 95 in 1954–55. The statistics from the two accredited schools verify Dorey's 1954 statement. At Gammon a general decline was recorded until 1954–55 when there was a remarkable increase. The figures are as follows:

| 1945–46 | 71 | 1949–50 | 66 | 1954–55 | 71 |
| 1947–48 | 64 | 1952–53 | 46 | | |

During this period the proportion of students with college degrees has increased from 63 per cent to 100 per cent. At Howard University the comparable enrollment trend is as follows:

| 1945–46 | 73 | 1949–50 | 60 | 1954–55 | 46 |
| 1947–48 | 66 | 1952–53 | 41 | | |

It is too early to judge the significance of the recent upward turn at these two schools.

Professor Dorey estimates that 1,132 new Negro ministers are needed each year for the Negro denominations and for Negro churches in dominantly white denominations. All studies indicate that not many more than 100 Negroes are being graduated from theological schools with the B.D. degree each year. If Dorey's estimate is even roughly accurate, approximately one thousand Negroes a year may come into the ministry with less than a B.D. education for some time to come.

[16] Frank Dorey, "Summary Comparison of Five Surveys of Negro College Graduates in Schools of Religion," March 1, 1955, mimeographed, Howard University School of Religion.

V. How Can the Need Be Met?

Given this general picture of the Negro ministry and Negro churches, in what direction can American religious and educational institutions move to strengthen the situation?

First, American Protestantism needs to become acutely aware of the problems of the Negro churches and clergy. A study more extensive and intensive than the present staff has undertaken is necessary. The paucity of accurate and current information is clear from figures cited in this appendix. The Board of Directors of the Rockefeller Brothers Theological Fellowship Program has shown an interest in the Negro ministry, and the Department of the Ministry of the National Council of Churches has taken steps to explore the needs of the Negro churches and ministry. Negro leaders in theological education have concurred in the need for a thorough study.

Second, the churches ought to lead the way with a policy of desegregation. It is clear that the development of independent Negro theological schools was predicated on church and educational segregation. The present financial poverty of these schools, the general lag in quality of secondary and college education for Negroes, and a host of other manifestations of the problem of the Negro churches have their roots in segregation. Nevertheless, the immediate needs of the Negro churches for ministerial leadership will not be met by desegregation. Opportunities for nonsegregated theological education are abundantly available at the present time in Northern schools and in a growing number of Southern schools. What excludes Negroes from nonsegregated theological education at the present time is not a bar of segregation at the level of admissions policies of schools, but the consequences of segregation at previous levels of educational achievement. Frequently Negro students are not able to meet the academic standards, the financial costs, and the social and psychological pressures that are involved in nonsegregated theological education.

A third direction in which we must move is to strengthen the quality of performance in Negro theological schools. The accredited theological schools serving a Negro constituency ought to be given more assistance financially and in the recruitment of good students. There is no question about the high quality of theological training at Howard, for example, but by virtue of its standards and the quality of its faculty it competes for students not so much with other Negro seminaries as with nonsegregated seminaries. Howard and Gammon, as well as the Negro associate member schools of the A.A.T.S., are forced to operate uneconomically with reference to all financial and human resources. The standards and quality of faculty of other Negro schools training men for the ministry ought to go up through the years. The immediate answer, however, does not appear to be the imposition of the four-year college, three-year seminary pattern according to A.A.T.S. standards on all schools. If all the Negro seminaries conformed immediately to these standards the problem of recruiting and training the Negro ministry would be more complicated than simplified. Students who have the financial resources and academic preparation to attend Howard University School of Religion, for example, can attend major Northern university-related theological schools just as easily. Both the accredited Negro schools are now facing a serious problem of recruitment. To raise the minimal standards immediately for all Negro seminaries would intensify and extend this problem.

The fourth and perhaps most important direction in which to move in the improvement of theological education for the Negro ministry at the present time is to strengthen undergraduate faculties of religion, and the campus religious life programs in colleges attended by large numbers of Negroes. More and more Negro ministers are getting four and five years of training in the various programs of the Negro colleges. To strengthen these faculties might have at least a threefold consequence. First, men entering the ministry immediately after graduation from college would be better trained theologically than they are now. Second, strong departments of religion might attract young Negro college students who are now recruited for other professions. A campus ministry of high quality could concretize an idea of the ministry different from that associated with Negro churches in the minds of the students. Thus the basis of recruitment for leadership in the Negro churches might be broadened. Third, students who have prepared themselves in strong undergraduate departments might be stimulated to do B.D. work at accredited theological schools.

A fifth step might be taken immediately. The Southern Baptist Convention and other groups have sponsored training institutes for Negro ministers in local communities. Both denominations and seminaries need to explore the possibility of extending and strengthening such programs. Ordained ministers with parishes but without professional education could improve the effectiveness of their work. Lectures, seminars, and workshops directed to the capacities and problems of the Negro ministers might bear early fruit in the lives of their churches.

Index